ERIK WIKLUND

INTERNATIONAL MARKETING

MAKING
EXPORTS
PAY OFF

McGRAW-HILL BOOK COMPANY

New York St. Louis San Francisco Auckland
Hamburg Johannesburg London Madrid
Mexico Montreal New Delhi Panama
Paris São Paulo Singapore Bogotá
Sydney Tokyo Toronto

For Kathy, with love

Library of Congress Cataloging in Publication Data

Wiklund, Erik.
   International marketing.

   Includes index.
   1. Export marketing. I. Title.
HF1009.5.W55   1986   658.8'48   85-23162
ISBN 0-07-070171-7

1234567890   DOC/DOC   8932109876

ISBN 0-07-070171-7

The editors for this book were William A. Sabin
and Rita Margolies, the designer was Dennis Sharkey,
and the production supervisor was Teresa F. Leaden.
It was set in Century Schoolbook by Williams Press, Inc.

Printed and bound by R. R. Donnelley & Sons Company.

CONTENTS

Preface   V
Introduction   1

PART ONE Starting from Scratch   13
ONE Products You Can Export   15
TWO A Low-Cost, Bare-Bones Plan   23
THREE How to Find Markets That Pay Off   37
FOUR A Lean, Sharp Team   53
FIVE Running Your Own Show   69
SIX How to Find Foreign Agents   81
SEVEN Promotion on a Shoestring   95
EIGHT When Is an Overseas Order for Real?   109
NINE Getting Into the Right Spirit   119

PART TWO Polishing Your Act   129
TEN The Art of Travel   131
ELEVEN The Personal Touch   147
TWELVE Plain-Talk Communications   159
THIRTEEN Profits and Commissions   169
FOURTEEN Bonus Sales through Foreign Aid   175
FIFTEEN The Saudi Experience   183

PART THREE What Next?   189
SIXTEEN New Technology as an Export Tool   191
SEVENTEEN The Bottom Line   195

Appendix   201
Index   213

ABOUT THE AUTHOR

Erik Wiklund, independent international marketing consultant and analyst, specializes in market research for educational and training products and in advising U.S. and European organizations seeking export expansion. He is also publisher and editor of *WEM Newsletter—The International Report for the Education Industry,* which has circulation in the U.S., Europe, and Japan.

Mr. Wiklund is fluent in or has working knowledge of six languages—French, Spanish, Portuguese, Italian, Swedish, and Arabic. His experience in the export business ranges across more than 80 countries, from the Americas to Europe and Asia.

PREFACE

Exports offer bright opportunities to large and small companies for expanding their sales and profits. With reasonable effort and minimal investment in time and personnel almost any firm can go after international sales successfully. The rewards often are greater than trying to scrape extra business out of a domestic market which has already been thoroughly worked over.

I hope this book will convince you that there is no special magic to finding and developing overseas sales outlets, and that any business person able to function in the domestic market can do the same anywhere else. You don't need special skills. As in any other business situation, successful international marketing has a lot to do with common sense and the ability to mix with people.

If you have never done business abroad, you will find this a practical, down-to-earth guide on how to set up your own operation and make it work.

If you are already active in the international marketplace, use this book as a checklist. It may reinforce your own strategy and possibly give you new hints on how to sharpen it. The book should also be a useful basic training manual for new administrative and marketing personnel.

I began learning about international marketing in my childhood. My first teacher was my father. He was a supersalesman, a real pro. He left Sweden at the age of eighteen, lived and worked in Germany, France, Austria, Spain, and Italy before moving on to Latin America, where he established a hard-hitting, prize-winning marketing network from scratch. He trained door-to-door salesmen, sales and branch managers, and dealers in Brazil, Uruguay, Argentina, Chile, and Peru.

By the time I finished high school I had accompanied him on many trips. At home, businessmen from half a dozen countries were always popping in for Sunday dinner. I grew up in an atmosphere where national boundaries seemed to have little importance.

My father's basic marketing philosophy was simple: "If you can sell it in your country, you can sell it anywhere."

My own work has taken me all over the world for the past twenty-five years. This book comes from the rich experience of having met hundreds of business men and women in Europe, Africa, Latin America, the Middle East, Asia, Australia, Canada, and, of course, the United States.

U.S. businesspeople are often criticized as being internationally naive and inexperienced. This is not true. They are no worse, and no better, than anybody else. No country in the world has a monopoly on international marketing excellence—or on international incompetence.

All the business men and women I have met in my travels have made a contribution to whatever I know about international marketing. I am grateful to all of them, as well as to my brother Edgard, an expert on handling international orders, shipments, and payments.

The anecdotes and examples cited in this book are all real. The names of individuals and companies are not, for obvious reasons. Statistics and forecasts are based on official reports from the U.S. Department of Commerce.

My father's simple philosophy still works in most of the world. I have seen it happen time and time again, whenever a company is determined to venture into foreign markets. Today's business world is far more complex than it was in the 1920s and 1930s. On the other hand, modern communications now give you access in minutes to almost any city in the world and you can fly anywhere in less than twenty-four hours.

In the 1920s a U.S. business executive on a tour of branch offices and dealers in Rio de Janeiro, Buenos Aires, Santiago, Lima, and Caracas would have been traveling by ship and by train for seven or eight weeks. The same trip today could be done comfortably in twelve days.

There is every reason and every convenience available to go after foreign markets today. The markets are there. Finding and developing them is within your capabilities. All it takes is determination.

Erik Wiklund

INTRODUCTION
The premise of this book is that, with extremely rare exceptions, there are receptive, ready, lucrative foreign markets for the exact product you are now selling in your home market, and that you can reach them through straight export sales without any need for complex schemes.

And get your money up front to boot!

Forget licensing and joint ventures. Forget intricate ball bearings-for-bananas barter formulas. Forget export-finance plans. Unless, that is, you are already exporting to the hilt and you are looking for other ways to cash in on foreign markets.

This is a book about exports, the simplest and most direct form of international marketing.

Find your best foreign markets, crack them, and build them up, and you will add a healthy chunk of profits to your bottom line. But first you may have to get rid of export apathy. If you are like tens of thousands of business executives around the world, you may be suffering from at least a touch of this worldwide malady.

In the United States, government reports have been reminding us, month after month, of the steady deterioration in the country's balance of trade. Sales of U.S. merchandise abroad are lagging far behind purchases, and the gap keeps getting wider. The U.S. 1984 trade deficit in manufactured goods was $88.5 billion.

All sorts of reasons are given for this ominous trend—the overvalued dollar, the federal deficit, the flow of foreign capital into the United States, low wages outside the United States and, of course, "The Japanese." Politicians and corporations clamor for more pressure on Japan and other countries to open their markets to U.S. products. But

1

one of the biggest obstacles to greater U.S. exports is the incredible extent to which export apathy prevails among U.S. firms.

Government figures show that over the years only about 5 percent of U.S. manufacturers have gone after non-U.S. markets seriously and actively.

It does no good for governments to try to "open up" countries if not enough firms jump into the breach!

On the surface U.S. businesspeople give a far different impression. Take a map of the world and pick out any city. It's a safe bet that nine times out of ten you will be looking at a place where U.S. businesspeople are trying to sell something to someone. From Bangkok to Buenos Aires, U.S. salesmen and saleswomen are a sight as common as Coca-Cola billboards.

Tens of thousands of hotels, restaurants, souvenir stands, bars, cab-drivers, car rental agencies, interpreters, translators, nightclubs, and massage parlors around the world would be out of business tomorrow if it were not for the globe-trotting hordes of U.S. salespeople.

This massive effort brought the United States a sum total of $217.9 billion in export sales in 1984.

Impressive? Not quite, when you realize that for every U.S. firm aggressively hustling for business around the world there are twenty back home whose executives cringe at the mere sight of a foreign stamp on an incoming letter. Or, not much better, executives who go about promoting exports erratically and inefficiently, hoping to pick up a little "gravy" here and there but not really taking foreign markets seriously. The result: U.S. exports are less than 10 percent of the gross national product.

Spoiled by a vast, affluent, easy-to-reach domestic market, too many U.S. firms have traditionally turned their backs on other business, giving the distinct impression among importers, distributors, and end users abroad that most U.S. manufacturers don't give a damn about world markets.

The phenomenon, however, is not limited to U.S. firms. Export apathy is also a common malady in several West European countries because *the larger the country, the less pressure on manufacturers to export.* West German, French, and British firms have ample domestic markets to keep them happy.

A good indicator of European export apathy is the number of manufacturers one runs into who have no literature in anything but the local language. There are German firms that have no catalogs in French for a market which is closer to them than Chicago is to New York. There are French companies that ignore the Italian or Spanish markets.

Japanese firms don't get off scot-free, either. If you are a Japanese manufacturer whose products are marketed in the United States and elsewhere, did you actively go out and seek foreign markets or did you sit and wait until a trading company came along and took you by the hand?

The main reason to export is the lure of new sales and profits, particularly after the domestic market is well established and your company is committed to growth. For thousands of companies around the world, however, the prospect of added profits, strangely enough, doesn't seem to be enough incentive.

Blindness to international profit opportunities is the chief and most devastating symptom of export apathy.

Export apathy comes mostly from fear of sailing into unknown waters, ignorance of what the rest of the world is all about, suspicion of "foreign" business situations, and just plain laziness. Some of the more commonly heard reasons for not exporting are fluctuating exchange rates, economic cycles, tough competition, unstable economies, too many revolutions, too much red tape, shipping problems, the risk of not getting paid, and the expense of traveling around the world.

None of these reasons is valid. They are flimsy excuses which reflect either an unjustified distrust of foreign markets or very poor homework in evaluating overseas opportunities.

The U.S. dollar, the Swiss franc, the Japanese yen, and other "hard" currencies may be high one year and low two years later, making some products more expensive or cheaper depending on which currency you are using. The balance of trade may be up or down. Economic cycles are a fact of life everywhere. If you wait for things to be exactly the way you want them to be, you will never get anywhere, abroad or in your own home market.

Firms experienced at international marketing have learned that the world is a vast, highly diversified marketplace. It may offer you a much wider range of opportunities than you would find in your own homogeneous home market. As a matter of fact, by combining domestic and international markets, you will gain a degree of flexibility in adapting to changing business conditions that you will not have if you limit yourself to the domestic market.

There are always opportunities to open new markets somewhere in the world—sometimes they are untouched territories offering outstanding rates of return on your investment.

As for competition, since when has it kept you from selling? Competition is tough all over. There aren't many order takers about, domestically or internationally. Any modern-day business executive knows this. Sales and profits are something you have to fight for, even in your own home market.

The United States, Canada, Australia, Japan, and Western Europe do not have a monopoly on relative economic stability. There are many other countries around the world where political and economic conditions are good for business and where rising wages and standards of living are creating large demands for consumer and other products.

Many countries have gone through political and economic changes, sometimes sudden and drastic, but continue to offer excellent opportunities for a broad range of imports. Since 1945 everybody has been waiting for Brazil to "settle down," with occasional exceptions. While their competitors continue to wait, dozens of U.S., Japanese, and European firms have found Brazil to be an attractive market for their products, political problems and economic slumps notwithstanding.

There are several other Brazils where you can keep on waiting forever for conditions to be exactly the way you would like them to be. And while you sit and wait, a lot of good business will be passing you by.

The need for export documentation is the weakest of all excuses. Anybody trained to do invoices and packing lists will be able to handle export forms. Red tape is not alien to businesspeople! Do you know anybody who decided not to go into business in the domestic market solely because of the need to fill out tax, unemployment, and insurance forms?

Travel expenses are a bit higher than those for domestic sales if you figure on trips to distant markets, but this applies only to airline fares. Daily hotel and other travel expenses are not higher than in your home market. In some countries they may be lower.

Airline fares alone are not an adequate reason for staying out of exports. And when you start planning your export strategy, you should not choose markets on the basis of what it costs to fly to them.

The only time when I am somewhat sympathetic with someone suffering from export apathy is when I am told: "Look, I'm happy with the way things are going. I know I could sell my product in Madagascar and the Maldives, but why bother?"

The trouble with this sort of reasoning is that it clashes with the "growth ethic." Stop growing and you die! Or, as an old boss of mine used to put it, "To stand still is to regress!"

There is, of course, another reason why you could be suffering from export apathy. *Perhaps the thought of selling outside the U.S. simply never occurred to you.*

Often it takes a major effort by an export agency, a trading company, or a foreign distributor to convince a manufacturing company that it should go international. It no longer surprises me when businesspeople in southeast Asia or the Middle East show me negative, discouraging answers from U.S. manufacturers to serious inquiries. Or when, even worse, they report that such inquiries go totally unanswered.

Many foreign firms are today successfully buying from German, Italian, Japanese, Swedish, or Canadian suppliers only because they were repeatedly turned down by the U.S. firms they first contacted. Talk about throwing business out the window!

This carelessness is not quite as prevalent elsewhere. Even European manufacturers who suffer from a touch of export apathy will at least answer foreign inquiries and make an effort to develop a business relationship. Japanese firms will usually send out a brochure and even a firm quotation.

The malady of export apathy is more widespread in large countries like the United States, Japan, Canada, West Germany, and France than in small ones like Denmark, Norway, Sweden, Switzerland, the Netherlands, Israel, Taiwan, and Singapore, where for most manufacturers international sales are a basic necessity for survival.

Consider Bent Simonsen, Danish manufacturer of computerized research oscilloscopes. He knows that the Danish market alone can never support his operation. (The total population of the country is less than 3 million). Simonsen simply must find enough foreign markets to justify going into minimum initial production.

In Simonsen's company the key marketing person will be the export manager. If Simonsen is to make a profit on his oscilloscopes, he will have to rely on foreign markets for as much as 90 percent of his sales. In Denmark this is not unusual. The figure can be as high as 98 percent, as a manufacturer of office machines in Copenhagen once told me.

In short, for manufacturers in small countries it is often a question of export or die!

Now let's go to the other extreme and look at a small manufacturer in the United States, the world's most affluent and biggest market, 100 times bigger than the Danish market. The company's customers and prospects speak the same language, have the same buying habits, read the same consumer and trade publications, go to the same conventions, and respond to the same direct-mail advertising. The marketing VP can hop a plane and fly anywhere in an area more than twice as large as Western Europe without visas or a passport. The factory can ship merchandise without filling out or authenticating a dozen forms. Market conditions don't change too drastically, and the political scene is reasonably free of explosive upheavals.

Why should this small, successful company take foreign markets seriously?

Why should *you?*

The answer, quite simply, is that export sales can be good business. They can add to your bottom line. You owe it to yourself and to your company to seek new markets for your product and to keep your competition from picking up this business by default.

The top twenty U.S. exporters in 1984 reached total export sales of from $480 million to $4.8 billion each. For a few of them this represented from 4 to 7 percent of total sales; for most of them this number was between 14 and 29 percent.

What will it mean for your company to increase its sales by 15 percent, even by 25 percent? How much will this contribute to your bottom line, considering that it will all be add-on business requiring only a modest investment?

Let's look at six good, positive reasons for going international.

First, foreign markets are new, profitable, unexploited territory. In the domestic market you face a daily challenge to reach out for new customers. If the market has been thoroughly worked over, any new promotional investment may produce no more than marginal results.

Overseas markets may give you a much better return for less money, and it will all be new business.

Super-Fi Inc., an Alabama manufacturer of stereo components with domestic sales in the $20 million bracket, never bothered with foreign sales. Foreign orders were routed to an order clerk who would send back cold, impersonal, we-couldn't-care-less form letters. Just the same, occasionally someone placed an order. This unsolicited business, usually regarded as a nuisance, brought in about $50,000 a year in sales.

One day Thurmond Hazelhurst, president and sole owner of Super-Fi, decided to attend the Hanover Trade Fair in Germany. He was overwhelmed by the thousands of exhibits and the crowds of foreign buyers and distributors.

"Where the hell have we been all these years?" wondered Thurmond, sick with the thought of all the business he had been passing up.

At the bar of the Hanover Intercontinental he met Gianni Ferri, export manager for a small Italian electronics firm, with years of experience covering European, Middle Eastern, and southeast Asian markets. Unhappy with his job, Gianni was looking for an opportunity to go to work for a U.S. firm. Two days later Thurmond hired him to cover the world for Super-Fi.

"I must be free to travel as much as I want and wherever I think we can do some business," Gianni insisted.

"Travel to your heart's content," Thurman replied. "In fact, go ahead and take your wife with you. I'll cover your expenses. But send me orders. If in one year you haven't produced half a million in sales, I'll kick your ass out!"

The first year Gianni (and his wife, who worked just as hard as he did, handling correspondence, helping with demonstrations, attending audio shows, researching markets and distributors) barely made it. The second year they brought back $1.2 million in orders.

Today Gianni heads a team of six full-time international salespeople who last year produced $21 million in orders. Thurmond never misses a European trade fair, takes pride in visiting some of his best overseas dealers, and buys his clothes on the Via Condotti in Rome.

Second, exports mean money up front. Would you like to make sure the money is already in the bank before you ship an order? Then go international. Virtually all export business around the world is done by letter of credit (L/C). An L/C quite literally is money in the bank. You are paid by a bank when you ship the merchandise. There are several other ways to do business abroad. You can spend weeks poring over government and financial manuals explaining barter, export finance, and other schemes. You don't need them. You can build up a healthy export business on a straight L/C basis.

The hundreds of exporters I have known over the years operate strictly by L/C—and this includes giant multinationals. This is because doing business by L/C means you take no risks, grant no credit, and suffer no delays in getting paid if you deliver as promised.

Many U.S. firms often wish they could handle their domestic business the same way. I have known some that would often fill foreign orders with merchandise originally intended for domestic dealers—particularly when the domestic dealers were among those who take their good time paying their bills and the manufacturer had a bit of a cash flow problem.

Third, exporting keeps you on your toes. Watch out when your company becomes smugly convinced that it sells the world's ultimate mousetrap. Someone abroad may already have something better. Competition is healthy. Venture into the world and find out what's happening. Nothing will sharpen your operations better than pitting your product and sales force against a tough competitor.

Not all foreign products are being exported to your market. Export apathy, remember?

Going into foreign markets may even give you ideas for products to market or manufacture on your own. It took a U.S. airline pilot on the Tokyo run to realize that there was a big potential market in the United States for the small, portable kerosene heaters the Japanese have been using for years in their homes, offices, and factories; he set up a U.S. marketing operation that has now become a multimillion-dollar business.

Fourth, Third World projects are big buyers. Internationally financed projects in the Third World generate hundreds of millions of dollars in purchasing every year. Most of the money is used to import all sorts of products. Table 1 provides a sample list of recent or ongoing overseas development projects offering multimillion-dollar opportunities for thousands of imported products.

Table 1
Recent Overseas Development Projects

Country	Type of Project
Angola	Cold storage complexes
Argentina	Agricultural education
Bangladesh	Port development
Benin	Education
Burma	Hydropower
Cameroon	Harbor Construction
Central African Republic	Construction of major hospital
Chad	Reconstruction of an airport
China	Petroleum and aeronautics
Colombia	Small hydroelectric plants
Cyprus	Construction of a dam
Dominican Republic	Rehabilitation of unproductive sugar cropland
Egypt	Harbor construction
Ethiopia	Urban development
Gambia	Urban development
Greece	Sewerage
Guatemala	Rural water supply system
Hungary	Industrial energy
India	Water supply, railway improvement
Ivory Coast	Electrification
Jamaica	Power plant and education projects
Jordan	Electrification
Kenya	Telecommunications
Korea	Science instruments, civil aviation
Liberia	Highway construction, education
Malaysia	Hydropower, health care, population control
Mozambique	Hoof-and-mouth disease control
Nepal	Agricultural development
Nigeria	Fertilizer project
Pakistan	Reservoir maintenance, oil and gas
Papua New Guinea	Road improvement
Philippines	Traffic signal system
Saudi Arabia	Housing project
Senegal	Rural development
Syria	Construction of science research unit
Tanzania	Coffee development
Thailand	Rural electrification
Tunisia	Improvement of a railway system
Turkey	Livestock breeding and sewerage
Uganda	Postal system and telecommunications
Yugoslavia	Hydroelectric, drainage

This business is highly competitive; nonetheless, it involves purchases of vast quantities of equipment, services, and supplies from firms around the world. Specifications are usually broad enough to encourage multiple bids.

Fifth, your product is already known. Businesspeople and end users outside the United States are avid readers of consumer, professional, and trade publications. If you advertise in any of them, you are already getting a fair amount of coverage around the world. The more removed the readers are from major urban centers, the more likely they are to save back issues zealously and refer to them when they are ready to buy. This explains why from time to time a product which has been obsolete for two or three years may turn up in a bid request from a remote country.

Your product will also have been seen by visitors from abroad, possibly even purchased from retailers and taken back home by them. And don't forget large multinational companies with purchasing offices in your domestic market. They may be buying your product regularly and shipping it out to subsidiaries all over the world without your knowledge.

All of this gives you exposure to many potential foreign buyers.

Sixth, large construction firms are involved in multibillion-dollar projects worldwide, and they buy a lot of merchandise back home. International development projects attract the world's largest construction companies as well as architectural and engineering consultants. Most of the business explosion in Saudi Arabia since the oil boom of the mid-1970s has been fueled by gigantic construction projects which generate the purchase of billions of dollars of products of all types.

The projects invariably are designed by U.S. or European consultants. As a rule their specifications reflect the products with which the consultants are already familiar.

In a typical case, the government of Saudi Arabia decides to put up a new building for one of its ministries. The design contract goes to Youngman & Sons, a Utah firm of architectural consultants specializing in international projects. The final specifications contain detailed lists of furniture, fixtures, office equipment, air-conditioning systems, water fountains, elevators, intercom systems, and hundreds of other items—all "similar or equal" to specific U.S. products and models. Construction is awarded to a Korean firm which in turn sets up a purchasing office in the United States to buy all the equipment specified by Youngman & Sons. Similar projects have been awarded to Italian, French, German, British, Canadian, and Japanese firms.

You may already be selling your product to construction contractors' home offices. You may even be promoting your product among architectural and engineering firms. But unless you are organized to go after this business systematically, you will barely scratch the surface of this lucrative market.

ENGLISH IS THE
WORLD'S BUSINESS LANGUAGE.
Companies in the United States, Canada, Australia, the United Kingdom, and any other English speaking country have a major advantage when they go international.

Millions of businesspeople, professionals, government officials, end users, and consumers around the world read and understand their literature, their advertising, their instruction manuals, and their correspondence. This is a powerful, built-in international marketing tool.

Japanese, German, French, Swedish, and Italian firms, for instance, don't enjoy this advantage. Their export managers and support staff must learn to do most of their work in English, a foreign language.

Imagine what would happen if before exporters in English speaking countries could go out and promote their products around the world, they had to learn how to speak, read, and write Finnish, Greek, or Urdu, and then produce literature and make all their presentations in the same language? They would indeed have cause to succumb to export apathy!

THE WORLD IS GETTING SMALLER.
The world is shrinking. Travel time continues to decrease; in less than 24 hours you can be on the other side of the world. Instant communications by means of international direct telephone dialing, electronic mail, the computer, and overnight courier delivery is bringing the world market practically to your front door.

If you limit your thinking and goals to the domestic market, you will leave the rest of the world open to your competitors.

Why give this business away?

You may have to start from scratch, or you may just need to get serious about exports. In either case an export department need not cost you an arm and a leg.

You can go after foreign markets selectively. Don't let the world map overwhelm you. Nobody covers all countries. It makes no difference how many markets you reach as long as you develop a systematic, sensible plan and concentrate your resources where they will produce the highest return.

You will definitely waste a lot of money and resources if you start roaming all over the world indiscriminately, reaching out for as many countries and distributors as possible without regard to quality and end results. This sort of haphazard, sloppy approach can be as devastating abroad as it is domestically.

The secret is to find those countries where your product stands the best chance of success. Zero in on markets which are ripe for your product, and learn how to break into them on a low, affordable budget.

The number of countries you set up as initial targets should be related to your level of staffing and other resources—unless you think you can do business mail-order style, without budging from your chair. What counts is not how many countries you go into at first, but what kind of a start you make and what sort of long-range plans you develop.

The purpose of this book is to help you find export markets that pay off and show how you can get into them in a professional manner, with only a modest investment in money and personnel.

Even if you have already stepped into the international arena, why not see what it takes to start from scratch?

PART
ONE

STARTING
FROM
SCRATCH

CHAPTER
ONE

PRODUCTS YOU CAN EXPORT
The overwhelming majority of the manufacturers I have known in the past thirty years were able to find and penetrate attractive foreign markets without having to make any changes in products they make for their domestic buyers.

Their products? Just about everything you can possibly think of.

For U.S. products, the biggest export markets in 1984, in order of importance, were Canada, Japan, the United Kingdom, Mexico, West Germany, the Netherlands, France, South Korea, Saudi Arabia, Belgium and Luxembourg, Taiwan, Australia, Italy, Singapore, Venezuela, the U.S.S.R., Hong Kong, China, Egypt, Brazil, Switzerland, Spain, South Africa, Israel, and Malaysia. Exports from the United States to these countries ranged from $46.5 billion (Canada) down to $1.9 billion (Malaysia).

Other important markets for U.S. products were Sweden, Algeria, Nigeria, Colombia, Chile, New Zealand, Indonesia, Thailand, Pakistan, India, Jordan, and Turkey.

With rare exceptions there will be a market for your product in virtually all of these countries.

(For exporters outside the United States, all of these were also attractive markets, though not necessarily in the same order. And exporters from other countries can add the United States to the top of their list of possible markets.)

Acceptance of your product will vary. But at this stage keep an open mind. Don't take anything for granted or start making wrong assumptions. The international marketplace is full of surprises! California wines are selling in Europe. Who would have thought a few years ago that French bottled water would be a hot seller in bars, restaurants, and supermarkets across the United States? Or that the streets of Saudi Arabia's top cities would be jammed with cars built in Brazil? And did you know that Japanese schools are buying scales made in the United States?

In some of the top markets you will face impossible odds because of local manufacturing. But these markets are more than offset by others which are wide open to imports, with few restrictions or none at all.

The list of ordinary consumer products being successfully exported around the world includes everything you would find in a modern shopping center: linens, bathroom items, glassware and tableware, housewares, disposable diapers, lingerie, ready-to-wear clothes, costume jewelry, menswear, giftware, books, toys and games, sporting goods, home and office furniture, patio furniture, swimming pool accessories, carpeting, cosmetics, stationery items, do-it-yourself tools, greeting cards, kitchenware, refrigerators, blenders, mixers, toasters, vacuum cleaners, washing machines, dishwashers, electric can openers, canned food, soft drinks—you name it!

Department stores everywhere attract masses of buyers whenever they put on special displays of imported products. "America Week," for instance, a program sponsored by the U.S. government, is always a big event wherever it takes place, whether at Harrod's in London, Les Galeries Lafayette in Paris, or Takashimaya Department Store in Tokyo.

Some countries will accept your product exactly as it is, even in its original packaging. You would be surprised how many U.S. and British products are sold in continental Europe and other non-English speaking countries in their original English-language packaging. Of course, this does not work all the time. You may need packaging in German if you really want to go after the full potential of the West German market. Anybody seriously trying to get into the U.S. and Canadian markets will definitely have to offer packaging in English (which could be produced by the firm's North American distributor).

Some products, for example textbooks, at first glance would seem tough to export. An extreme example might be a primary school math text that was published in Japan for Japanese children and follows the official curriculum of the Japanese Ministry of Education. Yet, even for this apparently limited product there can be reasonable export markets. Consider the large Japanese communities in the United States, Canada, and Brazil, and the expanding "colonies" of Japanese businesspeople and their families stationed in all the major industrial cities in the world.

British and American textbooks are being sold to private schools around the world where English is the language of instruction. Universities are big buyers of scientific and technical books in English, and occasionally also in German and French.

Electrical requirements can be a minor problem if you produce an electrical product. Most of the world operates on 220 V 50 Hz, which for U.S. and Canadian manufacturers means changing motors. (Don't try to talk foreign customers into using a transformer. It works, but it is not a good solution. Your end users will go along with it if they want your product very badly, but they won't be too happy about it.)

Some countries, notably the Scandinavian countries, West Germany, Australia, and the United Kingdom, have tough electrical requirements that often call for changes in wiring and safety features. It won't do to tell them that your U.S. product is Underwriter Laboratories approved.

On the other hand, firms wanting to get into the North American markets have to deliver products with 110 V 60 Hz motors and comply with U.S. and Canadian requirements.

The list of "good export markets" is extensive enough to give you a choice of where to start. If you find, through research, that a highly prized market will offer you an outstanding potential but that you will have to make a change or two in your product, you will then have to figure out if the increased sales are worth the cost and effort. You may decide that at least during the early stages of your export operation— say for the first one or two years—it may be easier to seek markets which will take your product "as is."

The larger and more complex the market, the more demanding the consumers and end users may be.

This is why many European manufacturers are doing well in Europe, the Middle East, southeast Asia, and Latin America, but have made no serious effort to break into the U.S. and Canadian markets. And it is why many U.S. manufacturers have stayed away from some of the largest European markets.

A word of caution about product changes and "special models for export." From time to time you will indeed run into foreign distributors who insist that your product is unsaleable without changes to meet local needs. This may not always be true. You've run into the same problem in the domestic market. Who hasn't known dealers who promised to sell carloads if only the product was green or blue or bigger or smaller or had round knobs instead of square ones?

When foreign distributors ask you to change your product, they may just be making an excuse for not doing their job. Other distributors in the same countries might do just fine. If, however, you are convinced that there is definite market resistance to your product, shift to other markets *unless you are willing to invest in product conversion.*

The world is an enormous marketplace. My experience has been that distributors, consumers, and end users will usually insist on buying the same product you sell in your domestic market, and on occasion may resent being offered a different version.

Your type of product, then, and the extent to which you may have to adapt it to users' likes and dislikes, will dictate where you look for markets.

Some equipment and machinery categories for which there is a high demand all over the world are listed below.

Biomedical equipment
Computers and peripherals
Computer software
Electronics production and test equipment
Printing and graphic arts equipment
Electronic components
Metalworking and finishing equipment
Avionics and aviation support equipment
Process control instrumentation
Food-processing and -packing equipment
Air and water purification equipment and pollution control equipment
Laboratory instruments
Business equipment and systems
Electric energy systems
Communications equipment and systems
Building products and construction equipment
Farm machinery and equipment

Let's take a closer look at some of these categories, starting with biomedical equipment. Biotechnology is creating a vast new field with dozens of specializations. Opportunities for any product in this area will be excellent virtually everywhere in the world. It will be difficult not to find a country which does not already have a critical need for products used in emergency medical care, hazardous waste treatment and disposal, radiation therapy, biomedical electronics, biomolecular engineering, nuclear medicine, industrial hygiene, bionics, radiology, dialysis, and implants.

Needs will be widespread not only among industrialized nations but also in underdeveloped countries where funds are scarce but where the need to improve health conditions is critical. International lending agencies such as the World Bank, the Asian Development Bank, the Latin American Development Bank, the African Development Bank, and the European Economic Community are already giving high priority to financing large health improvement projects throughout the world, most of them involving multimillion-dollar procurements.

The information and telecommunications revolution is opening up markets for finished products, services, components, and software. New electronics industries are sprouting in many countries outside the traditional "industrialized" areas. Among them are Brazil, Argentina, Mexico, Singapore, Indonesia, India, Pakistan, Egypt, and Turkey.

While the growth of indigenous industries may prompt governments to shut down imports of similar products, the new manufacturers themselves become big buyers of critical components, systems, and research instruments. You may not be able to export your finished computer product to India, but Indian computer manufacturers could well be interested in importing one of your subassemblies, giving you a total sales potential much larger than you could have expected if you were marketing a finished product.

Furthermore, the sale of a locally produced system can create a market for a peripheral which has to be imported.

In fact, expanding indigenous industries in developing countries—not only in electronics but also in appliances, transportation, and many other areas—are creating a big demand for imported components, subassemblies, and other technology. Many of these nascent industries would not be able to survive without imports.

Similar situations will be created as more firms switch to computer-aided manufacturing (CAM). CAM will broaden a manufacturer's traditional line and sales potential. An appliance maker will market washing machines, but will also market the robots that manufacture, operate, and service them; the software to make the entire production system function; and the training to program and maintain machinery, computers, robots, and peripherals.

The company's combined know-how will open up business opportunities in countries which today may be closed to its washing machines. In some markets the company will sell everything: finished product, production robots, process control software, training programs, and services. In others sales will be limited to robots, software, or training services. Even countries with appliance-manufacturing plants of their own will be prospects. Brazil, for instance, unlikely to import washing machines, will be a prime prospect for CAM-related products and technology.

The same intensive worldwide demand will exist for products and services related to computer-aided design (CAD) and computer-aided engineering (CAE). Both are rapidly emerging as major new product areas. If your product is in any way related to the vast information and telecommunications area, including CAM, CAD, CAE, and robotics, you will have a wide range of possible markets to choose from.

In the United States, the seven industries with the highest predicted growth between now and 1990 are semiconductors, electronic connectors, electronic components, x-ray and electromedical equipment, computers, radio and TV, communications equipment, and lithographic platemaking devices. Products in all these categories will be highly exportable.

Office automation, already a huge part of today's $500 billion informatics market, will continue to generate demand for an endless stream of computers, peripherals, software, videodiscs, laser cards, robotics, information storage and retrieval systems, and communications systems. Big buyers of new office automation systems are governments, private industry, and hospitals in every country.

One of the biggest new markets for office automation systems in the last ten years has been Saudi Arabia, where entire new ministries and industrial complexes had to be built and equipped virtually from scratch. Imports ranged all the way from simple filing cabinets and staplers to remote information retrieval systems.

Household products are big business worldwide. They also are highly competitive business because there are so many countries now producing appliances. There are also more people earning better wages than ever and enormous new markets offering opportunities for every imaginable household product. Household automation will before long rank as high as office automation as a new product area. The world market for modern household products is no longer limited to a handful of the more affluent countries.

Opportunities are also attractive for any product related to education and training. Universities and technical schools are buying laboratories, workshops, research instruments, audiovisual systems, language labs, computers, planetariums, and closed-circuit TV systems.

In countries where local funds aren't available, universities are turning to foreign aid and international lending institutions such as the World Bank for long-term loans. Practically every major university in Latin America, as well as many in the Middle East and southeast Asia, has been a big buyer of imported equipment and instruments, its purchases financed as a rule by aid from the United States, Canada, Germany, France, Italy, Sweden, or Japan, and increasingly by the World Bank and other big international lenders. This market keeps growing year after year, providing excellent sales opportunities for many U.S., Japanese, and Western European manufacturers.

Looming even larger is the training market—both industrial and military. The high cost of training operators of sophisticated machinery and systems is creating a big need for modern simulators utilizing computer and videodisc technology. The biggest immediate markets for modern training technology are the United States, Canada, Australia, Japan, and all of Western Europe.

With such diversified worldwide opportunities before you, the first thing to do is ask yourself: *Exactly what is my product?* Of course you know what your product is, so this is a silly question! Not really. What are you really selling? What is it you can offer when you start opening up overseas markets?

Let's take an example. Assume you are a U.S. manufacturer of language laboratories. Here is what you are selling:

1. A complete language laboratory. (Obvious!)
2. Individual student recorders for language training. (Also obvious.)
3. A teacher's laboratory console which can also be used in other installations, such as a computer learning lab. (New product?)
4. A console control panel and subassemblies which can be sold to "manufacturers" in countries where you can't sell your finished product because of import restrictions.
5. Expertise in designing and planning language labs and similar learning systems. (You could sell this as a service to educational authorities, architects, and construction firms.)
6. Your brand name and dealer organization in the United States. (This is a highly valuable "product" for any manufacturer who would like to market a related but noncompeting line in the United States. And why not? If you can sell a foreign company your marketing strength, you will be adding to your profits.)

We could stretch this list and include components, peripherals, and all sorts of related products. No need to get carried away. This is just an exercise to show you how important it is to be totally flexible in your approach to international markets. (By the way, none of these five suggested "products"—including the language lab manufacturer's domestic marketing organization—constitutes a "special model" or modification of an existing product. Every one of them is a specific, existing, logical, saleable product.)

Go through this exercise with your own sales staff. Brainstorm it, if just for the hell of it. *You may have much more to sell than you think!*

Chances are that in the beginning you won't have to do much more than go out and sell your finished, packaged product. You'll be busy enough! Besides, it isn't a good idea to dilute your efforts.

You will be able to pick out several good, receptive markets for your product from the list of countries we looked at earlier in this chapter. (Our hypothetical language lab manufacturer, by the way, should find at least ten good markets for a complete system among those countries.)

But keep an open mind. Stay alert for *any* promising situation. If you are a small- or medium-size firm, one of your strongest assets is alertness.

Having clearly settled in your own mind what it is you are going to market internationally, you are ready to start developing an aggressive export sales strategy.

CHAPTER
TWO
A LOW-COST, BARE-BONES PLAN

How much are you willing to invest in international markets? What commitment are you willing to make in personnel? What can you reasonably expect to get out of overseas business?

There are three ways to get into export sales. Take your pick.

1. You can set up systematic direct sales to organizations in your own home market which together purchase billions of dollars in merchandise to be shipped overseas. In the United States this market consists of:

   - head offices of giant U.S. multinational and construction firms
   - purchasing offices in the United States of foreign department stores and governments
   - the U.S. military PX and Commissary systems
   - purchasing offices of the United Nations
   - foreign visitors

   Similar markets exist in Canada, Japan, Australia, and the Western European countries. You may already be involved in some of this lucrative business. How deeply and how professionally? Is anybody in your company going after this business systematically, or is it handled haphazardly by "whoever has the territory"? Covering this market requires no foreign travel, no major investment, no changes in or additions to your sales staff.

2. You can export your product through international trading companies and exporters who will sell it to specific countries or worldwide. There are thousands of exporters and trading companies in the United States, Canada, Western Europe, and Japan. Exporting is their business. This is a favorite option for many small firms who don't want to bother setting up their own export departments. It is *the least expensive way to export.* It isn't necessarily the best.

3. You can establish your own export sales department, no matter how small your company may be, become actively involved in overseas markets, and remain in full control of your exports.

In this chapter let's look at the first two options. Together, we'll call them the home-for-export market. The home-for-export market is a real and lucrative market, yet it is often ignored even by large international operators because it gets somewhat confused with domestic business, and it is therefore difficult (sometimes impossible) to decide who is responsible for it.

You can develop an attractive and profitable export business merely by recognizing the home-for-export market and doing what it takes to make it pay off.

DIRECT SALES.   The direct sales market is made up of many segments. Any one of them can mean big business. Look at them carefully and decide where your product fits best.

Consultants.   Architectural, engineering, agricultural, industrial, educational, data processing, telecommunications, health, transportation, and many other specialized consultants are designing projects and acting as advisors to governments, international organizations, and institutions all over the world.

In the Middle East, architectural consultants, particularly consultants from the United States, have played a key role in multibillion-dollar development projects. Virtually every important construction project in Saudi Arabia has been designed under the management of the U.S. Army Corps of Engineers, which for years has maintained a special "Middle East Division" on a mountaintop in the Virginia countryside. The Corps turns over the design of projects to prequalified U.S. consultants.

European consultants have also been very active and successful in the Middle East.

Projects designed by international consultants include schools, universities, hospitals, roads, traffic systems, government offices, military bases, airports, industrial plants, hotels, high-rise residential quarters, and complete new cities.

The specifications for construction materials, machinery, vehicles, furniture, supplies, appliances, teaching aids, instrumentation, hospital equipment, and the countless other products required by these projects are invariably based on those for products with which the consultants are familiar.

If you promote your product persistently among U.S. consultants, for instance, results may come from the most unexpected sources. A typical example: a Korean construction company wins a contract to build kindergartens in Saudi Arabia and immediately turns to a score of American manufacturers of preschool teaching aids and playgrounds whose products were specified by the U.S. firm that designed the project.

Competition for big construction projects around the world is pitting U.S., Canadian, European, and Asian companies against one another. In practically all cases, however, to promote your product among the construction companies themselves is to enter the fray too late, because the company will already have obtained specifications and equipment lists from the project designers.

It will be practically impossible for you to cover all consulting firms in your domestic territory who may have influence on foreign projects. You can start at least with the large, more obvious architectural firms. Study architectural and construction publications and newsletters; find out who is active overseas.

In the United States check also with the U.S. Army Corps of Engineers, the State Department, the Department of Commerce and the U.S. Agency for International Development. From these sources you should be able to create a good list of prospects.

International Companies.   Some 5000 U.S. companies, through overseas subsidiaries, have overseas operations including factories, branch and regional offices, and in some countries elaborate residential compounds for American personnel. (American compounds with more than 1000 residents are not unusual in the Middle East.)

There are also hundreds of European and Japanese firms with their own subsidiaries worldwide, many of them with giant operations and compounds in the Middle East and other developing areas.

Not all of these companies are committed to buy products from their own countries. Usually they do, however, for three important reasons: (a) their staff is familiar with products from the "home country"; (b) purchasing of major items can be done in the home office; (c) it is cheaper to consolidate purchasing and buy the same brand for all subsidiaries (which is why the towels, soap, ashtrays, and shampoos in some hotel chains all look the same).

The "international company" market generates massive demand for plant machinery, supplies, testing equipment, vehicles, spare parts, process control systems, training equipment, computer systems, appliances, office machines, furniture. . . . The list is endless. Requirements of residential compounds include all types of household appliances, fixtures, food and other consumables, educational equipment and materials, entertainment and leisure products. Including soap, ashtrays, and shampoo!

Draw up your own list of international companies. You can get their names from business magazines and newspapers, chambers of commerce, government. Approach their purchasing departments and find out if there is a special section for overseas procurement. Try to meet the people in charge. They may not necessarily know about your product.

The Overseas Military Market.   More than $3 billion annually in consumer goods, not all of them made in the United States, is sold by U.S. military PXs and Commissaries overseas. The bulk of this market is made up of the joint Army–Air Force PX system. PX managers abroad decide what to buy. Commissary managers are restricted by a "brand name contracts" list but still have considerable discretion. All PX and Commissary orders are placed through central headquarters in the United States.

Your best approach to the PX and Commissary market is through specialized military representatives (reps). They generally work against commissions but on occasion will buy on their own for resale. Some reps handle all types of consumer products; others are specialized.

Keep in mind that the PX and Commissary system primarily serves young consumers, that ethnic products are popular, and that purchases are invariably in bulk at top discounts.

Foreign Governments.   Governments account for substantial purchasing abroad. Big items on governments' overseas procurement lists include high technology systems, spare parts, and avionics, telecommunications, data processing, and military products.

Foreign embassies are seldom involved in actual purchasing, but do play a role in identifying and contacting manufacturers in response to requests from their countries. This activity is usually handled by the office of the commercial attaché.

Adding all foreign embassies to your mailing list will cost you a pittance. Send them your catalogs and frequent announcements. This is good public relations and can bring you good leads from time to time.

Some countries also maintain military purchasing offices attached to their embassies. If you have a product of interest to the military, send literature to the attention of the military attaché at each embassy and ask to be placed on the embassy's military vendor list.

Foreign government purchasing is also advertised regularly in government trade publications. In the United States the best source is *The Commerce Business Daily*, published by the U.S. Department of Commerce. Other countries have similar publications, released daily or weekly by their ministries of commerce, boards of trade, or other agencies involved in international trade.

Department Stores. The world's largest department stores do their buying abroad through trading companies or specialized independent purchasing firms. Some of them have their own purchasing offices.

Department stores are a big market for consumer goods and a major target of special promotions such as "America Week" or "Made in the U.S.A. Week," both sponsored by the U.S. Department of Commerce. (This type of promotion, by the way, is usually accompanied by heavy local advertising.)

The United Nations. The U.N.'s purchasing is spread out among a number of agencies. Some have headquarters in the United States, others in Europe. Any member nation can compete for this business. Each agency is specialized.

The U.N. agencies themselves do not generate the same magnitude of procurement as do projects financed by organizations such as the World Bank. The U.N. agencies often act as advisors rather than actual buyers.

A good example is UNESCO (the United Nations Educational, Scientific, and Cultural Organization). A $50 million educational development project in Zaire, for instance, may be jointly financed by the government of Zaire, the African Development Bank, and the World Bank, but designed (including product specifications) by UNESCO advisors. Purchasing and contracting will be done by the Ministry of Education of Zaire, most likely with advice from the same UNESCO team which helped write the specs.

Other U.N. agencies operate in much the same manner. A notable exception is UNICEF (the United Nations Children's Fund). UNICEF maintains in Copenhagen a large warehouse with substantial stocks of basic equipment and teaching aids for primary schools in developing Third World countries. UNICEF ships from Copenhagen and issues replacement orders as stocks are depleted.

In the United States all UNICEF buying is done through the U.N.'s New York headquarters. To qualify as a vendor you must submit catalogs and specs, and sometimes samples for evaluation. UNICEF has very strict requirements governing the types of products included on its basic list and carried in its regular inventory.

Foreign Visitors. Foreign visitors do not always generate immediate sales, but their visits often lead to important business. These visitors may include potential overseas distributors, end users, government officials, buying delegations, foreign aid project directors, and consultants. Regardless of where they come from, be prepared to welcome them. Alert your telephone operator, receptionist, and secretaries to be particularly courteous and helpful.

You can encourage foreign visitors by periodically sending announcements to exporters, trading companies, foreign embassies, and government foreign aid offices. Include catalogs, details of your product line, and information on how to get to your office or plant. If you are not within easy reach of a major airport or station, you may want to offer to pick up important visitors provided you are given enough advance notice.

It is common practice in most countries to send out specialists to visit the offices and plants of manufacturers around the world before writing specifications for a major project.

TRADING COMPANIES AND EXPORTERS.

Trading companies and exporters constitute another portion of the home-for-export market. Here, however, you will be dealing not with end users who have offices in your home territory, but with organizations who will buy your product on behalf of foreign buyers, or who will help you sell your product abroad.

Trading companies deal both ways: They promote exports as well as imports. They range in size from giant operations like Japan's Mitsui to small, independent agencies which act mainly as buyers on behalf of a few large companies in a particular country. The amount of business generated by trading companies can be quite staggering. Japanese trading firms buy more than $15 billion annually in U.S. goods for export to Japan.

Since the top trading companies are Japanese, it will be worth it for you to look into them as possible openings into the Japanese market. One of the functions of these firms is to promote and export Japanese goods around the world. But the other, equally important, function is to import on behalf of Japanese clients who lack the know-how, facilities, budgets, or inclination to do it on their own. (There are, indeed, Japanese firms that make a living out of selling imported products, and who therefore need experienced organizations to find sources for them abroad.)

In Japan, the clients of Japanese trading firms include national distributors; wholesalers; jobbers; retail chains; department stores; manufacturers who need imported parts, machinery, or supplies; and specialized sales organizations.

Needless to say, a Japanese trading company is often the best outlet for a small Japanese manufacturer who wants to crack some of the biggest world markets, particularly the United States, Canada, West Germany, France, and the United Kingdom. But to date most Japanese manufacturers are not actively involved in overseas business. The main source of their export apathy is their inability to communicate except in Japanese.

The largest Japanese trading companies usually maintain offices in New York, Chicago, Houston, Los Angeles, San Francisco, London, Brussels, Dusseldorf, Milan, Paris, Copenhagen, Hong Kong, and many other major business centers. Purchasing is assigned to specialized departments by product.

A common criticism of Japanese trading companies is that they are not really promoters, merely buyers and sellers. This is not entirely true. Trading companies do make a serious effort in some cases to promote a Japanese product abroad or a non-Japanese product in Japan. The problem is that a trading company may carry quite literally thousands of products and cannot possibly promote every one of them aggressively. Usually a Japanese end user will identify a foreign product and then send an order to a trading company. The trading company will purchase the merchandise, then arrange payment, shipment, and delivery to the end user in Japan.

Merely being represented by a large trading company is meaningless and will not in itself generate orders. The sight of the trading company's fifty-story headquarters in the Shinjuku section of Tokyo may be quite impressive, but the individual charged with handling your account may occupy a small cubbyhole of an office on the thirty-seventh floor, five corridors removed from the nearest elevator, with minimal staff and facilities.

On the other hand, making foreign trading companies aware of your product is good business, as long as you don't give away territorial exclusivities. Build up a list of foreign trading companies with offices in your domestic territory. Get names and addresses from embassies (starting with the Japanese). Send catalogs, prices, and specifications.

European trading companies are not as numerous as Japanese trading firms, but a number of them operate actively worldwide and can help open up new markets. Several of them are strong in southeast Asia, with offices in Taipei, Singapore, Hong Kong, Jakarta, Manila, and Kuala Lumpur. They deal in products from any source—as long as there is a market for them. Some have been in the area more than a century.

A variation of the trading company is the exporter. Exporters are independent agencies who buy merchandise from manufacturers or wholesalers and ship it abroad. There are some 6000 independent exporters in the United States alone, about as many in Western Europe, and more than 2000 in Japan.

In the United States, the Department of Commerce has a directory of several hundred export agencies. Similar lists are published by government trade organizations in all major industrialized countries.

Exporters play a key role in international marketing. Cultivate them carefully and selectively even if you plan to set up or expand your own export department. Exporters are helpful in developing sales in countries where you are not particularly active. They can be an asset when they carry a fair variety of products similar to but not in direct competition with yours, since if they add yours they have additional products to sell to their established overseas agents and end users.

Exporters may specialize in a narrow range of products or be open to any interesting deal. Some exporters may have traveling reps who either cover many countries regularly or concentrate on a few countries where they have good connections. Others may do minimal travel and promotion, acting essentially as order takers who work on narrow profit margins.

Exporters usually buy on their own accounts. You ship to the exporter's warehouse, and are paid under normal domestic billing.

The biggest disadvantage in dealing with an exporter is that you probably will not be in control. Some exporters may try to get alternative quotations from your competitors, and if they are determined to offer your product and you refuse to quote prices, may try to get around you by contacting one of your domestic dealers or wholesalers.

Your policy toward exporters depends on your product. If you don't need after-sales service and you market your line on an open, nonexclusive basis, you should develop a broad list of exporters and keep them supplied with catalogs and net export prices. *Your list need not be limited to exporters in your immediate area.*

There is no reason why a U.S. or a Canadian firm with an open-line product should not also try to offer it to exporters in Japan and Europe—or why Japanese and European companies cannot try to do business with U.S. and Canadian exporters.

Otherwise, deal with exporters gingerly. Evaluate their capabilities, credit, and experience before submitting quotations. Decide whether you want to work through a few well-chosen ones or throw your line wide open to one and all.

A slight variation on the exporter theme is the export management company (EMC). The EMC is an exporter who undertakes to actively promote your product in one or more countries, travels abroad regularly, and supposedly has expertise in specific markets and types of products. The EMC will require an exclusive arrangement for a particular territory; an EMC may work with you on a commission basis (you do the billing and shipping to the overseas account) or purchase from you for resale in the territory.

EMCs usually will carry several noncompeting lines in the same broad product area. This allows them to offer a measure of specialization. Wise EMCs will try to do a good job with all lines carried rather than put too much effort into any single one. This is a good way to make the most of their investment in travel expenses, time, and overhead.

An important function of EMCs is to pioneer products of companies still unknown in international markets. The expertise they have accumulated over the years gives them a good idea of favorable countries, market segments, and potential agents. The best EMCs are not, therefore, order takers waiting for end users to discover your product.

EMCs with established networks of overseas agents will take on new lines mainly with reference to the capabilities of their agents. This of course saves you a lot of time. You don't have to go into extensive market research, and you gain the advantage of an existing marketing organization at little or no cost to you.

To their overseas agents, EMCs and exporters offer the big advantage of one-stop shopping. They carry a fair range of noncompeting lines and will also handle agents' inquiries and orders for other products. The agent outside the United States who works with an EMC in New York, for instance, in effect has the benefit of a full-time buying office in the United States. This gives the agent a wider product line to sell and therefore a much broader market to go after in his or her own country. The price the agent pays for this benefit is higher merchandise costs, since EMCs must add their profits to the manufacturer's factory price.

But things are not all that neat and rosy. EMCs have to keep looking over their shoulders and stay two jumps ahead of the game for their own self-protection. Ideally an EMC wants to handle enough lines to avoid excessive dependence on any single manufacturer. To represent a large, well-known domestic manufacturer is always a feather in an EMC's cap, but can be very risky. A smart EMC will always try to carry a good balance of different products, because he or she can never be sure when one of them may be lost.

Here are three reasons why an EMC may lose a particular line: (a) not selling enough; (b) the manufacturing company has decided to do its own international marketing; (c) selling beyond the manufacturer's expectations.

The first reason is obvious. The second and third usually go together. An EMC is probably about to lose a client when an officer or director of the manufacturing company raises the question: "Why don't we take over the job ourselves and earn the extra profit?"

If you now work through an EMC or plan to do so, *you will yourself raise this question sooner or later!* Scratch a big multinational today, and you may discover that way back it got its start overseas through the efforts of an EMC!

Also dangerous to EMCs are the successful overseas distributors who do such a good job selling your product that they begin to wonder why they cannot deal directly with you, bypass the EMC, and get themselves a better deal.

You, the manufacturer, will find it difficult to resist the temptation of added profits if you cut the EMCs out, or of the extra sales you may be able to generate if your overseas distributors can buy at a lower price.

These are facts of life. No amount of loyalty to EMCs (or vice versa) is going to last forever.

Don't blame EMCs, therefore, if for their own protection they keep looking for new lines, particularly from small, inexperienced manufacturers, and aim at developing a high volume of business spread out among various products—and not just yours.

One or more EMCs may give you easy access to a number of lucrative foreign markets. First you must decide what specific role you want the EMC to play; then try to find the company or companies that best fit your needs. Check references. Ask questions. What countries are covered? How many lines carried? Major manufacturers represented? How long in business? How many people on the road?

If you sell a consumer-oriented product on an open, nonexclusive basis with no protection to anybody, you should encourage exporters and EMCs equally by building up a mailing list and bombarding them frequently with product announcements, price updates, and other promotion.

Don't underestimate the capabilities of exporters and EMCs. Work with them aggressively. Follow up frequently and don't just sit back and await results.

Remind exporters, EMCs, and trading companies of your existence! Make noise!

If you have to deal with them selectively and you can't avoid talking about territories and exclusivity, memorize these two vital rules:

1. Don't be in a hurry to give away big chunks of the world.
2. Avoid long-range commitments.

You may already have identified some countries which you would like to handle on your own. If you haven't, you will very soon! Either save them for yourself, or let an EMC cover them with the understanding that eventually you may want to move in. This may force the EMC to neglect these markets and concentrate elsewhere, but at least it will keep everybody honest. It will be best for both of you if the EMC focuses on territories you don't see yourself moving into for several years.

If you should decide to develop your *entire* export business through exporters and EMCs, try to keep your hand on the tiller. Take a serious interest in overseas markets, ask for reports, discuss promotional schemes and new approaches. Show that you really care about this business and consider it important.

Assign specific responsibility to an individual in your company who will identify and systematically promote sales to all segments of the home-for-export market.

Don't give the job to a domestic sales manager.

Anybody whose prime target is domestic sales is not going to take exports very seriously and will cover the home-for-export market whenever time allows. In other words, never! Lists of exporters will quickly be filed away and forgotten.

Create a new position—an export salesperson who reports directly to your top marketing V.P. or the CEO. If you expand and create your own full-fledged export department, this person could become your export manager or an overseas regional manager.

Lines of responsibility will not always be neat and straight. Overlaps will be inevitable, and you will not always have a straight answer for who should be doing what and when. For instance, if you have a government sales department, you may already be doing some promotion among military PX and Commissary buyers. This may or may not be aimed also at overseas installations.

Domestic dealers or salespersons may already be calling on U.N. offices, foreign embassies, international construction companies, and consultants, but not as part of a systematic, well-conceived marketing plan.

The extent to which you will want to go into the home-for-export market *without the support of overseas agents* will also depend on your type of product. If your product requires installation and maintenance by trained personnel, you could be in serious trouble if you don't know where a shipment is going.

When you make a sale to a foreign government or a U.N. agency, for instance, you will know the destination. But suppose a multinational firm places an order through its regular procurement channels, and you don't even know that the requisition came from abroad?

There are three ways to handle a sales situation which requires technical installation and training.

1. You can send a technician at your expense, if the value of the order allows it, to make the installation and train one of your customer's technicians. (On a $200,000 sale, for instance, $3000 for travel expenses should not be prohibitive.) If the unit value is low, you will have to charge extra for your services. If the customer refuses to pay, drop the business.
2. You can train the customer's technician at your U.S. plant free of charge. This is a common approach in sales of sophisticated equipment such as military systems, telecommunications, and hospital instruments.
3. You can refuse the order. Tough to accept, but in the long run your best bet even when buyers insist they can do the job. Usually they can't, and you end up having to send one of your own people to clean up, at your expense.

If eventually you set up overseas agents, some of your home-for-export sales may cause conflicts between them and domestic dealers or salespeople, unless your product requires no after-sales service and is sold on an open basis without protection or exclusivity to anybody at home or abroad.

For instance, you make a sale to a construction firm for shipment to Indonesia. Your Indonesian agent claims that he had called on the local branch of the firm. A domestic saleswoman claims the sale because the customer's head office is in her territory. You don't want to antagonize either the Indonesian or the domestic saleswoman. You don't want to discourage promotional efforts at either end. You may never know who really played the key role in clinching the sale.

How do you handle this can of worms?

You play it by ear!

I have yet to find a company with a formula that makes everybody happy in this type of situation. You can divide the overall commission in two parts: two-thirds or more for any required after-sales service and maintenance, payable to the Indonesian agent, since he will have to look after the equipment; the balance of the sales commission should be split between the Indonesian agent and your domestic saleswoman. Or you can try any number of other similar formulas.

(If the Indonesian is not responsible for service but under the terms of your agreement is entitled to a sales commission, you divide the commission between him and the domestic person.)

Let's make it a bit more complicated.

Suppose you appointed three nonexclusive agents in Indonesia and all three claimed the account? Or suppose the contact in Indonesia was made directly by your own traveling regional manager? Or your domestic salesperson never really did any business with the customer's home office but nipped over at the last moment when she got word that a big order was in the offing?

There are no hard and fast rules for settling any of these squabbles. You will run into them as often as you do in your own home market.

HOW MUCH WILL IT COST ? If you can sell your product in the home-for-export market without any fear of after-sales problems such as installation and maintenance, you can run a tight and profitable operation on very little money. Figure on the costs shown in the table below.

Full-time salesperson	$35,000
Travel to major cities every three months for personal calls on exporters, EMCs, and trading companies	6,000
Monthly mailings	1,000
Total	$42,000

These figures are based on travel within the United States. The costs should be about the same if you are a European manufacturer, assuming that you are reaching exporters not just in your own country but elsewhere throughout the continent.

If you are a Japanese manufacturer, you have an advantage because exporters and trading companies are all overwhelmingly concentrated in Tokyo and Osaka.

Mailings should be to a select list of no more than 1000 addresses. The list, again, depends on what type of product you are offering. For a highly specialized product you will be able to narrow down the list considerably.

If the salesperson comes from your existing sales force and does not have to be replaced (try dividing the territory among the remaining salespeople), the investment will be negligible.

Even if you opt for this low-cost, bare bones type of export plan, you would be wise to consider some overseas travel to make personal contact with end users and agents and also to attend major international trade fairs, conventions, and seminars. One or two trips a year may be enough. Each trip could be short, no more than a week or ten days.

This minimal amount of travel is important, not merely as a show of support to the exporters and EMCs who are promoting your line abroad, but also to give you a personal feel for overseas markets, your competition, and market conditions.

The more you are exposed to overseas markets, the more control you will have over your exporters and EMCs.

Developing a strong home-for-export promotion is good business, but don't lull yourself into thinking that this is all you really want out of international marketing. You can do much better!

Lucrative as it may be, look at the home-for-export market only as a first step, because it really isn't all that difficult to pick out and develop international markets that pay off!

THREE

HOW TO FIND MARKETS THAT PAY OFF

In 1928 my father was sent to Brazil by a Swedish manufacturer of household appliances with a simple directive: "Get some door-to-door salesmen and start ringing doorbells."

Market research would have shown that the price of a floor polisher or vacuum cleaner in Brazil was twice as much as a servant's yearly wage, that most Brazilian middle class families had at least two servants to do their cooking and cleaning, and that no salesperson would ever be allowed into a home for a demonstration. In short, any direct sales effort would be a total waste of time.

Within days of getting off the ship my father was labeled by local businessmen as yet another crazy foreigner who couldn't tell the difference between black beans and smorgasbord. Door-to-door selling in Brazil? Preposterous!

Armed with missionary zeal and five years' smashing success leading door-to-door salesmen in Italy—where it had also been said that it couldn't be done—my father wasted no time evaluating the market or assessing economic conditions. Instead, he rented a small office, and bought an expensive desk, a deep leather armchair, and a box of the best available Bahia cigars. Dozens of men responded to a newspaper ad promising instant and unlimited success in "a challenging new business venture."

The interviews were simple. No forms to fill out. A brief chat revealed if the candidate was aggressive or timid, pleasant or pushy, easy with words or tongue-tied.

Anyone who passed the test was gently pushed into the depths of the leather chair and offered a cigar. His captive audience of one thus safely cornered and bedazzled, my father proceeded to make his pitch with the contagious and vigorous enthusiasm that would keep his sales forces hypnotized and rarin' to go until he retired thirty years later.

In a few days he had forty green but eager salesmen ringing doorbells up and down Copacabana and Ipanema. Two years later Brazil was competing successfully in the company's worldwide sales contests, and it remained a consistent trophy winner until the outbreak of World War II.

International marketing in the 1920s and 1930s was a lot different than it is today, and success often depended more on faith and enthusiasm than on research and analysis. Fired up salespeople like my father saw themselves as upholders of a simple and straightforward principle: get out there, do your job, never mind the odds.

Manufacturing was limited to a few industrialized countries. There were few problems of foreign exchange and international payments. Import controls were rare, and business procedures and regulations in most countries were not too complicated.

Try now to export a household appliance to Brazil, and it will take you only two or three phone calls to learn that the country produces refrigerators, freezers, washing machines, vacuum cleaners, floor polishers, irons, toasters, blenders, electric can openers, and automatic potato peelers—and that imports of any of these items are not allowed.

Establishing yourself in markets around the world today requires much more than gut feeling, enthusiasm, good cigars, and a rousing pep talk. Conditions vary widely from country to country. You can no longer afford to plunge into world markets without serious research to identify countries where you have a chance of success.

However, finding markets that pay off is not a complex job. Ample information is readily available, usually free of charge, from government and other sources. In most cases it will not be precisely what you are looking for, and you will have to refine and interpret the data on your own. But this does not call for any particular expertise, just a measure of common sense and prudence.

If you fail to do adequate market research, you can easily end up in the wrong markets, and this in turn could cause you to turn sour on international marketing as a mistake you should have avoided. You will then either retreat back to the domestic market or maintain a lukewarm, ineffectual, sloppy international operation—and that is no way to run a business.

Done systematically and thoroughly, market research can help you identify markets and develop fairly accurate projections. If you are already involved in overseas markets, you may be able to improve your sales and profits substantially by going back to basics and taking a fresh look at the entire world marketplace. Are the countries you initially targeted really the best ones? Or have you overlooked a prize plum or two?

GATHERING THE DATA. Eventually a personal computer and telephone line will be the main tools for accessing international market data. But until enough databases are available, you will have to do the initial tedious job of digging up statistics and shaping them into a format that makes sense to you.

The best source of international trade statistics is the government. Most of the research data needed by U.S. firms is available from the U.S. Department of Commerce (DOC). Similar government organizations in other countries offer the same service to local manufacturers and suppliers.

Government export figures are the basis of all statistical market analysis. Product categories, however, are frequently large, and you may have to do a bit of additional digging on your own to come up with more precise figures.

Official statistics usually give only a partial picture. Department of Commerce figures will tell you how much the U.S. panty hose industry exported worldwide and to which countries, but if you want to know how much Australia, for instance, imported from all sources and how much was locally manufactured, you will have to look up Australian panty hose statistics. You can do this at the Australian desk of DOC or at the Australian Embassy in Washington. (As a rule, DOC will have the latest foreign government import-export statistics.)

To make government statistics more meaningful to their members, some trade associations have foreign departments and on occasion hire consultants to do detailed overseas market studies and to develop statistics for more narrowly defined product categories. Your own association may be helpful in refining your initial set of government figures.

Before you start looking up statistics, you need to know that some countries have done away with product descriptions and switched to international trade codes. If you deal in two or three products, this is no problem. If you have to look up twenty or thirty items, you may have to constantly shift back and forth from a reference list.

There are three international codes: the Standard International Classification (SIC), the Standard International Trade Classification (SITC), and the Brussels Tariff Nomenclature (BTN). The United States uses a fourth system, Tariff Schedules of the United States, to report its own import-export figures.

A "harmonized system" now being developed internationally among industrialized countries may go into effect in 1987, clearing up much of the current confusion and making identification of product categories much easier and quicker.

Early in your research you should get into the habit of using product codes. Eventually they will come in handy when you are entering your research data into computerized databases and spreadsheet projections. By computerizing data, you make it easier to standardize research, reporting, and forecasting procedures, particularly as new data are culled from reports submitted by your regional managers, overseas agents, support staff, and consultants.

Statistics from the major industrialized countries, particularly the United States, Canada, Australia, Japan, the United Kingdom, West Germany, Italy, and France, are usually broken down into narrow product classifications. Figures are fairly recent, seldom more than six to nine months old.

Reports from smaller countries are of limited value because figures are for broad, and therefore meaningless, product classifications. However, these reports give you at least two important items of information: size of the country's exports or imports, and their destination or source.

Some countries' statistics may be two or three years old. Which is why, for instance, you will get a much better picture of Bolivia's imports of optical binocular microscopes by looking up exports to Bolivia from the United States, Japan, West Germany, East Germany, and Switzerland than by referring to Bolivia's own statistics.

The minimum data you need before you start putting together a list of tentative target countries include:

1. Exports of your particular product for the last three or four years, with breakdown by country of destination
2. Country share of leading markets
3. Exports by other leading manufacturing countries (with breakdown by country of destination)
4. Total imports of leading importing countries

For a start let us look again at the top twenty-five markets for U.S. products in 1984. They are listed in Table 2.

To the data in Table 2, we should add a few more countries which are also important markets for U.S. exporters: Sweden, Denmark, Norway, Finland, Colombia, Chile, Argentina, New Zealand, Indonesia, the Philippines, Thailand, India, Pakistan, Jordan, Algeria, Morocco, and Nigeria.

The priority markets on which you will focus for the initial phase of your export operations will be among those on these two lists.

(If you are not a U.S. manufacturer, the United States, the most attractive, if also the toughest, export market for manufacturers throughout the world, must obviously be placed at the very top of your list.)

You may want to make your starting list even longer, but all you will accomplish is to clutter it up unnecessarily. Much can be said for the strategy of going after small, out of the way countries which everybody ignores and quietly cultivating a cozy, private market. But this is expensive and risky, and you cannot afford any wild adventures

Table 2
Twenty-Five Largest Importers of U.S. Goods (1984)

Country	Total Sales (in billions of dollars)*
1. Canada	46.5
2. Japan	23.6
3. United Kingdom	12.2
4. Mexico	12.0
5. West Germany	9.1
6. Netherlands	7.6
7. France	6.0
8. South Korea	6.0
9. Saudi Arabia	5.6
10. Belgium & Luxembourg	5.3
11. Taiwan	5.0
12. Australia	4.8
13. Italy	4.4
14. Singapore	3.7
15. Venezuela	3.4
16. U.S.S.R.	3.3
17. Hong Kong	3.1
18. China	3.0
19. Egypt	2.7
20. Brazil	2.6
21. Switzerland	2.6
22. Spain	2.6
23. South Africa	2.3
24. Israel	2.2
25. Malaysia	1.9

* As reported by the U.S. Department of Commerce

at this early stage. Several small countries can add up to attractive sales, but for a company just getting started, sales success will depend on sales to fairly substantial markets.

Developing sales in a small country can take just as much of your time and effort as going after a large one with 100 times the potential!

For U.S. manufacturers, Canada is quite clearly a unique and special market. By considering it as an adjunct to the U.S. domestic market, you give it the status of a "regional" territory, in which case Canada ends up being given lower priority than the U.S. northeast or west coast areas.

On the other hand, to put Canada in the same category as any other export market is to ignore the many things this market has in common with the U.S. market and the relative ease with which business can be done across the U.S.-Canadian border. Promotion, travel, selling, shipping, and payment have more in common with U.S. domestic marketing than with regular export procedures.

This neither domestic nor international status often results in Canada not being given the importance it deserves. The answer for a U.S. firm is to put Canadian marketing under a separate export division whose sole concern is to develop a strong marketing organization in that country.

Canadian firms trying to do business in the United States should do the same, establishing a separate U.S. export marketing division.

The same special status should be given by a European manufacturer to neighboring markets, even though the similarities and ties between them are not nearly as strong as those between the United States and Canada. A West German manufacturer, for instance, should treat France, Austria, Switzerland, and the Low Countries differently from markets in the Middle East and southeast Asia.

For any manufacturer, Japan is a special case. It is unquestionably a top market. It is difficult, but not closed or impossible. Too many North American and European firms are intimidated by what they see as unbeatable odds against penetrating the Japanese market. As a result, they don't even make an effort to see what this market can offer.

Other large, stable, and affluent markets for any manufacturer are Western Europe and Australia. They are also the most sought after by your competitors and offer highly developed marketing and distribution facilities. Your final target list may include four or five of these countries. They could eventually account for the bulk of your exports.

Unless you have a highly developed export department, don't be too eager to seek sales in the U.S.S.R. and China. (The same goes for most of Eastern Europe.) These are all very difficult markets to crack. To do so requires much time and patience, and often lengthy negotiations with state authorities and trading companies. Worthwhile, yes. But not when you have a number of other easier choices before you.

The most industrially developed countries of the Third World, countries where many imports are either banned or drastically curtailed to protect local industry, are India, South Korea, Brazil, Argentina, and Mexico. They produce the widest range of products, including high technology such as sophisticated electronics, computers, and space systems.

These countries are difficult markets for consumer products, but at the same time they are expanding their purchases of components and subassemblies for their industries; they also buy scientific and medical equipment and instruments as well as many other advanced products.

The more industrialized a developing country becomes, the greater its need for new technology. For these markets, products with the best potential are those which are expensive to produce and do not lend themselves to mass production.

Other countries with expanding local industry (mainly consumer) are Thailand, Malaysia, the Philippines, Pakistan, Indonesia, Chile, Colombia, and Venezuela. Most of them are good markets for many types of consumer products from Japan, North America, and Europe.

Mexico should be a high-priority market for any U.S. or Canadian manufacturer.

Saudi Arabia is an excellent market for consumer, agricultural, industrial, health, office, military, education, or training products. Its neighbors along the Arabian Gulf—Kuwait, Bahrein, Qatar, the United Arab Emirates, and the Sultanate of Oman—are all affluent but small markets which take up as much marketing time, investment, and effort as larger countries. You may not want to include them in your list of first-phase priority markets, but keep them in mind for later, when you are well established in Saudi Arabia and have reason to go back to the area frequently. You should also consider Jordan and Egypt when you start expanding into the Middle East.

The entire Middle East is an importing area, with little local manufacturing of any kind.

Taiwan, Singapore, and Hong Kong are unique markets open to imports. Conditions are extremely competitive, but keep in mind that although local manufacturing is highly developed, it is not all-encompassing. Take a look at these three markets selectively.

South Africa, Algeria, Morocco, and Nigeria are the four top markets in the African continent (Egypt is usually considered part of the Middle East). Conditions vary substantially from one to the other. Product needs in all of them are quite diverse. Algeria is making a major investment in development projects, particularly technical education and health.

The list of countries receiving loans from organizations such as the World Bank keeps increasing as more territories become independent. Except for the oil-rich countries of the Middle East, the list includes most of Africa, south and southeast Asia, the Pacific area, and Latin America.

Some of the largest recipients of World Bank and other economic assistance for development are Indonesia, Thailand, Korea, Pakistan, Egypt, Nigeria, and Brazil. However, keep in mind that internationally financed projects don't offer opportunities for steady, month after month imports.

You should not select a country as a first-priority market purely on the strength of internationally financed development projects. You will need more than that to make a market pay off. Big projects are a sink or swim proposition.

The U.S. market constitutes a particularly attractive but somewhat frightening market for manufacturers outside the United States. It is usually seen as overwhelming, demanding, complex, and extremely costly to get into. The vast territory and large population of the United States have discouraged many European firms from getting into this market. They just don't know where to start. There are any number of firms throughout Europe with active and profitable operations in southeast Asia, Africa, and Latin America (in addition to Europe itself), and virtually no sales in the United States.

Others have approached the United States the same way they would approach any other market: paying short visits, appointing an "agent" to look after the entire country, and making no effort to find out exactly what makes the market tick.

The United States, however, has become today the world's biggest market for imports. A far cry from the early 1950s, when I was trying to sell European office machines in midtown Manhattan and kept running into a solid wall of resistance. Our toughest objection to overcome was: "No thank you. We buy American!"

Ignoring the United States is a mistake still made by many manufacturers and suppliers abroad. The top 1984 sources of exports to the United States (not including countries that are predominantly oil exporters, such as Saudi Arabia and Venezuela) are listed in Table 3.

Export-import data from all countries are readily available from government sources, including embassies. Becoming familiar with the many services and publications offered by these sources is a must. Most of it is free or available at nominal cost.

The U.S. Department of Commerce, in addition to carrying U.S. trade statistics, also has the most recent trade reports from countries all over the world, as do equivalent government departments in most other industrialized countries. These are usually located at "country desks," where a visitor can also obtain other data on the particular country.

As a U.S. manufacturer you should visit the country desk at DOC handling each of the major exporting countries in your product group to obtain the latest information on their exports.

When you visit government offices in the course of your research, find out what plans there may be for official, government sponsored events and exhibitions abroad in your product category. These promotions are usually preceded by a fair amount of research by consultants hired by government, and will give you a very good clue as to which countries are seen as having a good potential for your product. *Take advantage of this free research!*

Ask also for information on any promotions which may have taken place within the last year or two. Research and reports produced before

Table 3
Chief Exporters of Goods to the United States (1984)

Country	Total Sales (in billions of dollars)
1. Canada	66.9
2. Japan	60.4
3. Mexico	18.3
4. West Germany	17.8
5. Taiwan	16.1
6. United Kingdom	15.0
7. South Korea	10.0
8. Hong Kong	8.9
9. France	8.5
10. Italy	8.5
11. Brazil	8.5
12. Netherlands	4.3
13. Singapore	4.1
14. Sweden	3.4
15. China	3.4
16. Belgium & Luxembourg	3.3
17. Switzerland	3.2
18. Australia	2.9
19. Malaysia	2.8
20. India	2.7
21. Spain	2.6

and after these events by government sources and consultants should be still valid and definitely valuable.

Visits to foreign embassies can also be useful; they may reveal information and opportunities you have overlooked. Most embassies maintain commercial reference libraries which are open to businesspeople regardless of nationality or of whether you want to buy from or sell to the particular country.

Japanese and Italian manufacturers interested in doing business in the United States, for instance, can visit the commercial libraries maintained by the U.S. embassies in Tokyo and Rome or the U.S. consulates in major Japanese and Italian cities and obtain information on distributors, competition, and other aspects of U.S. market conditions.

U.S. businesspeople interested in Japan and Italy can do the same by visiting the Japanese and Italian embassies and consulates in the United States.

When you visit the embassy of a country which is also an exporter of your type of product, find out also about any special international promotions the country may have sponsored around the world or has in mind for the next year or two. This will give you an idea of where that country's industry is concentrating its efforts.

ORGANIZING THE DATA.   What to do with import-export statistics and how to make sure they are put to good use—in other words, how to convert them into a practical tool of international marketing—has always been a problem. Invariably this type of information is so boring that it is filed away and seldom used.

If you are able to put your statistics into simple computer spreadsheets your task will be enormously simplified and you will end up with a format which allows you quick updating and retrieval at any time, as well as a simple formula from which to work out projections.

Total Exports.   To analyze export markets it should be enough to identify the top six to ten exporting countries in your product group. Look up, for instance, total exports of the United States, Canada, Japan, West Germany, the United Kingdom, and France. From this you can get an idea of world-market shares.

If you compare figures for the last three or four years, you will be able to establish trends. If you carry this a step further and work out growth or shrinkage ratios, you can also create rough projections for the next three or four years.

In the United States, information on the top exporters can be obtained by visiting the various country desks at DOC or the countries' embassies in Washington.

Once entered on a computer spreadsheet, this sort of data can be easily updated every three months, whenever new official statistics are made available by the top exporting countries.

Destination of Exports. For each exporting country draw up a list of the countries of destination. Figure out what percentage of the exporting country's product went to each country of destination. A quick study of these lists will reveal the best and worst markets for each exporting country. If you want to make the analysis more elaborate, you can go to the trouble of figuring out how each country of destination performed over the last three or four years.

This information can also be handled quickly and effectively if you enter it into a computer spreadsheet format. However, a word of caution: These lists will become too cumbersome if you include too many countries. The number of exporting countries can usually be kept down to five or six—and this list will probably take care of the bulk of world exports in your product line.

On the other hand, you can easily end up with a list of 100 or more countries of destination. Any statistical analysis of more than 20 countries is difficult to manipulate. Frankly, you don't need it. Statistics have a way of getting complex and unmanageable. The smaller the number of countries you list, the easier it will be for you to update the information and put it to work for you.

Country-by-Country Imports. You can also organize import-export data in the form of a more-detailed analysis of a particular country's imports. That is, you can look at imports from the viewpoint of the importing and not the exporting country. This is a good way to see how a particular country has shaped up over the years and where it has done most of its buying.

To be useful this information should cover a period of at least three or four years. If the importing country is also a manufacturer of your product, you should add to your tabulation some data on local production and determine what share of the total market it covers.

Gathering and evaluating this information requires considerable work and initiative when countries report import-export figures in broad categories or when reports are delayed a year or more. The best sources of information will be the exporting countries rather than the countries of destination. For instance, if you are trying to compile total Venezuelan imports for your product, it may be wiser to find out what Venezuela imported from the major exporting countries and create a Venezuelan trade profile from these data.

End User Population.   You may want to back up your trade statistics with an evaluation of the size of specific overseas markets. Government and embassy sources will be helpful, as will trade associations and chambers of commerce. Specialized government agencies will also have significant data. For instance, if you sell transportation equipment, the U.S. Department of Transportation or a ministry of transportation in another country is likely to have data on types of end users, standards, and equipment used.

CRITERIA FOR TARGET COUNTRIES.   Having gathered your basic

statistics, you must now decide what basic requirements a country must meet in order to qualify as a specific target for your particular product. In addition to special criteria related to your type of product, consider the following general ones.

Volume Potential.   Your object is to seek the highest sales with the least investment, promotion, and personnel. Other factors being favorable, it therefore makes sense to go after those countries which have been importing the largest quantities of your type of product.

High Market Share.   If U.S. exports have a significant share of a particular country's market for a particular type of product, U.S. manufacturers should have a reasonable advantage there.

Location.   You will save travel time and expenses if you can concentrate on initial-priority markets that are in the same general region.

Language.   For U.S., Canadian, Australian, and British manufacturers there is definitely an advantage in choosing countries where English is an official or widely understood language.

Steady Import History. Be wary of countries with erratic import histories. You cannot rely on them year to year. A sudden burst of imports may have resulted from a massive international loan for one or several projects, creating a distorted picture of a country's import volume. A great year could easily be followed by a long dry spell.

Also question any country showing a decline in imports from a particular country even though the overall total still keeps it among the top importers on your list. This decline may be caused by increasing competition from other exporting countries or from local manufacturing, or by a steady depletion of foreign exchange reserves and tighter import restrictions.

Stability. Be particularly careful of any countries which may have gone through major economic or political upheavals in the last few months. This will not yet be reflected in official trade statistics.

COMPLETING YOUR RESEARCH.   When your list is down to twelve to fifteen countries, try to talk to people who can give you information about local conditions and outlook based on their own experience.

Your trade association is a good place to start. Some of its officers may have personal knowledge of these countries. They may also refer you to manufacturers of noncompeting products who may be happy to lend a hand. This sort of advice is by far the best. In the course of an informal chat you may pick up priceless information on competition and hints on potential agents. You may even decide to restore to your list one or two countries you had already discarded, and cross out some which are not as promising as statistics may have indicated.

Major banks with foreign departments are a good source of information on economic and political conditions, payment procedures, and shipping problems.

For a U.S. businessperson a two- or three-day visit to Washington is a good investment at this point. Call on the various country desks at DOC, and call at foreign embassies. But don't allow yourself to be carried away by enthusiastic DOC officials. Some of them view export promotion as an idealistic crusade to "sell America," and may ignore the truth about conditions and opportunities in certain countries. At the other extreme are those extra-cautious officials who go strictly by the book.

Either viewpoint is quite different from that of the businessperson, who must look at markets outside the United States in terms of cold, hard profits.

At the embassies you visit, the person you want to see may go by the title of commercial attaché, commercial officer, economic secretary, or one of several other variations. Some embassies have excellent reference libraries.

In addition to verifying or refining your statistics, on an embassy visit you have a chance to look up trade publications, newspapers, and directories, *including classified phone books, among the most valuable sources of information anywhere in the world.*

Allow yourself enough time to browse around an embassy's reference library. You will come out with a great deal of practical, useful information including names and addresses of possible agents and major lines they currently handle (easily obtained from a classified phone book).

There is one more important step you can take before you settle on a list of target countries: *Attend a major trade fair.*

Find out which is the biggest and most important international fair for your product, then go and browse around. It will probably be somewhere in Europe, most likely West Germany. See who is exhibiting. Note how much effort and money your competition is investing in the event. Get a feel for the types and numbers of buyers attending the event from all over the world.

Don't rush the visit. Stay the entire time. Stop for a chat with competitors. Introduce yourself to exhibitors and to the officials responsible for the fair. Pick up catalogs and reports. Attend meetings, get yourself invited to a cocktail party or two, mix with foreign visitors in your hotel's bar and restaurant. Be nosy!

You will come home with a wealth of information and may even have been lucky enough to meet important visiting agents from other countries.

You will not have been the first or the last businessperson to become excited about international markets as a result of attending a major fair.

If you represent a business outside the United States, and have an eye on the U.S. market, you will garner the same wealth of information by attending national or regional shows in the United States.

Information on important trade fairs is readily available through trade associations and through embassy and other government sources.

Your research need not take more than a month. This should give you ample time to identify your priority markets.

The out-of-pocket cost will include the items listed in the table below.

If the research is done in-house, it will need one full-time person. Find a meticulous (within reason!) person who can do all the preliminary data gathering and tabulation. If you have an idea of whom you would

Allowance for reports (many of them will be free of charge)	$ 250
Phone calls, telexes	500
Ten days' travel to visit embassies, government offices, trade associations (not counting airline fare)	2500
Optional: five days' visit to major international fair (not including airline fare)	1250
Total	$4500

eventually choose to run your export department, you may want to give this person responsibility for the research. It will give him or her a good opportunity to start learning about foreign markets and conditions.

Another possibility is to give the job to an outside consultant—someone who is familiar with government and embassy sources and who has personal overseas experience. A consultant will charge you a fee but may be able to give you a list of the ten best markets fairly quickly, without tying up any of your staff or executives.

A reliable consultant could also be useful later on in helping you take your first steps in your own export operation. Or, if you are already into exports, in helping you redirect your efforts where they will produce the greatest benefits.

You may even be lucky enough to have the research done for you free of charge. Years ago Mohammed Helmi, an Egyptian friend of mine about to get his M.B.A. degree, offered to do an international market survey free of charge, as part of his thesis, for a small midwestern manufacturer of woodworking machines. All he asked was the company's cooperation in supplying him with some information about the product, distribution patterns and prices, and the industry in general.

The manufacturer readily agreed ("What the hell, why not?").

Mohammed wrote his thesis (which earned him his M.B.A.) and sent a copy to the company. Within the week he got a phone call from the president.

"Mohammed, how about coming over and practicing what you've been preaching?"

Mohammed became the company's first international sales manager. (Know any aspiring M.B.A.s?)

Allowing enough time for research pays off when, finally, you get a picture of the international marketplace and are able to put together a workable market strategy. Your decision on which countries to sell to need not be a momentous one. You could make a mistake on one or two and eventually have to drop them. The main thing is to make a reasonable start.

At this point, don't make your list of possible targets too tight. Let the person who will eventually become your export manager have some say in the final decision.

No matter how thorough and systematic your research may have been, when the time comes to pinpoint initial markets, you and your export manager will still face a calculated risk as in any other business decision. Facts and figures may look good, and opinions may all be positive, but all they really tell you is that you have a reasonable chance to succeed in the markets you have selected.

Beyond this you still need a touch of that pioneering zest and faith which guided my father when he landed in Brazil on his door-to-door selling adventure back in 1928.

There are always different ways to look at statistics—and at a market.

Two shoe salespeople came to a remote country the world had seldom heard of, and spent several days trekking from village to village to see what sort of business could be had.

The first cabled his home office: "Outlook hopeless. Returning home tomorrow. Nobody here wears shoes."

The second salesperson, a competitor, saw things a bit differently. Her cable read: "Outstanding opportunity. Market wide open. Nobody here has bought any shoes yet."

Different individuals have different outlooks. It shows you that who you pick to go out there and do the job still means a lot.

What kind of person do you want to run your export sales department? What kind of regional managers? Where will they come from? What should they know? What will be their roles and responsibilities?

CHAPTER

FOUR

A LEAN,
SHARP TEAM
The irreducible, minimal export department rests on the shoulders of a one-person sales force focusing on a very small, carefully defined overseas market. This market is made up of no more than the number of countries one salesperson can cover effectively.

After a couple of years this embryonic operation can quickly grow into a three- or four-person sales team working fifteen or more productive markets around the world.

In either situation the key individual is the export manager. Your success in developing and sustaining an export organization depends, then, first and foremost on the caliber of the person you choose as export manager.

The export manager, even when you start with a one-person sales department, will need the support of a full-time assistant. Most of the internal administrative work, processing of orders, invoicing, collections, and shipping will be handled by your existing staff. Until export sales become substantial, this work should be manageable; you may need to add staff later.

Top priority at all times must go into selecting the men and women who will be responsible for selling your product overseas. In addition to the export manager these will eventually include one or more regional managers.

From the very beginning you should also consider the services of a competent consultant to help guide your export and regional managers at least until they have each taken two or three trips abroad and have begun to get a feel for the international marketplace.

Your export manager should be appointed *before* you draw up an international strategy. You may have done considerable initial research ahead of time and developed a good idea of which markets to go after. You may also have started to put together an export budget you can be comfortable with.

But don't try to serve a finished package on a platter to whoever takes on the job of running your export show. Let the export manager participate in the final planning and feel that she or he has made a personal contribution to overall strategy.

THE EXPORT MANAGER.   The person responsible for running an international marketing operation goes by any of a number of titles: international marketing manager, vice-president in charge of international operations, international sales director, export director, and variations on all of these.

Let's simply label the position "export manager." Whatever the title, the responsibility of this person is to:

1. Identify overseas markets
2. Appoint overseas agents
3. Promote export sales
4. Visit foreign markets regularly
5. Appoint regional managers
6. Organize and run an efficient export department
7. Keep up with market research

The bottom-line goal of the export manager is to produce profits for the company.

Being export manager is a full-time job. Between traveling abroad, covering sales possibilities in the home country, and following up on orders, mailings, and international promotion, the export manager has no time for anything else.

Therefore, to give export management responsibility to someone whose main job lies in another area, such as domestic sales, is a total waste. The export job will never get done.

What should you expect of an export manager? Who should you consider for the position? How should the export manager's position fit into your existing corporate structure?

First of all, the export manager should report to the company's top executives, such as the president, managing director, and vice-president for marketing. Under no circumstances should an export manager be subordinated to your company's domestic sales manager. This, unfortunately, happens all too frequently in countries with large domestic markets, such as the United States.

Having an export manager report to a domestic sales executive only spells trouble. Nine times out of ten domestic sales managers will favor their own traveling salespeople, reps, and dealers. They will consider their job much more vital than those of the international sales staff, and will eventually resent their foreign travel, particularly when it takes them to sunny shores and it's blizzard time back home. There are many other potential causes of friction.

The worst case of this kind I ever ran into was that of a U.S. electronics manufacturer who decided to go international and hired a competent export manager away from a competitor with the promise that the export manager would report directly to the company's president. The day the new export manager reported for work, he was told that the export department would operate under the supervision of the company's mid-Atlantic regional manager.

The arrangement did not last long.

Essentially an export manager must be a hardworking and adaptable individual capable of selling to a diversity of customers abroad and at home (don't forget the home-for-export market!).

In the beginning most of the export manager's time will be spent contacting overseas agents, planning trips, and actually traveling. As sales expand the export manager will hire regional managers to look after new territory. While the export manager will continue to go out into the field and may even retain his or her own territory, he or she will have to devote more time to planning and to the business of running a tight ship back home. Therefore, you are also looking for a person with administrative and management ability. Your company's export department is not a one-shot, occasional effort, but a professional operation with long-range goals.

Let's assume that you are the newly appointed export manager of a company with a fledgling international marketing operation. Who are you? Most likely, you are either someone who has been promoted from within your company or an outsider with personal international marketing experience.

Promotion from Within.   Frankly, I hope you came from within. For a company in the early stages of an export operation, it is important to send out into the field someone who is thoroughly familiar with its product, personnel, and procedures.

If you came from within, you may have been a salesperson, a regional manager, or a technician. Your company knows your strengths and weaknesses, and does not have to waste time on product training and company indoctrination.

If this is your first job as export manager and you were promoted from a lower position, you are probably starting at a lower salary than your company would have paid an experienced outsider.

An aside: Your company may have had another important reason for giving the job to a loyal and competent employee—the positive effect on company morale. A company should not hire outside talent unless there is nobody inhouse who can either do the job or be groomed for it. This rule is basic to Japanese business thinking, but is not always followed in Europe, much less in the United States.

As the export manager you must get along not only with clients but with company staff. Because of the kaleidoscope of cultures, traditions, and personalities you will need to deal with, you must be someone who comes across as low-key and not as a bulldozer or a spoiled prima donna.

Tact and diplomacy are your stock in trade. If you know an important foreign language, so much the better. Spanish, French, German, or Arabic, for instance. But this is not an indispensable requirement, except for export managers in non-English speaking countries, in which case English is indispensable if the company wants to be active around the world.

A German export manager who speaks nothing but German can function quite well in a central European, German speaking area which takes in West Germany, East Germany, Austria, Switzerland, and parts of Czechoslovakia, Hungary, and Poland. He or she can also be understood by enough businesspeople in the Netherlands and the Scandinavian countries to function there.

French export managers with no foreign languages have a slightly larger but not necessarily more affluent Francophone market consisting of France, Belgium, Switzerland, Algeria, Morocco, Tunisia, and many countries in central and west Africa.

A Japanese export manager who speaks nothing but Japanese is out of luck.

Hiring from outside the Firm.   If you are new to the company, you may be an experienced export manager with a proven record; if so, you probably will ask for more salary and incentives than someone who is being promoted from within the firm. To the company doing the hiring, some of the disadvantages are obvious: As an outsider, you don't know the company or the product; you have to be trained from scratch; you may not have had recent direct-sales field experience. The larger the export department you ran in your most recent job, the more time you had to spend on managerial tasks, the less on selling. If you headed a multimillion-dollar operation and a team of seven or eight regional sales managers, you may be too expensive for a newcomer company.

Your foreign experience would probably allow a newcomer company to dispense with the services of consultants or advisors in the initial stages of its export activities. On the other hand, such a company at first may be more interested in a salesperson than in a manager.

Chances are better, then, that you are someone whose last job was as an overseas regional sales manager or traveling salesperson, someone with recent direct-sales experience who is seeking a long-term career opportunity.

Possibly you are a retired foreign service officer or a professional in another field who has lived abroad. Some newcomer firms may consider such candidates. However, these possibilities must be looked at by the company with long-term growth in mind. Having lived abroad is an asset but not a critical one. Experience as a military or foreign service officer or teacher is not necessarily a qualification for the export manager's position.

You may be one of the thousands of recent immigrants who have arrived in the United States from Latin America, Lebanon, India, Pakistan, Taiwan, and many other countries. In that case you probably had business experience where you came from, and, of course, you know at least one foreign language. (The same influx of experienced immigrants, mainly from the Middle East, has hit West Germany, France, Switzerland, and the United Kingdom in recent years.)

However, as a recent arrival in the United States looking for work in international sales, you may find that a newcomer company looking at your credentials will wonder if you shouldn't be considered as a regional manager, so that the company can take advantage of your expertise in your country or region of origin, rather than for the export manager's job.

Opportunities for Women. Are you, the newly appointed export manager, likely to be a woman? At this time, perhaps not. Women have yet to make a major impact in international sales, and you don't have to go to Saudi Arabia to learn why. *It's still a man's world.*

In twenty-five years I have met fewer than a dozen women export or regional managers. They were all American, Australian, German, Italian, Swedish, Norwegian, or British.

However, changes are inevitable. If you are a woman interested in a career in sales or management, you will find alluring opportunities in international marketing. You could well be one of the increasing number of women who in coming years will be cracking this very tough nut. If so, an understanding of the obstacles you will face can be a real asset as you enter the field.

Regrettably, male chauvinism is alive and well in too many countries, without even taking into consideration the Middle East. Acceptance of women in anything other than the traditional secretarial or clerical role ranges in most countries from *poor* or *reluctant* to downright *nonexistent.*

A woman traveling on business needs to be aware of the fact that except in the United States, Canada, and *a very few other western countries,* opportunities for women in truly executive positions are extremely rare. She must prepare herself to accept cultural differences which in some countries can be quite drastic and in some cases revolting to a staunch feminist.

The most difficult area is the Arab World. But women will also encounter resistance in Asia, Africa, Latin America, and parts of Europe. It is more common for women to hold executive and sales positions in the Scandinavian countries than in central Europe or along the Mediterranean shores.

Yet, in spite of obstacles, women stand to play an increasing role in international sales; they represent a vast storehouse of talent, talent which so far has made a negligible impact on the international scene.

In fact, women are already involved in international marketing. Many women in the United States and other western countries are for all practical purposes the managers of international divisions, even though in some cases male executives may be nominally in charge.

Male chauvinism is still a potent force but on the whole is not making any progress. It is an insurmountable obstacle in only a handful of countries, and it should be easy for an international business executive who is a woman to work around these countries.

A woman with a realistic understanding of cultural barriers and problems can operate effectively as an export or regional manager almost anywhere in the world. The exception: a few remaining male bastions in the Arab World.

A female export manager can handle the overall management function for a company's international operation, while reserving for herself a territory which includes the countries which are more receptive to women sales executives. This will work quite well even in a one-person export sales department. Among the priority markets revealed by market research will be many where a female executive will be able to function without any problems.

The more obvious "open" areas are Western Europe, Australia and New Zealand, and southeast Asia. Add to those the United States and Canada.

Markets where women are totally barred or at least significantly discouraged can be covered by male regional managers. In a one-person department starting from scratch, any closed markets which may be on a priority list can be saved for the time when the company is ready to hire regional managers and expand. Latin America is still "macho" territory, but more women are winning executive positions in business and government. Women traveling on business will invariably be treated courteously, but will not always be given the same importance that would be accorded a man.

In southeast and south Asia, although women executives and company owners are becoming more visible, women traveling on business still encounter resistance.

The Arabian peninsula on the whole is forbidden territory for female salespeople and executives. In Saudi Arabia women are not allowed a role in business—not even that of typist. This restriction applies also to women who come into the country to accompany husbands on contract to Saudi firms. A woman caught doing a bit of discreet typing or other office work for her husband's office could be thrown out of the country, along with her husband, and never allowed to return. And let us not go into the many social restrictions and prohibitions women have to put up with!

Conditions in the Arabian Gulf, though not quite as poor, are still bad enough to make it virtually impossible for a female export or regional manager to visit the area.

The international vice-president of a U.S. manufacturer of office machines has found a way around this problem by bringing her son on her visits to the Middle East. He handles all business discussions while she ostensibly plays a quiet, ceremonial role.

Elsewhere in the Middle East and Africa women traveling on business will be accepted reluctantly. The best that can be said is that this is not an easy area.

In Japan, female executives are rare. Formal to the extreme, most Japanese are not prepared to deal with business executives who are female.

But even in conservative, tradition-bound countries, a woman will not be prevented from functioning effectively as an export or regional manager. There are plenty of territories to choose from outside the Arabian peninsula.

If you are a female export manager, remember that Saudi Arabia may be closed to you personally, but that this does not prevent you from meeting and discussing business with your company's Saudi agent outside the country—at an international fair, at a sales meeting, or when the agent comes calling on you.

As with your male counterpart, much will depend on your courtesy, on your appearance, on your ability to deal tactfully with cultural differences—in short, on the *personal touch.* The same basic rules of personal and business behavior will apply to both of you. Except that you will be confronted by the ever-present demand that you prove yourself to be up to the job. However, this should come as no surprise to any woman who has been exposed to the business world, in the United States or elsewhere!

A further caution: Women's rights is a subject to be avoided at all costs in business and social conversations, even with men and women who on the surface seem to be fully "liberated."

A woman able to put on a business presentation and in full control of her facts, as any well-trained professional sales person should be, will gain the admiration and respect of the most conservative man she must deal with.

Another point to remember is that, while a woman must cope with discrimination in many forms abroad, she will also receive a great deal of attention and may be more readily remembered by overseas agents and end users. She can be an asset to her company simply because she *is* still unique.

The idea of bringing more women into international marketing has not been sufficiently promoted. Too many firms still fail to understand the benefits a female export or regional manager can bring to her job. She, the female export or regional manager, may well look back after several years on the first "sale" she made—the one to her employer— and realize that it was one of the most difficult.

Educational Requirements.   What about a college education? A degree? You, the newly appointed export manager, almost certainly do have one.

But when it comes to academic background the question is not so much *where* you studied or what sort of degree you have, but *what* you know and *how open you are to learning about foreign cultures, habits, languages, and business methods.*

Having majored in international business or business administration is obviously a plus. But does it carry more weight with a potential employer than a major in international relations? European or Far Eastern history? Foreign languages? Science? Engineering?

As a matter of principle, most employers will require an export manager to have a college education. Yet even this should not be a hard and fast rule. The company's chief executive officer has to judge each candidate for the job on the basis of individual merits and product requirements.

Willingness to Travel. Willingness to travel is obviously an indispensable requirement for an export manager. You may be abroad a good four months out of twelve. Even when as an export manager you have developed a competent team of regional managers, you will still have to take frequent long trips. For a regional manager the pressure is even worse.

This can involve significant strains on personal relationships. It takes a well-adjusted couple to cope with long trips abroad by either partner. I have known sales executives who could travel six or seven months a year on a steady basis without apparent ill effects on their married lives. And I have known some who refused to be away more than once or twice a year on short trips—and who eventually had to drop out of export sales altogether.

The smaller the export department, the more pressure on the export manager to travel. Obviously this pressure is greatest in the one-person department. As the organization grows through the addition of regional managers, the export manager becomes more of an administrator and less of a salesperson out on the road. The need for personal travel diminishes somewhat.

However, few men or women ever become export managers without having gone through years of steady overseas exposure.

For men or women who reject steady travel, running the administrative side of an export sales operation may still be an attractive proposition. The job can encompass overseas promotion, research, order processing, evaluation of overseas agents and prospective regional managers, submission of offers, handling of communications, and any number of other functions within an export department.

It can also include the responsibility for keeping in touch with trading companies, exporters, and the other sectors of the home-for-export market. Travel can be limited to special events such as international trade fairs or sales meetings, plus occasional visits to overseas agents in order to keep in touch with actual market conditions.

Travel, therefore, need not be entirely eliminated. There can be enough of it to make the job attractive and diversified, but without creating a steady, year-round obligation to go on the road at regular intervals.

However, opportunities can be far more attractive if a salesperson does not mind putting up with the travel problem and looks ahead to a career in active international sales.

Computer Literacy. As a newly hired export manager one of your functions will be to try to take full advantage of the personal computer as a marketing tool. This can multiply your effectiveness many times over. You don't have to be a computer expert. Just be aware of what the computer can do in terms of storing and updating data, and what benefits you and your regional managers (when you hire them) can get out of it.

The smallest, one-person export operation can now, with an inexpensive personal computer, develop and utilize masses of information. Until a few years ago this sort of facility required expensive systems which only huge companies could afford.

Some basic but important computer applications worth keeping in mind as you develop your export operations are listed here.

1. Current trade statistics and other figures showing market conditions, particularly in your priority target countries
2. Lists of potential agents in these and other countries you may expand into later
3. Data on your overseas agents, such as performance and background
4. Standardized "forms" for quotations, allowing your office or your regional managers in the field to produce quotations quickly, on the spot
5. Computerized field reports from regional managers
6. "Situation board" showing status of pending quotations and orders

These applications are all possible with existing inexpensive computers and software packages.

Information can be a strong weapon for your export sales staff, but only if it is readily and easily available when needed, particularly while they are traveling. The wider the range of situations and problems which a traveling export or regional manager can handle without checking back with the home office, the sharper the edge the company will have over the competition.

THE EXPORT ASSISTANT. The export assistant performs an important support function without which an export manager cannot get the job done effectively. It is not a "typical" secretarial job. Somehow whenever a new executive position is created, the first thing that comes to mind is that "you will need a secretary, of course." The job invariably consists of taking dictation, typing letters, answering the phone, and making airline reservations.

I would hope that companies starting an export operation from scratch would try to break away from this pattern by doing away with archaic office routines and giving "secretaries" more important responsibilities. Figure out the personnel and time involved in producing a letter the conventional (dictation) way, and compare it to what it would take you, the export manager, to produce the letter yourself on a computer screen, and you begin to see why so many companies are still in the horse and buggy era!

Your assistant must be someone who can be trained to learn enough about your ongoing export operations so that he or she is able to look after the office when you are away on a trip. It's not as if you just flew overnight to Boston and will be back tomorrow. People are going to call and ask questions. If there is no one available to provide the answers, your export operation will not last very long.

The advantage for a company starting from scratch is that export manager and assistant can together develop routines and planning without being bound by established office procedures which might not work very well internationally.

Another important function of the assistant is to constantly gather and update trade and other statistics. In fact, the six computer applications we looked at a while ago could all be the responsibility of the export assistant.

Other important jobs for the assistant are the following.

1. Mailings to potential agents in new, untouched markets
2. Keeping up with government sponsored overseas promotions
3. Liaison with trade associations, chambers of commerce, government officials, and embassies
4. Gathering data on potential agents

The export assistant should be encouraged to contribute new ideas, including suggestions for new markets to be penetrated.

THE REGIONAL MANAGER.   Next to the export manager, one or more regional managers are the most vital elements of any aggressive export department. You don't have to appoint regional managers at the very beginning, but once you are ready to expand, this will become a priority.

Economy-minded companies, when faced with the need to send people out into the field, immediately start thinking in terms of commission reps, traveling salespeople who handle several noncompeting lines, get paid a commission on actual sales, and cover their own travel and other expenses.

On the surface this arrangement looks good. The rep plan works for some types of products, particularly fast-moving off-the-shelf consumer items. However, the rep inevitably ends up pushing the lines that move the quickest. And reps are not particularly interested in a company's long-range plans and development. Like everybody else, they have to look after themselves first.

If your product can indeed be promoted by reps, just the same consider having them report to regional managers who are fully employed by you and who are directly responsible for organizing overseas territories.

The regional manager is the "face" of your company which an overseas agent or end user will see. In most cases the regional manager is the only person from your company the overseas agent will ever meet.

Personal contact is vital to any international operation. There is no substitute for building up close rapport with agents. Of course, business is business, and if someone comes along with a better deal, your overseas agent could be tempted to drop you and switch lines, friendship or no friendship. However, it is always easier for agents to desert you when you have neglected them.

Here's a complaint from the Korean agent of a large U.S. manufacturer of machinery: "We have sold millions of dollars of their equipment in the last five years and they have never bothered to come to Seoul."

The only reason this agent keeps selling the product is that nothing better has turned up yet.

The company going international has about the same choices open to it when hiring a regional manager as when choosing an export manager: promote someone from within—preferably a good and loyal salesperson—or go outside and pay more for someone with international experience.

Essentially the regional manager is a salesperson who must systematically cover a territory, calling on agents, helping them on calls to major end users, introducing new products, submitting quotations, and explaining new demonstration procedures, pricing, and the many other aspects of a regular selling job.

A person who has done this type of job successfully in a domestic territory has the best qualifications. If on top of that the regional manager speaks the most important language in the territory, so much the better!

Where should you base a regional manager?

This depends on the territory. Regional managers are most effective if in addition to covering their territories frequently they maintain close, direct contact with the home office, personally follow up on their pending projects and orders instead of leaving things to the office staff, and generally look after the interests of their overseas agents.

As the export manager you cannot have close control of your regional managers if they are based abroad and only come home on short occasional visits.

Basing a regional manager in Singapore, Hong Kong, London, Geneva, Paris, or any other strategic regional city can cost a small fortune, particularly if the regional manager is married. The company ends up having to pay living allowances and exhorbitant rentals for modern housing, in addition to moving expenses. All of this can easily cost more than the regional manager's annual salary.

It is nearly always much cheaper to base regional managers back home and put up with the expense of added airline travel every time they go out to their territory. This actually is a fraction of what it would cost to maintain them abroad.

There are exceptions. If you hire foreign regional managers who already live in their territories, they will not need any special allowances and there are no relocation expenses. On the other hand, chances are they will find it difficult to really "join the team" and will always be outsiders.

And despite the added expense, any firm seriously interested in developing major markets like the United States, Canada, Japan, or West Germany should consider a full-time resident regional manager, whether a native of the country or not. These markets are important enough to call for a permanent, day in, day out presence.

If yours is a small operation being created from scratch, you, the export manager, will be your own regional manager as well. You will spend considerable time on the road, responsible for the company's initial overseas sales territory. You should not be in a hurry to give up this dual function, even when you start appointing regional managers.

It will take a few years before you can honestly tell yourself that you have complete international coverage. Even then, it will be to your advantage to hold on to at least part of your original territory. Direct selling will keep you in touch with field situations; you will have a much better understanding of market developments and the problems faced by your regional managers and overseas agents than if you leave the field entirely.

You should encourage your regional managers to make use of portable computers as early as possible, not for any sophisticated programming, but as a means of carrying with them valuable market information and putting it to use while traveling.

Eventually your regional managers should be able to send you daily computerized reports via phone lines. They will also find their computers handy for keeping files of personal notes and comments on markets, foreign agents, end users, VIPs.

OUTSIDE CONSULTANTS.   If you are the executive in charge of launching an export operation, you probably sought out a consultant before recruiting your export manager.

You did the right thing. A consultant with overseas experience can be a big help to any firm starting from scratch or reassessing its export operations. This is a good and economical way to minimize your initial risks, capitalize on your investment, and speed up the process of developing foreign business.

The best time to hire a consultant is when you decide to go international and before you reach any major decisions.

A good consultant can help a company pinpoint priority markets, evaluate candidates for the export manager's job, establish procedures for finding and appointing overseas agents, organize travel schedules, work with an export assistant in establishing contact with sources of trade data, plan overseas promotions, conduct training sessions for support staff, and explain overseas markets and strategy to your top executives.

Consultants who regularly spend time abroad, exposed to markets and conditions, are even more useful. They can be alert to new opportunities for a product, and they are able to meet with competitors and end users much more freely than one of your own regional managers could.

In important major markets such as the United States, Canada, Japan, and the largest Western European countries it pays to consider the services of a full-time resident consultant thoroughly familiar with the local market for your type of product. A consultant can complement the work of a regional manager assigned to the territory, particularly if the regional manager continues to be based in your home town rather than in the territory itself.

The terms and conditions of consultants should be carefully spelled out in advance. There is no need to have a consultant sitting for days on end in your office. The initial research and planning stage will probably take up to thirty days of a consultant's time. Afterwards you can try to settle for a few working days per month.

As your operation expands, a consultant's assignment can be shifted to new areas. A person with a good nose for business can be a very effective and inexpensive bird dog, helping you to uncover new markets.

The services of a consultant will be most useful when there is close, two-way communication with you and when you are able to focus on the essence instead of the frills.

When dealing with a consultant remember: The consultant is not all-knowing and infallible. Listen to the advice but don't take it for granted. Ask questions. Don't be afraid to appear ignorant!

Brainstorm as often as you want. Consultants welcome a chance to toss an issue back and forth across the table. It is much better and more challenging for them than submitting a report and not knowing if it will ever be acted upon—or even read! Consultants worth their salt will tell you that some of their best advice and ideas come out of personal exchanges with clients.

Don't be impressed with pretty binders. Consultants quite often (no doubt encouraged by receptive clients) make their reports look voluminous and impressive. Typing is double- or triple-spaced, with margins as wide as the lapels on last year's jackets. The whole thing is neatly submitted in fancy binders.

All of this costs you money and is meaningless. Ask for concise advice, not necessarily written. Make sure the consultant understands you want to get to the point and are not interested in the adornments. You want substance! Leave out the sauce, please!

Avoid theory. Go for the practical. Consultants are good at painting a picture of a market, its conditions and overall outlook. But there's a time for generalities, and there's a time for facts.

Keep your eye on the target. When you trim off all the nonessentials, the consultant's task boils down to helping you find specific markets and specific agents who will sell your product and make money for you. Remind yourself (and the consultant) of this basic fact of life whenever discussions begin to wander far afield!

To launch your own export operation with an irreducible staff, then, you need a full-time export manager, a full-time export assistant, and the services of a part-time consultant. This gives you the basic elements of a lean but potentially sharp team with which to open up a few key target countries.

These are the basics that you need to plan the strategy that will allow you to run your own show.

CHAPTER
FIVE
RUNNING YOUR OWN SHOW

When your lean, sharp team is in place, you will be ready to work out an international strategy. Here are its four vital ingredients.

1. First-phase priority markets
2. Second-phase priority markets
3. Liaison with home-for-export market outlets
4. A budget

Your strategy should be mainly the responsibility of the export manager, who at this point should have all the facts, figures, and consultant advice necessary to make decisions and recommendations.

FIRST-PHASE PRIORITY MARKETS. Once again, suppose you are the newly hired export manager of a firm which is going international. The first step in your strategic planning will be to pick out the specific markets you plan to develop during the first phase of your export activities, a phase which should last at least one, and possibly two years.

For a start, get a good world map, tack it on the wall, and stick pins wherever you have identified a market worth going after. Your final choice of first-phase priority targets will have a lot to do with geography.

Aggressive exporting requires plenty of travel. The number and size of the markets you choose as your first targets will therefore depend on your available sales personnel. If you are starting from scratch and going into markets where your company has had no marketing efforts whatsoever, follow this simple rule of thumb: *One traveling salesperson is worth six markets.*

A regional manager cannot effectively develop more than six markets from scratch at one time without diluting the sales effort. (This applies also to you, the export manager, assuming that you will have a full territory of your own.)

What constitutes "a market"? Sometimes a country, sometimes a part of a country; size, number of major commercial cities, and distance between them are the deciding factors.

Obviously the United States, Canada, West Germany, and Japan will take much more time and effort to develop than Singapore, the Philippines, Bahrein, or Ecuador. If you plan, therefore, to include one or more of the big industrialized countries in your first-phase priorities, you may have to consider each one of them the equivalent of two, three, or four "markets."

A regional manager assigned to develop sales in West Germany may have no time for more than two other countries, for instance.

Travel planning and allocation of time for business trips can be a problem when you target a country that has no single predominant business center. In a country that is largely decentralized you are forced to include more than one major city when you make your regular rounds. The agent you select may not be able to cover the entire country. You may need several agents. You will in any case want to call on major end users and perhaps subagents in more than one city.

Later we will look in more detail at specific travel problems in some countries. For now, as you consider your final list of market priorities, make a note that decentralized countries include Canada, West Germany, Italy, the Netherlands, Spain, Sweden, Switzerland, Brazil, Colombia, Australia, New Zealand, Japan, India, Turkey, Saudi Arabia, the United Arab Emirates, Nigeria, and South Africa. In each one you may need to visit several cities. (The most decentralized of all markets is, of course, the United States.)

Among the most centralized countries, countries where a visit to a single city may be sufficient, are France, England, Norway, Denmark, Finland, Greece, Austria, Portugal, Egypt, Mexico, Argentina, Chile, Venezuela, South Korea, Thailand, Indonesia, Malaysia, Singapore, Taiwan, and the Philippines.

When making your final choice of first-phase priority markets, you should also take into consideration the pros and cons of doing business in a highly developed, industrialized, sophisticated country as opposed to a newer market—a country, as the French would say, *en voie de developpement.*

A sophisticated market may have recognized the need for your type of product years ago. You could be stepping into a bloody arena where every imaginable competitor is fighting primarily for replacement sales and market expansion. Overall business volume may be high, but the number of companies trying to get a slice of it will also be high.

In contrast, there may be markets on your list where the need for your type of product did not exist until recently, possibly because of import restrictions or lack of funds. Such a market could provide disproportionate and outstanding opportunities for a few years. The best example of this type of market in recent history is Saudi Arabia.

Whether to go for developed or developing markets is a choice you will have to make; it will depend on your product and your competition. A balance between the two may be the wisest approach.

For practical travel, planning, and cost reasons it makes sense to cluster target markets by region. But don't get carried away with the regional concept. Executives with orderly minds often like to get fully established in one region before moving on to another. Is it worth it? Usually not.

It will take much longer to get a region fully organized than you anticipated. For the sake of having a neat regional organization with an agent properly established in each country, you will waste valuable time, money, and personnel in many unimportant markets within the region. Meanwhile, you will have overlooked profit-making opportunities in other parts of the world.

For instance, if you plan to develop business in Latin America, concentrate on Mexico, Brazil, Argentina, Chile, Colombia, and Venezuela. They include more than 80 percent of the Latin American market. Put the other countries on the back burner until you have more traveling salespeople.

The "export regions" which include enough priority markets to make them good working territories for individual regional managers are:

1. North America
2. Western Europe
3. Southeast Asia
4. The Middle East
5. The Far East
6. Australia and New Zealand
7. South America

8. South Asia
9. Africa

Not all can be kept in neat, separate compartments. Try to combine two or three regions into a single territory. This tactic gives you a foothold in each so that when you are ready to expand you will already have a foundation from which to build a territory for a new regional manager.

For a U.S. firm, the North American market is limited to Mexico (assuming that Canada gets special status). Obviously, Mexico is not enough to keep a regional manager fully occupied. You may want to complement Mexico by adding parts of South America to the territory, or even giving the regional manager responsibility for a distant region like Australia and New Zealand. Since Mexico is so close to home, there should be no serious problems in working out travel schedules.

For a Canadian firm it will make sense to cover the United States and Mexico before moving into any other country.

If you are launching an export operation from a country outside North America, you may well decide that the United States, Canada, and Mexico are just too much for a single regional manager. You may want to cover Mexico later, when you expand your export sales team, and concentrate at first on the United States and Canada in view of the similarities between these two markets.

Western Europe is a logical priority area for a U.S. manufacturer. As the export manager of a U.S. company most likely you will try to concentrate at first on the major markets there: the United Kingdom, West Germany, France, and Italy. A regional manager responsible for these four markets will have little time for anything else.

However, if you are not particularly bullish about all these European markets, you may want to focus on one or two and give your regional manager a mix which could include three markets in north Africa and the Middle East, Algeria, Turkey, and Saudi Arabia, for instance. This would not create a burdensome travel situation.

A combination of markets in Europe, north Africa, and the Middle East is in fact a good starting point for a one-person operation. Here is a territory that the export manager can partially hold on to even when the company has begun to hire regional managers for other territories.

Southeast Asia has become one of the most attractive new regions for exporters, in spite of local manufacturing. An initial-priority territory could include Indonesia, Singapore, Thailand, and Malaysia. The same regional manager, however, should be able to cover parts of another region. This region might be: (a) the Far East (mainly Japan and Korea), (b) Australia and New Zealand, or (c) south Asia.

You could even consider grouping parts of three regions into a single territory; for instance, you might lump together Korea, Thailand, Singapore, Malaysia, Indonesia, and Pakistan.

An initial Middle East territory should include Saudi Arabia, Egypt, and Turkey. However, rather than giving priority to some of the other countries in the area you would be wise to add parts of south Asia (Pakistan) and of Africa (Algeria), or to think about combining the Middle East with a European territory.

The Far East includes Japan and Korea, both of them very important markets but perhaps not candidates for an all-out effort if you are starting from scratch. Consider, however, adding at least Korea to your southeast Asia territory.

Australia and New Zealand in themselves constitute a large market, particularly for U.S., Canadian, and British firms. (Emphasis should be on Australia, which has by far the larger area and population.) Large as this market may be, however, it should at first be combined with another region, and the most logical one is southeast Asia.

As noted earlier South America, for a newcomer, means Brazil, Argentina, Colombia, Chile, and Venezuela. If your research tells you that in most of these countries you stand a good chance of marketing your product successfully, they make up a complete territory, enough for a regional manager. You can add Mexico to it. You can even consider adding South Africa to the same territory, taking advantage of travel connections across the South Atlantic.

It is risky to consider south Asia by itself as a territory. There are vast differences between the region's four countries, India, Bangladesh, Sri Lanka, and Pakistan. If any of these turns out to be a high-priority market for you, include it in the territory of a regional manager covering either the Middle East or southeast Asia.

Africa is too diversified and erratic to constitute a single territory. The three countries likely to turn up on your list of priority markets are South Africa, Nigeria, and Algeria. If you add South Africa to a South American territory, you can then include Nigeria and Algeria in the territory of a Middle East or European regional manager.

If you are starting from scratch and you, the export manager, will be the only salesperson traveling in the immediate future, my choice of territory would be a combination of Western Europe and the Middle East.

For a two-person sales force I would suggest the same territory plus a combination of southeast Asia with Australia and New Zealand.

For a three-person sales force I would add Algeria to the European territory, set up the Middle East as a full-fledged territory including one of the south Asian countries (perhaps Pakistan), and leave the southeast Asia plus Australia and New Zealand combination unchanged.

If you are planning international strategy for a European manufacturer, I would sugget North America as your top-priority region, followed by the Middle East and southeast Asia (with the additions suggested above). This assumes that you are giving special status to European markets.

Whatever territorial distribution you arrive at, make sure your sales team is used to develop business where you have the largest potential. Don't be afraid to skip countries offering at best marginal returns. Be flexible with territorial definitions. Adapt territories to your personnel and other resources.

Don't waste your efforts. You may identify a country with outstanding, high-priority potential sitting all by itself 5000 miles away from the nearest regional manager's territory. Go after it! The cost of an extra 10-hour flight every three or four months is not going to put you out of business. If the regional manager already has a full load, try to rearrange it or drop from the initial territory a country where things are not looking particularly good.

SECOND-PHASE PRIORITY MARKETS. Second-phase priority markets are countries which appeared on your original list of attractive markets but were not included in your first-phase priorities because you lacked the personnel or other resources. You may also add other second-phase markets once you start traveling, talking to agents, attending international conventions, and receiving letters and telexes from all over the world.

Prepare for expansion even when you don't have the personnel. Take it for granted that sooner or later you will be ready to go into more territory. You might be ready within two years of the start of your operations.

Develop a backlog of new potential markets as early as possible. Each salesperson, after having established and trained agents reasonably well in the initial territory, may be ready to take on additional responsibility. New markets will require as much individual concentration as the original ones, except that much of the preliminary evaluation of potential agents will already have been done.

What is the optimum number of markets a regional manager can effectively handle?

There is no straight answer except to look at potential returns and the need to utilize personnel and other resources *where the action is.*

More important than deciding on an abstract "optimum" is to ask yourself if you should increase a particular regional manager's territory.

It may not be a good idea. A British or Japanese firm with a North American regional manager would be foolish to expand this territory to include South America. The job of running North American sales could in fact require *additional* sales staff to support the regional manager.

This is also true of the large Western European markets, and of Japan and Australia.

In exports, as in your domestic business, sales expansion is not necessarily a matter of territorial conquest but of exploiting each market to the hilt.

If you are ready to hire additional salespeople, your first job is to find out where they can do you the most good. In the large markets we have looked at, this could mean dividing an initial territory in half, or appointing assistants to established regional managers.

Let's look at some regions.

Western Europe can and should be expanded, but you may need additional sales personnel to do the job. If you are off to a good start in any of the top four European markets, you should not dilute your sales efforts in them.

Southeast Asia is an expandable region which can continue to be handled by one regional manager. If you started with Indonesia, Malaysia, Singapore, and Thailand, you should add the Philippines, Hong Kong, and Taiwan. Eventually southeast Asia should be a self-contained, complete territory.

The Middle East is also expandable. From a satisfactory start in Saudi Arabia and Turkey, for instance, you should move into all of the Arabian Gulf countries as well as Jordan and make this a complete territory.

Australia and New Zealand should be worth increasingly concentrated effort. Whoever is responsible for this territory should not have additional countries thrown in. These markets eventually can be a complete, full-time territory in themselves.

South America is an expandable market and can become a complete territory. If you started with Brazil, Colombia, Argentina, and Chile, add Ecuador, Peru, and Venezuela, for instance.

You can also create brand-new territories for new regional managers. Go back and look at what I suggested for one-person, two-person, and three-person sales forces.

LIAISON WITH HOME-FOR-EXPORT OUTLETS. Trading companies, exporters, and export management companies (EMCs) should all be part of your international strategy. Responsibility for developing this business will be yours, the export manager's. Before you make any serious effort to promote it, however, decide how it will blend in with your overall plan.

Exporters and EMCs will ask you for exclusivity in one or more countries. Try to point them toward countries or regions which are not on your own priority list. The ideal situation is the one in which you can assign to an EMC a territory so far down on your priority list that you have no plans to go after it yourself for years. If the EMC happens to be strong in the particular market, everybody is happy.

Some of the most difficult areas for imports are central America, Africa, south Asia (particularly India and Bangladesh), and Eastern Europe. EMCs with particular expertise, contacts, and a good track record in any of these areas are certainly worth cultivating and working with. You should be ready to support them, protect their commissions, and turn over to them any inquiries coming from their assigned territories.

Don't be too quick to discount companies with particularly strong positions in some of the high-priority markets you have identified. If you are starting from scratch, with a one-, two-, or even three-person sales force, there are plenty of territories to go around! Assigning one or two of them to exporters and EMCs could be a wise move.

As your sales force grows, continue to work closely with successful and reliable EMCs. Find ways to cooperate rather than clash.

For example, an EMC may be doing a good job promoting your line in Argentina and Brazil, countries not included among your initial targets. Later you appoint a regional manager for South America. Should you drop the EMC? No!

Let your regional manager concentrate on the west coast of South America, while occasionally dropping into Argentina and Brazil to give the EMC a hand (trade shows, demonstrations, a bit of public relations among end users and agents).

The trading companies on your list most likely will be Japanese. Go after them even if you plan to appoint an exclusive agent or regional manager for Japan. Your Japanese agent will be the first to recognize the importance of cultivating trading companies. Many of this agent's customers, although contacted and cultivated directly by the agent, will in fact place their orders through trading companies. There is nothing unusual about this in Japan. It is fairly standard procedure. The order will come through the U.S. office of the trading company. This is all to your advantage, and all you need do is reassure your exclusive Japanese agent by including an agency commission in all sales to Japanese trading companies.

AN AFFORDABLE BUDGET. The budget is the one major element of the strategy that must be blocked out before the export manager is in place. The size of the export budget clearly depends on whether the company starts with a one-person sales force or decides on a more substantial operation. There are two ways to look at the final figure. As the executive in charge of initial planning for international marketing, you can ask either:

1. What is the total budget?
2. What is the *real* cost in new out-of-pocket expenses?

Let's consider the items that go into the budget of an "irreducible minimum" department.

Export Manager's Salary. The export manager's salary is the biggest single item in the budget and could range from $35,000 to $60,000 depending on whether you promote someone in-house or hire an outsider. As we saw earlier, there are strong reasons for promoting someone from within your company. One of them is that you can keep the initial salary low, with the promise of a raise after the first year and possible incentives on sales.

(Be careful not to emphasize incentives. This could give the idea that you are going after quick results rather than building up a solid, long-range operation. You can always reward someone with an occasional bonus depending on performance.)

However, trying to pinch pennies *too* much on export managers' salaries is false economy. Eventually you get what you pay for. The key to your international success will be the export manager. Take your time in appointing one and offer a decent income.

Export Assistant's Salary. The export assistant should also be carefully chosen from your existing staff. Set aside $20,000 for the first year.

Clerical Help. There is no need for special full-time clerical personnel the first year. The export department in the beginning should be able to make use of your existing staff. Allow $20,000 the first year.

Travel Expenses. Figure on $200 daily (hotels, meals, laundry, telephone, telex, local transportation, tips). This is a good rule of thumb which applies almost everywhere.

Airline fares will range from $1000 to $3000 per trip depending on which countries you choose to cover.

The export manager should spend about 90 days a year in travel abroad. This allows coverage of the initial priority territory three times a year but does not include unscheduled trips for following up on unexpected hot projects or reacting to new opportunities in countries not included in the initial scheme.

Communications Expenses. Telex and telephone will cost you about $8000 a year in the beginning. You cannot operate internationally without a telex or an equivalent computer-based system. Short of using the phone, there is no other way to respond quickly to urgent requests for quotations and other critical inquiries. Your company will not be taken seriously if you don't have a telex.

Promotion. Figure on a rock-bottom $25,000 allocation the first year. It will cover the cost of catalogs for overseas agents, mailings to prospective end users and agents worldwide, participation in some government sponsored events, and reasonable entertainment of visiting foreign agents.

Postage. Day-to-day postage and occasional use of courier services for quick delivery of bids or catalogs to meet tight deadlines should be well within $7000 the first year.

Domestic Travel. To keep in touch with trading companies, exporters, and EMCs may take up to thirty days a year. Much of this work can be done by telephone.

Budget Summary. The table that follows summarizes your export department's tentative first-year budget.

In your second and third years there will be increases in all categories, including salaries. The export department may have one or two full-time clerical employees. Allow for an overall 20 percent rate of increase from one year to the next. You may also want to figure on a two-person sales force. (Assume $30,000 for the regional manager, plus $26,000 for the regional manager's international travel.)

Export manager	$ 35,000
Export assistant	20,000
Clerical help	20,000
International travel	18,000
Airline fares (three trips)	8,000
Telex and telephone	8,000
Promotion	25,000
Postage and courier service	7,000
Domestic Travel	6,000
Contingency	10,000
Total	$157,000

The Three-Year Budget. Your total three-year budget, based on a ninety-day yearly travel plan for the export manager and the same for the regional manager, will therefore look more or less like this (in round figures):

First year (one person)	$160,000
Second year (two people)	248,000
Third year (two people)	290,000
Total	$700,000

What Are the Real Costs? We've looked at the estimated budget. Now let's look at what this really means in terms of actual new, out-of-pocket expenses for the company as a whole.

If export manager, export assistant, and regional manager are promoted from within, you may not have to hire anybody.

Take a critical look at your overall operating expenses, and you are likely to note a few lumps of fat here and there. Is your domestic sales department overstaffed? Are your office personnel making full use of modern technology? Is everybody really filling a need? If you give the export manager's job to a domestic regional manager or salesperson, can you reshuffle domestic territories among the rest of the sales force and make everybody happy without bringing in any outsiders?

If your domestic advertising budget can be trimmed by only $15,000, you will have taken care of most of your very modest export promotion needs.

Will $15,000 really make that much difference to your domestic sales? Look carefully at any new promotional expenditures you may be contemplating in your domestic operations—expenditures for personnel, advertising, travel, conventions, shows. Is it all really necessary? Or wouldn't it be better to invest some of this money in new overseas business?

The table that follows shows what your *real, new* outlays will be reduced to if you promote from within and transfer money from your domestic promotional budget.

International travel	$18,000
Airline fares (three trips)	8,000
Telex and telephone	8,000
Promotion	15,000
Postage and courier service	7,000
Domestic travel	6,000
Contingency	10,000
Total	$72,000

The second and third years these figures go up by 20 percent, and you must also add $26,000 in travel expenses for the regional manager for each of those years. This gives you a total three-figure figure of $310,000.

Developing a suitable international strategy and budget need not take more than two or three weeks, assuming that enough market research was done in advance. Don't let this be a lengthy and tedious process. Avoid written feasibility studies and don't bring too many executives into the decision making. The plan you have in mind is reasonable and certainly modest in scope.

While it is being worked out, the export manager will also have to start putting together a package of information and product literature for the next, all-important phase of the operation: finding, evaluating, and appointing the people who will carry your message to end users abroad—the overseas agents.

CHAPTER
SIX

HOW TO FIND FOREIGN AGENTS

On a flight from Paris to Riyadh in 1975, the plane packed with eager salesmen with visions of Eldorado and early retirement in Rolls Royce splendor, I ran into Pierre LeJeune, export manager for a French manufacturer of training equipment.

Well into its dramatic oil boom, Saudi Arabia had become a magnet which drew businesspeople from all over the world. Many of them were newcomers who had never before stepped into the international arena. "I am delighted to see you," Pierre said. "I am on my way to signing a contract with a fantastic Saudi agent. A prince—really high level. Royal family! I am meeting him tomorrow. Come and be my witness when we sign the contract."

The prince, a charming man in his thirties who had been involved in several multimillion-dollar sales, had a small, modest office in an old building close to the old bazaar section of Riyadh.

We met with him and his lawyer. A few changes were made in the proposed agency agreement, but there were no major problems. The contract signed and witnessed, we sat sipping tea and making small talk. In the course of the conversation the prince quietly asked, "How much business do you think we will be able to do?"

"We have high expectations, your excellency, very high indeed!" replied Pierre. "Five hundred thousand dollars a year in a fairly short time."

"In commissions?"

Pierre laughed. "Oh, no, your excellency! In sales. At 5 percent this will bring you about $25,000."

Nothing else was said about business. The prince took us to his palace for dinner, was most hospitable and friendly throughout the evening, and afterwards insisted on personally driving us back to our hotel in his Rolls Royce.

Pierre was ecstatic. As soon as the prince had driven away he said, "Can you imagine! With this man representing us Saudi Arabia will very quickly account for at least 15 percent of my entire export business. And I guarantee you that in a few months the prince will want to expand into the rest of the Gulf area."

Six months went by. I ran into Pierre at the Didacta educational fair in Hanover.

"How are things in Saudi Arabia?" I asked.

Pierre shook his head.

"I don't know what to tell you. I am astonished. I have been back to Riyadh three times and the prince is never there. I cannot even find his manager, his office is always locked, and nobody answers my telexes."

After one year of no activity whatsoever Pierre gave up in disgust, blaming it all on the prince. Notice of cancellation of the agency agreement was given, but Pierre had to wait several months before he could legally appoint another agent—although the prince didn't seem to care one way or another.

What went wrong?

To start with, the prince had no staff to go after business systematically. His manager was really a personal secretary who followed him everywhere with an attaché case full of cash.

The idea of making $25,000 a year in commissions meant nothing to a man who had to maintain a household of more than 100 relatives and servants. The mere suggestion that $25,000 might appeal to him was insulting.

A prince dealing in multimillion-dollar projects would never lose face by approaching a high-level official to discuss business which amounted to a pittance.

Pierre LeJeune took the prince's hospitality as an expression of eagerness to strengthen the business ties between them. In reality, by the time we sat down for dinner that evening, the prince probably had put the entire matter out of his mind, and was simply displaying the splendid hospitality that is typical of Saudi Arabia.

The mistakes of Pierre LeJeune are made daily by export and regional managers all over the world. The fault usually lies with the visiting executive. You, as the export manager of a new international operation, should be particularly careful not to repeat Pierre's mistake. Before you appoint foreign agents, make sure you have analyzed their sales capabilities, the level and quality of their government contacts, and their experience, and know how much time they can devote to your product.

Put things in proper perspective. What do you expect agents to make in profits and what will this mean to them? An attractive return or a mere pittance?

What do you expect from your agents? Which specific individuals in an agent's organization will actually be responsible for promoting your product. How capable are they? What will motivate them?

LOCATING AND CONTACTING AGENTS.

First, let's back up for a minute and get our terminology straight. What is a foreign agent?

For our purposes, the agent is the person or organization selling your company's product in a particular country. An agent can be any of the many types of sales organizations needed to move products: an importer, wholesaler, retailer, commissioned representative, jobber, distributor or dealer.

Your type of product will determine what category of agent you need in a foreign market. If your agents have to be importing wholesalers, supposedly it will be their responsibility to open up dealer or other retail outlets on their own. If they are to sell directly to major end users, they will actually be performing the functions of a dealer or commissioned representative.

Whatever the category, in each country you will be dealing directly with one or more individuals or companies we will call "agents."

As the export manager it will be largely your responsibility to identify and appoint overseas agents. You will also be heavily involved in the process if you are a regional manager. Finding, evaluating, and appointing agents is a complex process, particularly if your product requires aggressive, exclusive representation. *The worst thing you can do is try to rush it.*

Impatient European and U.S. firms make the mistake of appointing overseas agents without enough serious preparation more often than the systematic Japanese do. Export managers under pressure from management to come up with quick sales and profits are bound to make bad choices. In the long run they will have to spend too much of their time getting themselves out of bad situations and replacing agents.

They will not have accomplished anything except to create confusion in the target country and cast doubts on the reliability and wisdom of their companies.

The Japanese are not under such pressure. They think long-term and will not hesitate to go back to the country several times before making a definite agency commitment. Once made, however, the commitment is usually lasting.

Finding lists of potential overseas agents is not difficult. Making sure you appoint the right ones is something else. Lists of agents are readily available from several sources, mostly the same ones that produced the data for your market research.

The U.S. Department of Commerce (DOC) has business trade lists for almost every country. The larger the country, the more specific the list in terms of product categories. In small countries like Qatar or Fiji there may be a single, all-inclusive "business list" that doesn't tell you much about the types of products handled by the various companies. Keep in mind, however, that *the smaller the country the less specialized a local agent is likely to be.*

DOC lists not only give you names and addresses but also tell you how long a company has been in business and whether it is small, medium, or large.

Classified telephone directories are excellent sources of information on potential agents. Reading them is also a good way to find out which of your competitors are active and who represents them. Also look up related product categories to identify firms that may not be carrying your specific type of product.

You can look up telephone directories at government international trade offices or foreign embassies. However, having pinpointed specific priority markets, it may be a better idea to buy the directories of the major cities in those countries and have them readily available at all times.

In the United States, telephone directories from any city in the world can be ordered by calling (800) 222-0400. The same service is available in most other countries. (Or a businessperson in another country can always order directories through a friend in the United States who has a telephone.)

Your trade association may once again be an excellent source of information. Find out if it has a reference library with literature from member firms. Many firms like to publish complete lists of their overseas agents in their international catalogs. While at the trade association, ask for the names and addresses of counterpart associations in the target countries, then write them for lists of members.

If in your earlier research you obtained friendly and useful advice from firms in your industry with noncompeting products, try them again for names of possible agents. They may welcome the opportunity to help expand the line of one or more of their own agents.

Go over trade publications. Comb through at least one year's back issues. You may find references to important overseas agents.

From all of these sources you will be able to put together a good initial list. The simplest first step is to write everybody—or at least all the candidates that look best to you. Make the letter as direct and personal as possible.

Be positive and enthusiastic. Do a selling job! The best overseas agents are already successful and busy, most likely doing quite well with a competing line and not likely to jump with glee at the sight of your catalog. Good agents have to be convinced that selling your product will improve their business.

Try not to be excessively enthusiastic about an agent who responds to your letter eagerly. Ask yourself instead why this agent is not yet handling a competitor's line. Play the devil's advocate from time to time. It can be a useful game.

Your letter must stimulate agents enough to make them write you back. They may or may not know about you. If yours is like most companies throughout the world, you are offering a product which has plenty of competition and is not necessarily one of a kind. Why should an agent get excited about it? What sort of profits do you offer? How do you plan to support the agent? Can you deliver on time?

There is no need for an exhaustive letter covering all of these points. Make short but convincing statements. Short letters are easier to answer. You can elaborate later. Enclose your catalog, company background information, and any other material that will strengthen your letter.

If price is one of your main features, send a sample quotation.

Enclose a questionnaire but don't ask too many questions. Keep it simple. Don't scare the agent away with requests for lengthy forecasts and reports on local economic conditions and market shares. The sole object of this first letter is to get an idea of the agent's activities and possible interest in your line.

Here is some basic information your questionnaire should produce.

- Name, address, phone number, and telex number
- Name of owners or managing director
- Years in business
- Number of employees
- Type of products handled
- Manufacturers represented

- Branch offices and size of sales force
- Size and description of sales territory
- Warehousing facilities
- Service facilities
- Bank references
- Main types of customers
- Trade references

You should also ask whether agents buy on their own accounts or work on a commission basis.

Response to this mailing will be mixed. You may receive a phone call or telex from a company which insists on an immediate quotation and catalogs—along with an exclusive franchise agreement. You will hear from small, inexperienced companies and individuals more often than from well-established firms who are not at all convinced that they need your product. You will get letters from people who were not on your list and were referred to you by companies or friends that were.

Don't be overwhelmed or disappointed by the response. This is only the first step. Make no commitments. Proceed with caution when someone claims to have urgent immediate business for you. Try to get facts. You are not breaking into a new market for the sake of a quick sale. Your goal is long-range.

If you did not hear from the companies you had your heart set on, it does not mean they are not interested. There could be a number of reasons why they did not reply: the manager was out of town, the person in charge of English correspondence was sick, a big public bid took up everybody's time for ten days, the office was closed for summer or religious holidays.

Wait a month and write again. Don't give up too easily. If your second letter still produces no response and you still like the company's credentials, make a note to drop in for a personal assessment the first time you travel to the country.

Go over all responses. Look for specific statements rather than generalities. An agent who claims to market outdoor lighting for private swimming pools, patios, and restaurants will obviously show greater concern for a specialized manufacturer than one who is interested in all sorts of electrical appliances, as well as fixtures, machinery, scientific instruments, chemicals, disposable syringes, and hospital beds.

My all-time favorite response was from a one-man agency in Pakistan. This man's letterhead listed in the left-hand margin no less than thirty unrelated product categories in which the firm supposedly "specialized."

Check for references and brand names. Don't accept at face value statements such as "We are the exclusive agents of XYZ Inc." or "Our line is Eastman Kodak, Polaroid, and Bell & Howell." The exclusive agent could actually be a local dealer with a small territory. The other firm could be one of hundreds of retailers selling the same consumer products. These claims can be easily checked by contacting manufacturers or when you visit the country.

Attractive letterheads and company names can be misleading. Anybody can produce them. I have met individuals who carry half a dozen different company letterheads and business cards in their pockets, for whatever occasion may arise. In parts of West Africa they are known as "walking-about" companies because they may not even have a place of business.

Open a file for each firm which responds. Acknowledge all responses and don't underestimate anybody, even agents who may now seem unsuitable. You may need them later. Stay friendly with everybody.

Once you appoint an agent in a particular country, don't file away and forget the other firms you may have considered and contacted. *Your results in a given market will depend largely on the success or failure of local agents—yours and your competitors'.* Keep track of everybody. Build up a file of agents, update it frequently, and have it readily available for quick reference.

ANOTHER CAUTIONARY TALE. A cardinal rule of good international marketing is never to appoint an overseas agent until you have had a chance to visit him or her personally. Even then, don't be carried away by premature enthusiasm!

My first trip abroad as an export manager was to Africa. It was the early 1960s. The eyes of the world were on this enormous continent where colony after colony was becoming independent. The pace of events was dizzying. Here was a vast market of 250 million people, free at last to catch up with the industrialized world! A staggering potential!

"Wait and see! In five years we will be on a par with America and Western Europe," a euphoric young lawyer told me at a cocktail party in Lagos.

My choice of Africa as a major target was nothing but a hunch and not even a calculated one at that. No research, no logic, just the feeling that Africa most definitely was where the action would be.

From one of the bubbling new African nations came the sort of letter every export manager loves to read. David Obodeze, managing director of New Africa Enterprises, Ltd., saw an outstanding market for our product, was ready to introduce us to the highest government officials and the chancellors of all the universities, would gladly set up a special showroom for our line, and would we please immediately and most urgently send a responsible executive for at least a week of intensive promotion?

We exchanged several letters. The responses from David Obodeze kept getting more exciting. "Please bring demonstration equipment when you come," he pleaded.

I arrived on a Sunday morning. David had organized a press conference at the airport. My arrival was mentioned in several radio news broadcasts. The first evening David gave a huge outdoor barbecue to which fifty people were invited. For five days we went around from the office of one government official to the other, David proudly introducing his "new American partner" and leaving behind an engraved invitation to a reception on Friday.

Our demo equipment in the meantime had arrived at the airport, but whenever I urged David to have it cleared from customs, it seemed we had a very important government appointment to keep. At long last the equipment was released on Thursday. David, totally concerned with preparations for the next day's reception, had no time or inclination for demonstrations and had hardly glanced at my catalogs all week. He did, however, take me to his home one evening to show me his collection of twenty-seven hats.

The party was magnificent. There were undersecretaries and ministers, university chancellors and professors, brigadiers, managing directors, newspaper editors, a few ambassadors, an Italian advisor from UNESCO, and two poets. A band played nonstop for hours. On an enormous buffet, platters of a marvellous assortment of food were continuously replenished.

Any disappointment I may have felt over David's apparent lack of interest during the previous five days was quickly dispelled by the impressive list of guests. The following morning, before climbing into an Air Liban flight to Khartoum, I gladly signed an exclusive agency agreement with David.

The aftermath was as disastrous as Pierre LeJeune's experience years later with the Saudi prince. David proved to be totally incapable of promoting our product, partly because the actual work of promotion and selling was not really his cup of tea, partly because the country was not ready for the type of product.

There was no established, recognized need.

Rudimentary research would have saved us a lot of time and money. Except that in the early 1960s there was little to go by in Africa, and you ended up playing your hunches.

The point, however, is that you can be easily bedazzled by an agent's high-level contacts and social standing. Particularly when the agent assures you that a million-dollar order is virtually assured, so "Please let's not waste time, I need a very urgent quotation from your company."

You need more than agents' connections to get on a solid, businesslike footing in a market. The process involves setting up pricing policy, doing promotion, identifying end users, contacting the end users systematically, putting on effective and professional presentations, and offering after-sales service.

VISITING THE TARGET COUNTRY. When you visit a country for the first time, use all available local sources for additional research on possible agents and the market itself. The following guidelines should be useful as you arrive and plan the agenda for your visit.

1. If you did not have a chance to look up local telephone directories earlier, reach for the one in your hotel room as soon as you have unpacked. You may even want to buy one. Ask the concierge at the hotel.
2. Yours may be one of the increasing number of hotels with a business center and reference library with local trade directories. Take full advantage of the center's information and services.
3. At the hotel newsstand or bookshop buy local business magazines, guides, and directories, maps of country and city, the daily newspapers.

   Newspapers are excellent sources of commercial and market information, even when you cannot read the local language. Display advertising is easy to understand, and can give you a good feel for local market conditions. Are companies advertising imported products? If yours is a consumer product that relies heavily on advertising, which local firms are running the largest ads? Newspaper ads can give you interesting information on agents, competition, and prices.
4. Two hours at the U.S. embassy's reference library will give a U.S. visitor a chance to update or verify lists of prospective agents. Embassy commercial officers may not have much specific advice to offer simply because they are not specialists. They should be well informed, however, on overall business conditions, import regulations, payment problems, and other aspects of international trade, and their expertise in these areas will be of value to you. Embassies, by the way, are always located in a country's capital, which is not necessarily the country's biggest city. Such is the case in Australia (Canberra), Brazil (Brasilia), Turkey (Ankara), and South Africa (Pretoria). In most major cities, however, a U.S. visitor will find a consulate

equipped with commercial reference facilities and services comparable to those available at the embassy.

The same facilities are maintained around the world by almost all industrialized countries. In the United States, other countries operate consulates in New York, Chicago, and San Francisco, and often in Los Angeles, Houston, New Orleans, Miami, and Boston as well.

5. See if there is a government publications office where you can browse around and pick up reports, statistics, and other valuable information to complement what you already have. Language does not have to be a problem. While you obviously have to be conversant in the local language in order to read narrative reports, you may be able to figure out statistics easily with the help of someone who can translate headings and subtitles.

Even if it is all Greek to you, take the reports. Someone back home may be able to interpret them.

6. Try to visit some major end users, including a government agency. If you sell hospital equipment, for instance, visits to the health ministry and to a large hospital may reveal data on new hospital and clinic projects and statistics, and you may be able to make a presentation on your product and company, perhaps even find out who the most active local agents are and what brands they carry. An end user may on occasion be willing to make an off-the-record recommendation. An independent assessment of some end users should therefore be very helpful. Allow enough time for it on your first visit to a priority market.

Avoid being taken in tow by a David Obodeze from the moment you emerge from your plane because if you are, you will see only what *your* David wants to show you and you will leave the country with at best a foggy notion of what is really going on. Without antagonizing possible agents, try to have enough time to yourself. There is no harm in making the agent understand that you must do some research and evaluation on your own.

7. Some of the agents you are considering may be large companies with well-known names. They may look extremely attractive, but keep in mind that your product could be buried among dozens of other lines. This happens particularly with large import houses. You will have to determine precisely which department will be responsible for your product, and make your assessment based on the department's capabilities.

On the other hand, a small company with only a few lines to handle may look at your product as a unique opportunity for growth, and consequently might be willing to make a serious effort to promote it.

8. Discuss with an agent in detail what you expect in terms of facilities and promotion, initial investment, inventory, demonstration equipment, samples, literature. Concerns on commissions, prices, territory, exclusivity, and (if applicable) protection must also be fully aired.

Be straightforward when discussing competition and other obstacles which may appear in the course of a sale. If your price is higher than a competitor's, explain the reasons to the agent. Face up to possible objections. Most salespeople tend to gloss over potential problems. In the domestic market, problems can usually be settled with a simple phone call. Internationally, you may never hear about the problem and could end up with a disgruntled agent.

Don't paint a rosy picture only to have an agent lose face with an important customer because he or she did not have answers.

MAKING THE COMMITMENT.   The search for good agents in a major, highly developed market with a complex marketing structure follows the same pattern as in a less developed country, except that you have to be extra careful about an eventual commitment. If your target is West Germany and your product requires an exclusive national agent, it may take you months to reach a decision.

The same is true when a company from another country is looking for an agent in the United States.

A possible solution is to avoid a national commitment at first and go instead for local representation at the state or provincial level. This means doing a lot of groundwork: calling on dealers and reps, working with them directly, and establishing procedures to handle their orders and shipments.

This approach takes time. But it will give you an excellent knowledge of the market. Later, when you are ready to appoint a national agent, you will be in a stronger position. In fact, if you establish the beginnings of a dealer network, you may even decide to set up a small sales office of your own to supervise it, eliminating the need for a national agent.

I remember my Japanese friend Takao Murakami making the rounds of dealers in the United States for weeks at a time, calling on three or four a day from San Francisco to New York, taking orders no matter how small, until a couple of years later he had developed a network large enough to justify a full-time office in Chicago.

His British and German competitors in the meantime kept appointing exclusive national agents (and invariably dropping them after a few months), never spending more than four of five days at a time on their visits to the United States, and never making any headway. Occasionally they would stop in the United States on their way home from a tour of Latin America.

Every agency appointment that you do make is important. Which is why even when you are trying to set up representation in a smaller country, once you have met prospective agents, discussed your business with them, and gathered as much information as possible, you should try to go back home before making a final choice. It pays to wait until you are far enough from the trees to see the forest. Discuss your findings with others on your company's management team. They may not know much about export markets, but it helps to hear different viewpoints.

If you are impressed with a particular agent, you may want to reach a provisional agreement before you leave, subject to confirmation when you get home.

Eventually a choice is made, an agent appointed. The mechanism may be a simple letter or a formal contract, depending on your company's and the agent's requirements and procedures. The agent will insist on a written commitment, knowing full well, however, that what really will hold the marriage together is performance on both sides.

When an agency relationship deteriorates to the point that contract clauses have to be checked and quoted, a break is imminent. The contract will only serve to protect the agent on past business efforts and to tell you when you can go out and appoint someone else.

Before officially confirming an agent find out if there are any special legal requirements in the particular country. In some countries manufacturers have to officially register their agents with government procurement authorities, and only one "authorized agent" may be allowed. A U.S. firm should check with the U.S. embassy in the country, or with the U.S. Department of Commerce in Washington.

The performance of overseas agents depends a lot on how you treat and support them. One perennial source of concern among overseas agents is the ease and frequency with which U.S. executives switch jobs. Will a successor honor commitments to an overseas agent? Agree to pay commissions as previously agreed? Continue supporting the agent's sales efforts?

This concern on the part of agents can be a serious handicap for U.S. firms. Faced with a choice between a U.S. or a Japanese agency, an agent may feel much more secure with the more farsighted approach of the Japanese firm.

A commitment to an agent should be clearly understood and fully supported by every responsible executive in your company.

It is also important to remember that overseas agents work under conditions which would drive many domestic dealers up the wall. Consider these examples.

■ Overseas agents have to pay cash when they send you an order; their money is frozen at the bank the moment they open a letter of credit in your favor.

■ Agents may be thousands of miles away from you, entirely on their own, unable to pick up the phone to ask you to send in the cavalry to rescue them out of a tough presentation (something a U.S. company probably would not hesitate to do if a frantic call came in from a dealer in Savannah or Seattle).

■ Overseas agents may be unable to return defective merchandise for replacement without paying freight and clearance charges far in excess of what the goods were worth in the first place.

■ A shipment may be tied up in customs for weeks due to bureaucratic delays. It may take months from the time an agent places the order until the customer finally pays up; in the meantime the agent is paying prohibitive interest rates.

There are many other nuisances and obstacles; the upshot is that in some countries agents have to show far more initiative, inventiveness, and ingenuity than they would need to in a neat, well-organized business community.

Look at the case of Sami Saad, importer of home computers in a large but not particularly affluent Middle East country. He has to create a market among potential buyers who know nothing about home computers. A government committee classifies his product as a luxury consumer item because the committee associates personal computers with videogames. This means that Sami pays a prohibitive import duty, which of course has to be passed on to the consumer, making the product much more expensive.

Sami has to get an import license for each shipment. Once the license is granted, he has to apply for permission to buy dollars in order to open a letter of credit. Meanwhile Sami spends weeks trying to have his product taken out of the luxury category, hoping that this will substantially reduce the import duties.

In spite of these and many other handicaps, Sami keeps going and looks at the future with optimism. How many U.S., German, French, or British dealers would put up with these conditions?

It takes a lot of understanding to cultivate and handle foreign agents. They will look to you for training, ideas, help. They will welcome your efforts to promote your product and company in their markets—even if on a shoestring.

CHAPTER

SEVEN

PROMOTION
ON A
SHOESTRING
Your international promotion, no matter how modest, serves three main functions:

- To support your overseas agents
- To open up new markets
- To develop sales in the home-for-export market

In all large industrialized countries, a wide range of international promotions is available from government organizations, usually at nominal cost. If you plan to operate on a shoestring budget of, say, $25,000 the first year, get all the mileage you can out of these promotions.

In the United States international promotions are offered by the U.S. Department of Commerce (DOC). Let DOC know through its nearest district office which are the countries where you want to introduce your product. (You should contact DOC even before you make a final choice of target countries.) Find out how best to make use of DOC promotions and facilities in these countries.

Check also with your state's trade and business offices. Most states are becoming involved in export promotion schemes, often including special overseas trade missions and shows.

Outside the United States, similar programs are offered in all major exporting countries by national or provincial organizations. Canadian provinces, Australian states, and West German Pänder, for instance, usually help promote exports of manufacturers within their jurisdictions.

If you are dealing with a major trading company, find out what special international promotional events it may have planned, such as overseas seminars, exhibitions, and displays in department stores.

The U.S. Department of Commerce promotes U.S. products through four types of relatively low-cost promotions for specific industry groups:

1. Catalog shows
2. Trade missions
3. Trade Center shows
4. International trade fairs

These events are useful not only for newcomers but also for well-established firms. They are usually preceded by considerable promotion. Other industrialized countries all offer their own variations on more or less the same themes.

Remember that identifying government sponsored promotions abroad in your product group can be a valuable contribution to your market research, giving you access to information which government specialists have dug up at no cost to you. Therefore, don't wait to look into overseas promotions until after you have finished your research and worked out an international strategy. Do it *beforehand!*

THE CATALOG SHOW.   Every year, DOC sponsors a number of catalog shows around the world, each one for a specific product group and covering four or five countries. This inexpensive promotion costs only $175 to $250 and a supply of your catalogs. The catalogs are displayed for several days in each country. Local businesspeople are invited to view them.

Each catalog show is run by a hired independent consultant or trade association specialist whose role is to give "state of the art" talks and help explain the products of participating firms. The catalog show is an effective way to contact potential agents. It can produce ten good leads worth following up.

The disadvantage of this promotion is that your catalogs are exhibited side by side with your competitors'. Still, this is a very small price to pay. You are gaining exposure and the cost is negligible.

Occasionally DOC also puts on traveling videocassette shows for manufacturers who have invested in short demonstration programs and company presentations. This is becoming a popular and useful medium for manufacturers of heavy equipment and instrumentation.

Check with the DOC district office nearest you for possible catalog and videocassette shows in your product group. The catalog show is useful even before you have made serious efforts to identify possible agents. Keep this promotion in mind, therefore, for first-phase and second-phase priority markets. Plan well ahead.

THE TRADE MISSION. Trade missions are a good way to meet overseas agents and end users and to get a picture of local conditions. This promotion is usually heavily advertised in each country visited.

A mission is made up of from ten to a dozen business executives in a specific product group (such as scientific instruments, photo equipment, or printing machinery). Like the catalog show, it makes a tour of several countries within a region and is under the leadership of a trade association specialist or independent consultant.

DOC puts a lot of effort into advertising trade missions within the business community of each country to be visited. The idea is to sponsor direct contacts and meetings with prequalified local agents. There are also meetings with key government officials (ministers of commerce and industry, staff of government agencies with particular interest in the product group) and chambers of commerce.

A trade mission can be useful if the participant is the export or regional manager and not a chairperson of the board who takes it as a tax-deductible junket and semiholiday. Send someone who can get down to nuts-and-bolts business and who will be able to follow up, otherwise you will be wasting your time and money.

The trade mission will cost you a fee of from $2500 to $4000. This covers advance promotion, receptions, use of meeting rooms in hotels, seminars, and other activities. To this you must add airline and hotel expenses, bringing the total to about $7000.

For this you get the advantage of personal contact with several potential agents. If you have already identified some on your own, there is really no need to invest in a trade mission. If you are talking about a first-priority country, you will be going there anyhow.

However, a trade mission to a second-phase market, or one which you had not figured on in your original plans, could be a good investment. A trade mission can also be a worthwhile tour for a company executive who has not yet decided whether to go international and wants to get a feel for possible overseas markets.

THE TRADE CENTER SHOW. DOC operates full-time U.S. Trade Centers with exhibition facilities in Sydney, Vienna, Paris, Frankfurt,

Milan, Tokyo, Seoul, Mexico City, Warsaw, Singapore, Taipei, and London. Each puts on as many as ten shows a year. Each show is devoted to a specific industry group and lasts several days. Participants pay a fee which includes booth design and preshow publicity but not the cost of building the booth.

If you already have an agent in the country, a Trade Center show is a good way to reach end users, retailers, and other customers by taking advantage of the publicity usually built up by DOC around the show. The agent can staff your booth, saving you travel and hotel expenses.

The cost of participating in a U.S. Trade Center show will range from $2500 to $6000 depending on length and location. You should definitely consider this type of show in countries where you already have appointed agents. Many visitors will be important end users.

THE TRADE FAIRS. Every year the United States participates in a number of important international trade fairs. A U.S. section or pavillion may include exhibits of twenty or more U.S. firms. Each one pays a fee ranging from $3000 to $6000. The fee covers space, booth design, and promotion. It is much cheaper than going it alone.

When considering a U.S. section in a trade fair, DOC looks at short-range returns. The department invests in advance market research to try to figure out approximately how much can be expected in sales right off the floor during the fair and in the following twelve months. This implies making choices, usually in favor of shows which produce big-dollar results. DOC may decide, for instance, to go into an agricultural machinery show that could bring $30 million in short-range sales and skip a prestigious educational materials fair which at best might generate $5 million.

The best-known and most important of all trade shows is Germany's yearly Hanover Fair. Many international fairs are devoted to a particular field; they include DIDACTA (educational products), the Paris Air Show, ACHEMA (scientific instruments), and the Frankfurt Book Fair. These events attract buyers from all over the world. DOC will not necessarily participate in these events.

Participation in an international trade fair can be costly even when there is a DOC-sponsored U.S. section. You may have to send two or three people to staff your booth, and you may also need to provide material in foreign languages and hire full-time help and interpreters. You can easily spend $20,000 or more on a single four-day event by the time you add up travel, hotels, meals, taxicabs, local help, entertainment, cost of booth, and auxiliary services.

Be careful about which shows you pick, with or without DOC sponsorship. *An international event which attracts agents and end users from all over the world is a good investment only if you are able to follow up on most leads effectively.* This presupposes that you have enough experienced regional managers to pursue the leads.

If you start off with a selective but concentrated approach to only a few first-phase priority countries, with plans for expansion to an additional five or six markets after one or two years, avoid an international trade fair unless it takes place in one of your first- or second-phase countries and you are reasonably sure it will help you build up sales among local end users and consumers. Otherwise you are better off going to trade fairs as a visitor, to look, listen, and learn.

Before you participate in any overseas promotion, make sure it dovetails with your marketing plan. Give priority to your key target markets, and don't reach out for more than you can handle.

Sign up for a mission or show only if you seriously intend to follow up; otherwise you will disappoint many potential agents. This can cost you much in goodwill when you later decide to open up their markets.

In the early stages of your export venture, be careful how you spend your promotion money. Avoid one-shot schemes which will eat up your entire budget and offer only uncertain results. Six catalog shows may bring you more workable leads than a big, costly fair or a trade mission.

One problem, of course, is that government backed promotions may not target the markets you have decided to crack. There may be no U.S. Trade Center, for instance, in any of your first-phase priority markets. There may be no catalog shows or trade missions planned for any of these markets.

You can avoid being in this situation by getting advance information on government promotions and keeping them in mind when you put together your international strategy. If you know that your product group will be the subject of a show at the U.S. Trade Center in Milan next year, then you should take a look at Italy as a possible priority market, either first phase or second phase. Be discriminating, however. A trade mission to the Soviet Union or a U.S. Trade Center show in Warsaw may not be for you if you are a newcomer.

On the other hand, don't throw your plans out the window simply because no government promotions have been scheduled for your priority markets in the next year or two. If the government decides to put on a show in Italy, this does not mean there are no markets in Great Britain, Singapore, or Colombia. It simply means that there is a favorable market in Italy and a decision was made to put on a show there.

A catalog show or trade mission covering a particular area may be prompted by a report of real, significant opportunities or by a sudden awareness in government circles that the area has been unnecessarily neglected.

Balance your promotions; the mix should depend on what you want to accomplish. Catalog shows and trade missions are good for opening up new markets. Go into them when you have decided to expand your exports. Trade Center shows and trade fairs will support existing overseas agents. Make use of them particularly when you feel you are firmly established in a market and ready to make a big effort to expand local sales.

OTHER PROMOTIONAL TOOLS.   How else can you promote your export business, giving your agents some support and at the same time opening up new markets?

Domestic Advertising.   Your product may not be entirely unknown outside your domestic market. Many of your potential end users or consumers probably read well-known U.S. and other trade, consumer, and professional magazines regularly. Publications from the United States in particular are read all over the world. Any product—U.S., Canadian, European, or Japanese—advertised or mentioned in a U.S. publication will therefore benefit from this international readership.

Japanese publications are also widely read worldwide, but unlike U.S. periodicals they are indeed intended for international audiences and not just the home market.

Keep this free international bonus from your current advertising in mind when you plan your magazine advertising from now on. A slight change in copy may help draw interest from abroad. Instead of "Dealer inquiries invited" you may want to say "Domestic and foreign dealer inquiries invited" or "Write us for the name and address of our nearest domestic or foreign dealer."

The Press Release.   Send announcements about your expansion into international markets and the appointment of export managers, regional managers, and overseas agents, as well as news of important sales abroad to all the publications which carry your ads.

You should also develop a list of trade and professional publications abroad, particularly in major industrialized markets. (You can get names and addresses of foreign publications through embassies.) Send out product releases regularly. Keep them short and informative. Consider product releases in a few major languages other than English: French,

German, Italian, Spanish. It should not be difficult or costly to have an occasional short press release translated.

Direct Mail: Home-for-Export Market. The home-for-export market should be hit three or four times a year with direct mail. Include exporters, EMCs, military reps, U.N. agencies, foreign government purchasing offices. Other segments of this market, such as big international companies, purchasing offices of foreign department stores, and trading companies are best contacted directly and frequently rather than through mailings.

Your mailings need not be elaborate, but should be specific. Send a letter, a price list (particularly to exporters and EMCs), and literature. A mailing to 1000 addresses in the United States should cost you less than $500 including postage. Store the mailing list in a computerized database where it can be easily accessible for follow up, new mailings, and updates.

Direct Mail: Overseas Agents. Direct mail is also your main tool for reaching potential overseas agents. Build up lists of agents in every country where you expect to be active in the next two or three years. This will include first- and second-phase priority targets. Computerize and update the list frequently. Combine the list with specific basic data on agents (such as name of manager, years in business, and main lines carried).

Assign responsibility for direct-mail promotion to a specific individual in your export department, initially your export assistant. This responsibility should include creating lists, sending mailings on time, keeping track of responses, and following up.

Mailings aimed at potential overseas agents should consist of a short letter, one or two brochures, and a two-sided, one-sheet questionnaire. Pay attention to weights. Brochures designed mainly for the domestic market tend to be heavy and will cost you a fortune in overseas airmail— from the United States, $0.44 per half ounce, first class, and it doesn't take much to go over. Talk to your printer about using lighter paper for your brochures, your announcements, and even your letterhead. Look also for lightweight airmail envelopes.

Surface (sea) mail takes much longer but is cheaper—$0.37 for a full ounce. Quite often surface mail from the United States to Europe is delivered by air, but you can't be sure. Figure on three weeks for surface mail to Europe, four to six weeks elsewhere. With good advance planning you should be able to do most of your large overseas mailings by surface.

A Sales Manual for Agents.   The best way to support an established overseas agent is through frequent visits, particularly during the first year. Agents who have never sold a comparable product will know very little about yours. Assume that you will have to train your agents from scratch on how to introduce the product to potential buyers and explain its features, and that you will have to inform them about what objections to anticipate and instruct them on how to close a sale.

Even if you visit an agent three times a year and stay four or five days each time, personal contact is still limited. The danger comes during the long gaps between visits—out of sight, out of mind, out of answers. An objection comes up and a salesperson deosn't remember how to cope with it. The agent doesn't think it is worth phoning you for help. After all, it takes a little more change to call Chicago from Kuala Lumpur than from Kalamazoo.

You may want to consider developing a sales troubleshooting manual in which you try to anticipate every possible situation which may arise. You can do this little by little. If you have a computer or word processor so much the better. You can make frequent changes and additions, and produce printouts at minimal cost.

Bidding Specifications.   If your product is sold on the basis of project proposals leading to public tenders, make sure your agents are supplied with detailed suggested specs covering all contingencies and alternatives. Invest in translations of these specs into the languages of the countries you have targeted. Don't wait for an agent to do the translation. Anticipate situations and do as much as you can to support your agents, leaving them free to go out and sell your product actively.

The Newsletter.   A very useful promotional medium is a newsletter aimed at overseas agents and their salespeople, provided it is not just a glossy public relations exercise about people being awarded trophies at luncheons and dinners. Make it practical, useful, a forum for new ideas and successful experiences. Be honest. If at a stationery show in Chicago you sold a dozen staplers to a curious Japanese dealer, don't go about telling people that you are active in the Japanese market.

Try to produce the newsletter as inexpensively as possible. Use a word processor or computer to compose it, then print it out and photocopy it. Leave out fancy layouts, illustrations, and anything else that could delay an issue. The important thing is to get it out regularly. Keep it short and simple so that people will be encouraged to read it. Concentrate on content rather than appearance.

International Sales Meetings.   The international or regional sales meeting can be useful if you remember that conditions vary tremendously from market to market and that participants may not share the same problems and views.

In a vast country like the United States the problem does not exist. Here is a homogeneous market in which dealers and salespeople operate under more or less similar conditions from coast to coast. Outside the United States dramatic market contrasts are encountered in less time than it takes to fly from New York to Washington, D.C. A vast economic gulf separates Egypt from Saudi Arabia, Singapore from Indonesia, Japan from China, Brazil from Bolivia.

Overseas agents attend international meetings at great expense in travel and time. They want to learn about new products, and about how to increase sales in their respective countries. *They are not particularly interested in finding out what it takes to close a sale in Los Angeles, Montreal, Paris, or Tokyo.*

To run a worldwide or regional international sales meeting which pleases everybody is impossible. Combining one with a regular domestic dealer meeting is a mistake. In the first stage of your international operations, assuming that your priority targets are all bunched up on a regional basis, you may want to schedule a meeting in the region itself. If the group is small, it will not cost you much but will be a good way to show that your company is on the move internationally. Overseas agents like to feel that they "belong" to an organization. They like to be recognized.

Later, when you have established agents in several regions, your international meetings can be broken up into group sessions where you can try to bring together agents from countries with similar problems and economic standards.

Literature.   Much of your promotional budget will be used to ship literature to your agents. Manufacturers who do not hesitate to send cartons of literature to a domestic dealer become inexplicably stingy when it comes to shipping promotional material abroad.

Shipping literature can indeed be expensive, a fact which is frequently ignored by the overseas agent who expects you to ship vast quantities of brochures immediately and by air. The answer is to make a realistic assessment of agents' needs.

If someone asks for 200 copies of a catalog, is this an arbitrary figure or does the agent indeed have 200 prospective buyers or addresses? Is it necessary to send the entire lot by air? How about twelve or twenty pieces by air and the rest by surface? Will the literature be distributed all at once or gradually?

Literature is your company's business card. In foreign markets where you may not always be able to rely on effective, well-trained local salespeople, the impact of your literature is far more important than in the domestic market.

Brochures used in the export business are not always clear and self-explanatory. How many times have you looked at a brochure and then had to contact a dealer or salesperson to get some rudimentary answers? Perhaps those who wrote the material intended to leave some questions unanswered so that you would call.

What happens if you are 10,000 miles away? Does your literature really explain what your product is all about? Or does it raise so many questions that the prospect will not be able to decide whether to buy?

Literature often is written on the assumption that the prospective buyer already has a basic knowledge of the type of product and the technical jargon that goes with it. When promoting language laboratories around the world in the early 1960s, I had a problem with brochures which had originally been produced for the U.S. language teacher, who knew the difference between audio-active and audio-active–comparative labs and all the other terminology associated with this type of equipment. All of it, however, was extremely confusing in countries where language labs had not yet been introduced.

We overcame the problem by producing a two-page bulletin describing in condensed style what a language laboratory was, what types of units it contained, and how it was used. We also clearly explained all available options. We included sketches of suggested classroom layouts. Eventually this bulletin was incorporated into a four-page international brochure which became one of our most effective international selling tools.

A special international brochure need not be a major investment. If your company has a number of different brochures and catalogs for domestic sales, discuss with your overseas agents which ones carry your message best and consider combining them into a single brochure.

Make the brochure informative and key it to a reader who knows nothing about your product.

You can get much more out of a single, well-conceived international brochure than out of a selection of several. It is better to ship a larger quantity of one brochure than a little of everything. Too many different brochures are confusing and an agent never has enough of any one of them.

Brochures in English travel fairly well all over the world, particularly if yours is a high tech product aimed at advanced researchers, technicians, and other professionals. This condition of the marketplace obviously favors U.S., Canadian, Australian, and British firms.

Whether you should produce brochures in other languages depends on product and target markets. If you are going to cover the Middle East extensively, you will eventually need a brochure in Arabic. English is good for all of southeast and south Asia and a big part of Africa. But in Latin America you will sooner or later have to come out with brochures in Spanish and Portuguese (the language of Brazil).

If you are convinced that it's okay to stick to literature in English and decide to forget about translations (who needs them?), put yourself in this position: you live in Kansas City; a saleswoman drops by and tries to sell you a French lawnmower. She gives you catalogs in French. How would you react?

You'll think, well, this is different. After all, everybody understands English! I have news for you. Think again!

Translations of brochures should be done in cooperation with overseas agents. You can arrange your own translations of newsletters and other material which will be read primarily by agents and not by end users. But brochures are a different matter.

Translations made outside the target country, even by native speakers of the language, can be quite poor. Look at a lot of the business literature in English coming out of Europe and Japan, and you can quickly get an idea of how bad things can get, particularly when the translations are made by people whose native language is not English. Literal translations into another language are a disaster.

An educated native speaker is not necessarily a good translator or editor. When the same language is spoken in many countries—as Spanish and Arabic, for instance, are—there are enough variations in usage to produce hilarious and often embarrassing situations. The answer is to go to your biggest market in the area and have the translation done there.

If Brazil is one of your main targets and you want to create literature in Portuguese, have it done in Brazil by a competent Brazilian translator and not in New York by an erudite professor from Portugal who has never been to Brazil. Remember also that people who have been expatriates for many years may continue to speak their native language fluently, but may slowly lose their feel for the colloquialisms and new expressions used in everyday speech.

It is also important to provide operating instructions in several languages. If possible, try to produce a leaflet in three or four major languages rather than having separate versions and then running the risk of enclosing them in the wrong shipment.

Local Advertising.   Should you support local advertising? This decision depends on your product and the types of end users and consumers you are aiming at. In the first phase of your international operations, avoid local advertising commitments. For one thing, you won't have enough money to contribute unless you are prepared to set aside a lavish budget. Support your agents with material, layouts, camera-ready copy. Discuss classified telephone directory displays. But let them handle local advertising on their own.

Videocassettes.   By and by you can support your overseas agents with films, slides, videocassettes, and videodiscs. All are excellent media for demonstration and training purposes, and can also be offered for presentations to associations, business groups, and schools. The videocassette has become a popular and universal medium. Throughout Europe, the Middle East, southeast Asia, Australia and New Zealand, and Japan, the VCR is rapidly becoming a household appliance.

Remember that there are different standards. Except for North America and Japan, the PAL/SECAM standard is in use virtually worldwide. To avoid language problems, you should deliver cassettes with an English soundtrack, but send your agents copies of the script and suggest they arrange for recordings in the local language.

A SHOESTRING
PROMOTIONAL BUDGET.   You can get a lot out of your promotion
dollar if you stay away from extravagant schemes in the early stages of your international operation and concentrate on realistic goals. Here are some of the things you will be able to do within the $25,000 tentative budget we discussed earlier. Estimates are based on approximate current cost of promotions supported by the U.S. Department of Commerce.

3 catalog shows	$ 750
1 trade mission	7,000
1 U.S. Trade Center show	6,000
3 mailings to the home-for-export market	1,500
4 mailings to prospective overseas agents	4,000
6 issues of a newsletter to agents	1,500
Production of a new overseas brochure	4,000
Total	$24,750

The items listed below are not indispensable the first year.

- International sales meetings
- Foreign-language literature
- Participation in major international trade fair
- Promotional videocassettes

ESTABLISHING PRODUCT NEEDS.   Part of the purpose of your international promotion, of your personal contacts, newsletters, and mailings, is to help your agent establish a clear need for your product. This is crucial. Keep it in mind always, because it is too easy to assume that nobody has to be told what your product is all about.

Remember the shoe salesperson who came to the village where everybody went about barefooted!

The need may be obvious to you. But is it to the potential end user? Play it safe and assume that the need has to be explained and demonstrated. Taking things for granted can be costly. Home computer manufacturers are having a tough time keeping their sales up mainly because they assumed all along that every modern home needed a computer. Homeowners still have to be convinced.

And as you go through the never-ending process of training and retraining agents, contacting end users, explaining needs, and promoting your product, stop from time to time to remind yourself that all of this has only one purpose: to produce sales and profits for your company.

This means that you must work toward specific orders and know when an overseas order is indeed an order.

EIGHT

WHEN IS AN OVERSEAS ORDER FOR REAL ?

An overseas order is an order *only* when the money is in the bank.

The process of working up to a definitive order starts when you tell a prospect how much your product costs. You really cannot discuss business seriously with an overseas agent or end user until you quote a price. Western firms are not always willing to give out price information, preferring instead to qualify an inquiry and acting like a jewelry store which hides the price of its merchandise behind mysterious, cryptic labels.

The Japanese, Koreans, and southeast Asians take a different approach. Along with a brochure describing the product they will invariably send a price list and (to an agent) a discount schedule. Often a proforma invoice with freight charges included, good for sixty or ninety days, is also sent. Sending out a proforma invoice is standard procedure throughout Asia; western firms rarely do it.

Which method is best?

I favor the straight approach. Quoting a price will expedite the business of getting an order, or it will discourage someone who can't afford your product in the first place. Either way, nothing is lost by mentioning price.

If you are afraid your price will scare a buyer away, emphasize in your literature and covering letter, or in your presentation if you are talking to the buyer face to face, the reasons why your product costs more. Give the buyer reasons why he or she should buy your product.

It isn't always possible to quote an exact price. How much is a physics lab? A prefab school? A clinic? All you can do in these cases is give an approximate cost range or describe a hypothetical situation such as a lab for twenty high school students, a ten-classroom school, a fifty-bed clinic.

A price list which includes dozens of components and peripherals for comprehensive installations or turnkey jobs is often difficult to figure out when you don't know exactly what has to be included. Sample quotations can solve this problem. If you sell hotel kitchens, for instance, work out and have quotations for 50-, 100-, 500- and 1000-room hotels readily available for agents and end users. Spell out what goes into each installation.

Clear pricing, or a fair approximation, is the best way to start qualifying a prospect, also the best way to help an overseas agent figure out potential profit. The two critical prices in international business are the suggested list, or end user, price and the net export price.

The list, or end user, price should be high enough to allow flexibility in negotiating special discounts and other concessions but should not be too far out of line with retail prices in the domestic market. Final decision on local pricing should be up to your agents. They should know their markets a lot better than you ever will.

Ideally you should be able to refer to the same suggested retail price domestically and internationally, both for the sake of uniformity and to avoid problems with agents and end users who are familiar with domestic prices. Price wars in the United States and Western Europe are top news items in next morning's business newspapers around the world. If a big price reduction is offered to end users and distributors in the home market, you may have to extend it also to your other markets.

You won't be able to impose a uniform international user price, however, because of the many variables which affect prices in different countries, mainly shipping costs, import duties, value added sales taxes, interest on funds tied up in letters of credit, and collection expenses.

Salespeople's commissions and agents' overall profit margins also differ considerably, depending on local standards of living and income levels.

THE NET EXPORT PRICE.   The net export price is the price the manufacturer or exporter wants to get from a sale, after deducting any outside commissions. The difference between this price and the price the end user has paid is the overseas agent's commission or discount, and will also cover added expenses such as shipping costs.

Some manufacturers retain within the export price a small margin of 5 or 10 percent for possible third-party commissions or "bird dog fees." The bird dog could be a person who helped you identify a specific opportunity, or perhaps a consultant who recommended a particularly good agent. A slight extra margin or cushion comes in handy; it gives you the extra flexibility and allows you to encourage outside advice without sacrificing your real profit or upsetting your agent's prices.

You may also need the margin as an extra inducement to a buyer to close a big sale.

Overseas agents calculate their final end user price on the basis of your export price. They will add shipping costs and all other variables.

There are essentially two ways to set your net export prices:

- Make them identical with your domestic dealer prices.
- Calculate them on a cost-plus basis.

There are arguments in favor of each. Identical prices give you uniformity, for whatever it is worth. On the other hand, a domestic dealer price may have built-in reserves for promotion, yellow pages advertising, sales meetings, and other expenditures which are strictly domestic and of no benefit to the overseas agent. To make an overseas agent pay these domestic costs is not fair.

When pricing on a cost-plus basis, you start with your real costs and add only the overhead and selling expenses which can be directly tied to international sales, plus your profit. However, manufacturers unfamiliar with export sales often add excessive estimated charges to their costs, ending up with net export prices which are much higher than domestic dealer net. This is also unfair to overseas agents, who need all the breaks they can get and should not be burdened with extra handicaps.

A good compromise solution is to calculate net export prices on the cost-plus method *provided the resulting price is never higher than what you would charge a domestic dealer.* (Allowing, of course, for extra charges, such as cost of export packaging, which may apply to some shipments.)

Your net export price will be FOB your nearest and most convenient shipping port or international airport, for instance, FOB New York, FOB Houston, FOB San Francisco, FOB New Orleans. The FOB price has four basic components:

1. Net factory price

2. Inland freight to shipping port or airport
3. International freight forwarder fees
4. Export packaging

FOB means "free on board" and is the price you charge your overseas buyer for merchandise delivered and loaded onto a vessel or aircraft. *Never quote FOB factory.* The foreign buyer has no way to figure out your inland freight from the factory to the shipping port, or any international freight forwarder fees which may apply.

Your net export price for the same merchandise could vary considerably, depending on how the buyer wants the merchandise shipped. This in turn determines what type of packaging you need.

There are three basic shipping options.

1. You can ship by air, in which case no special packaging is needed. You ship in your regular cartons.
2. You can ship by sea in containers. You pay for a 20- or 40-foot container, which saves you money if you have enough merchandise to fill either size.
3. You can ship by sea in wooden crates (smaller than container size).

Freight forwarders and airline freight departments can give you estimated shipping costs so that you can work out comparisons between air, containerized ocean, and noncontainerized ocean shipments to your priority markets. If possible, try to work out at least approximate net export prices for each of the three options and pass them on to your agents.

The more you can do to standardize and anticipate price calculations, the easier it will be for your agents to submit quotations to their customers, and the easier it will be for them to get orders.

Your agents need to know your net export prices, but will seldom ask you for simple FOB quotations that do not include other export costs. One of the rare instances is when the country of destination insists that all merchandise be shipped on vessels of its own flag, in which case the buyer (agent or end user) pays for freight and insurance locally, in the country's currency. This regulation has two purposes: to promote the national merchant fleet and to conserve foreign currency.

THE DELIVERED PRICE. Normally the price that really matters to overseas agents is the cost of your merchandise *delivered to their port of entry.* This price includes your FOB cost plus freight (sea or air) and insurance, and is the figure an agent will use to open a letter of credit in your favor.

The two most common ways to quote a delivered price are CIF and C&F. Both CIF and C&F prices are quoted on the port of destination (CIF Rio de Janeiro, C&F Jeddah, CIF Bombay, CIF Frankfurt).

CIF (cost, insurance, freight) includes your FOB price, plus ocean or air freight to destination, plus insurance. C&F includes freight but not insurance; insurance is paid by the buyer in the country of destination.

FOB, CIF, and C&F are therefore the three most common international terms of sale. The choice is up to the buyer, and depends on the country's practices and regulations.

QUOTATIONS AND PROFORMAS.   After a few shipments you and your agents will have a good idea of CIF or C&F costs to their ports of destination. However, they will continue to ask you for specific quotations for each order. Agents do this for three reasons.

1. To confirm your net export price
2. To get a confirmed figure for shipping costs (or at least a very close estimate)
3. To give their banks the information needed to open an exact letter of credit

You can issue quotations to your agent by simple telex or in writing. A quick FOB quotation is good enough for ballpark estimates, but if your agent requires a firm and complete quotation, you have to specify a number of details; they might include the following.

- Quantity and product description
- Unit and extended prices
- Total FOB price and port of embarkation
- Ocean or air freight costs
- Export packaging costs
- Insurance
- Total CIF or C&F price to port of destination
- Terms of payment
- Validity of your offer

Sometimes an agent will ask you to specify the number of cartons or crates the shipment will consist of and their total weight and cubic dimensions. This information will be needed by the bank and by the insurance agency.

Manufacturers sometimes make the mistake of issuing international quotations with extremely short validity. A quote with a thirty-day limit, for instance, is useless in most international business transactions except for some commodities and other fast-moving items or for "special deals" which must be decided on quickly on a take it or leave it basis.

Sixty days is better but still unrealistic. Ninety days is really a minimum. An agent who orders for inventory will probably turn around and apply for a letter of credit within days of receiving your quotation. But if the order depends ultimately on decisions by an end user you may have to wait months, particularly if a government agency is involved.

Any delay can create problems. The buyer may decide to confirm the order six months later, well beyond the original validity of your offer, and still expect the same prices. You will then have to decide if you can live with the prices you quoted earlier. You will still have to issue a new formal quotation either reconfirming the first one or quoting new prices.

Agents or end users often require a proforma invoice. This is nothing but a complete, detailed quotation, usually done on a regular invoice form under the heading "Proforma Invoice." The proforma looks like a real invoice but isn't. You will still have to issue a real invoice when you get the order. The proforma is required by many banks before they open a letter of credit and occasionally also by customs authorities.

Agents may ask you to issue quotations directly to end users at prices higher than your net export. This happens in countries which require government agencies to purchase directly from foreign suppliers. In Korea agents are not allowed to issue orders on their own; only trading companies with a big volume of business are allowed to do so.

In a case like this the end user price should be decided by your agent. The difference between the quoted price and your net export (less freight and other charges) will be the agent's commission.

The process of submitting quotations can be simplified considerably if you make use of an international freight forwarder. The forwarder's function is to help you move merchandise to overseas destinations. The job includes submitting freight and insurance estimates, recommending suitable packaging, arranging container loading and export documentation, reviewing letters of credit, providing you and your bank with dock and airline receipts, and giving you advice on the best way to ship an order. The forwarder is one of the many specialists available to help grease the wheels of your export operation.

You can simplify the process of submitting quotations and proformas enormously by computerizing your prices, charges for packaging, and other reoccurring costs. Try also to code and store all proformas and quotations so that they can be quickly retrieved and used as models for future orders. This will save you a lot of time, particularly when you have to submit a quotation in a hurry.

THE LETTER OF CREDIT.   Now we come to the question: When is an international order a real order?

There is only one true test. An international order is a real order only when you hold in your hand a confirmed, irrevocable letter of credit (L/C).

Until then, all you have is the promise of an order. *Even when the merchandise is readily available, don't ship it until you have an L/C.* Refusing to ship does not mean you don't trust your agent. It is a simple and logical protection against the unexpected.

Several weeks may elapse between receipt of an order and the receipt of an L/C. The delay could be critical in terms of delivery. Should you take a chance and start processing the order before the L/C arrives? Here are two cases in which you will be justified in putting things in motion: (a) the order is for inventory, and comes from a reliable agent located in a stable country; (b) the order calls for standard merchandise which can be delivered to someone else.

Don't start processing orders for special equipment or those for which the buyers are end users, including government agencies. An order may be canceled for any number of reasons—some legitimate, some contrived, all very frustrating. A government decree may change import regulations overnight. An emergency austerity program may automatically cancel all foreign orders. A government department may learn that its budget is depleted, and its request for a letter of credit has been turned down by the finance ministry.

Whatever the reason, there is nothing you can do about it. If the order was for a standard product you can sell in New Mexico just as easily as in New Zealand, no harm is done. But if the product is nonstandard or a special model in limited demand, you may be stuck with extra, hard-to-move inventory.

Veterans of the Middle East oil-boom days will tell you countless stories of companies that got burned taking orders or letters of intent for granted. A letter of intent, issued usually by a government agency, is merely a statement that your offer has been accepted and that the agency intends to issue a confirming order.

A letter of intent definitely is *not* an order. Be happy when you get one, but don't open that bottle of champagne until you see and touch a confirmed written order *and an L/C that meets your requirements.*

To cover yourself against long delays between receipt of an order and of an L/C, state your delivery times in all cases as "120 days after receipt of a valid, irrevocable letter of credit."

The letter of credit, an instrument virtually unknown to firms doing business strictly in the U.S. market, is your guarantee that you will be paid in full and promptly even if the buyer should go broke. It is also the buyer's guarantee that you will deliver the specified goods under the specified conditions.

When your buyer opens an L/C, the buyer's bank is asked to transfer funds from the buyer's account to your bank for payment to you when you have submitted proof that the merchandise has been shipped as specified. Once the L/C is opened, the buyer cannot cancel it under any circumstances. There are two types of L/Cs.

The First Is the Irrevocable Letter of Credit. When an irrevocable letter of credit is issued, the buyer's bank guarantees payment to your bank, which in turn pays you. Your only risk is default of the foreign bank, which is highly unlikely. The irrevocable L/C is the acceptable method in most cases. Watch out, however, for countries with shaky finances and payment performance (banks and government sources can give you advice).

Also be aware that your bank may decide, before releasing the funds, to check back with the bank in the issuing country. This can cause delays.

The Second Is the Confirmed, Irrevocable Letter of Credit. On receipt of a confirmed, irrevocable L/C, your bank guarantees payment to your company. Your money is safe even if the buyer's foreign bank defaults. This is the safest method. Payment is entirely up to your bank once you have complied with all L/C requirements.

It is up to you to decide which type of L/C you want and to state this in your quotation. You must also tell the buyer which bank is to be "notified" (your regular bank, for instance).

The L/C actually will be opened through a "confirming" bank, which advises your regular bank when the L/C has been issued, and which pays your bank when the entire business is settled.

Let's look at a typical transaction. Your company, located in a small town in Vermont, banks with the First Municipal Bank. Your agent in Saudi Arabia is sending you an order; the agent opens a confirmed, irrevocable L/C in favor of your company at the Riyadh National Bank. The Riyadh National Bank works through the Chase Manhattan Bank of New York (its correspondent in the United States). Chase Manhattan receives the L/C, and notifies the First Municipal Bank in your home town. When all requirements are met, Chase Manhattan pays the First Municipal Bank, which in turn credits your account.

You should ask your agents to telex you details of L/Cs as soon as they are opened. You can then alert your bank and ask that you be immediately notified by phone the moment the L/C is received. You can also ask that the L/C be transferred from the overseas to the confirming bank by telex.

The charge for an L/C is between 0.25 percent and 1 percent of the total amount. This cost is absorbed by the buyer.

The L/C incorporates the full description of the merchandise, the prices, and all shipping details exactly as quoted in your proforma invoice. The L/C will contain precise shipping and billing instructions, down to how many copies of the invoice you have to submit and what other documentation must be attached. The L/C is prepared by the buyer's bank and sent to the confirming bank, which in turn sends it to you with a letter of confirmation.

Go over the L/C with extreme care. No error can be allowed, even in the spelling of your company's name and address. Make sure that the validity will cover you for the time needed to complete the order and to make a particular sailing date. Have your freight forwarder review the L/C as well.

If there is the slightest error, or a clause that you cannot live with, notify the bank and your buyer at once by telex. Ask for an amendment or extension of the validity, otherwise the confirming bank will *refuse to honor the L/C when you come back for payment.* Amendments to L/Cs are customary and usually easily complied with. They are a minor nuisance.

Don't under any circumstances deviate from instructions contained in an L/C. Follow them meticulously and to the letter, no matter how illogical and archaic they may seem. Otherwise you will not get paid.

When the merchandise has been delivered to the port of export your freight forwarder gets a dock receipt, prepares an ocean bill of lading, and submits it to the steamship company for signature. These and other required documents, such as your invoice and packing lists, are then presented to the confirming bank by your company or your forwarder. If everything is in order the bank pays you. The same procedure applies for air shipments.

Watch out for delays. The bank will not honor the L/C if you ship after a specified date. If you are not sure of actual shipping costs when you issue a quotation, you may submit an estimate. Ask the buyer to make sure to mention this in the L/C. The confirming bank may allow payment of up to 10 percent more than the original estimated freight.

The types of export documents needed for your target markets may vary somewhat. Your freight forwarder will know what they are. Generally you have to produce some or most of the documents on the following list.

■ Export license (In the United States this is required for merchandise which incorporates sensitive high technology which the United States does not want to make available to certain countries. Other countries have their own export licensing requirements.)

- Commercial invoice (This is a regular invoice.)
- Consular invoice (An invoice prepared on special forms and sometimes in the language of the country of destination, required by some importing countries.)
- Certificate of origin (Stipulates the country where the product was manufactured.)
- Inspection certificate (Usually applies to plants and other agricultural products and is required by most countries.)
- Clean on-board bill of lading (This document says that the carrier has accepted the merchandise for shipment without any exceptions noted.)
- Airway bill (Same as the bill of lading, but for air shipments.)
- Dock receipt (This provides proof that the merchandise was delivered to the pier.)
- Insurance certificate (An insurance certificate is required if insurance is provided by you, the seller, and not by the buyer.)

Handling export documentation at first seems complicated but soon becomes routine. It is no different from working with the many other forms any business enterprise learns to live with.

In a small export operation you will have to rely on regular company staff to do your export paperwork. Orders and L/Cs at first will not be coming in regularly. There could be occasions for complaints when someone who ordinarily does something else is given from time to time the job of dealing with export papers.

This is when it will become clear that your entire company, and not just your small export department, must have a positive outlook about your international venture and an understanding of what it is going to take to make it work.

NINE

GETTING INTO THE RIGHT SPIRIT

The factors that will contribute to your success in international marketing—or at least the most important ones—are the same in the computer age as 2000 years ago when a Phoenician exporter decided to set up a dealer network along the Upper Nile. They do not even include special international skills.

With occasional exceptions, the dozens of international marketing executives from the United States that I have met in a quarter of a century of world travel speak nothing but English, know little about the history of the countries they are covering, have a rudimentary knowledge of those countries' geography, seldom bother to keep up with political developments, often do not even know the name of a country's ruler (and if they do they mispronounce it atrociously), and on occasion expect a dealer in Bangladesh to know who won last year's World Series.

A few are outstanding executives with a knack for international business. The great majority are good, and do a reasonably effective job of promoting their company's business. A handful have been disastrous and probably would have been just as bad in the domestic market.

The many Europeans, Australians, Canadians, and Japanese I have also met over the years have no special international qualifications either, except that the continental Europeans and Japanese speak, read, and write English reasonably well.

What do these men and women, not including the occasional total incompetent, have in common?

- They know their company and its products.
- They can get along with agents and end users and do as fair a selling job as one would expect of any sales executive or salesperson. They are not better or worse salespeople than their counterparts back home.
- They are willing to travel and put up with all the inconveniences this usually implies.
- They feel secure and confident in their jobs.
- They are supported by home offices that understand what it takes to make an international marketing operation work.

Which of these requirements is the most important?

If I were to name one paramount requirement I would say without question: company support. Yes, the others are all important. Obviously you need to have a thorough knowledge of your product and company. But export and regional managers cannot do a good job when they are not fully supported by their company. Logical? Of course. But you would be surprised how often this rule is violated.

Company support is not tangible. It is not the same as a specific international strategy with clear targets and guidelines that can be jotted down on paper. Company support is something that must be developed: the right spirit, a frame of mind, a concept understood and accepted by everybody, from the chief executive officer to a production line apprentice.

Company support has five indispensable, basic components.

1. A positive attitude
2. A commitment to support the marketing group
3. Patience
4. Perseverance
5. Flexibility

If any one of these five key ingredients is missing in your approach to international marketing, your chances of success will be reduced or perhaps vanish.

A POSITIVE ATTITUDE. There is no point in going international unless your company's entire staff is sold on the idea, realizes how important it is to the company's growth and profits, and learns that a customer in a country with an unpronounceable name is just as important as your friendly dealer in Burbank or Biloxi. Without a positive attitude funny things happen. An important bid may be sent surface mail and miss its deadline because your mailroom clerk decides it is ridiculous to spend $9.75 on postage to some unheard of country. Your billing clerk sees no reason to make seven copies of an invoice as required by a letter of credit; doesn't everybody, after all, have a copier? Your shipping department sends out an incomplete shipment and puts the rest on back order, never bothering to find out that the letter of credit did not allow for partial shipments.

Other, more serious mistakes may be made, but unfortunately it is the small, insignificant ones that usually sneak through unnoticed, spelling disaster and giving export managers a few extra premature gray hairs.

All of this can be easily avoided if everybody in the company is made to realize that international business is just as serious as domestic business and is not to be treated as somebody's new hobby. Also that there are a few requirements that apply which are different from those of normal domestic business and, most important of all, that everybody should embark on this new venture enthusiastically. Your export sales team will not perform at their best if they do not have the support of a positive attitude back home.

COMMITMENT.   Once the commitment to go international is made, you must stick to it and give your export team a chance. The worst thing you can do is pull the rug out from under them prematurely.

All company officers and directors must be made fully aware of the commitment, of the plan, and of the objectives you hope to achieve. *Everybody should be warned against expecting quick results.*

A frequent mistake of newcomers to international markets is to back down on commitments to international marketing long before sales have had time to materialize. The absolute minimum commitment you should make when going international is three years. Experienced old timers will laugh at this suggestion. It will seem to them too short. Companies seriously determined to capitalize on foreign markets usually plan far beyond three years. However, three years at least gives you a chance to see trends and to analyze the capabilities and potential of overseas agents and markets.

To expect results earlier is unrealistic, also unfair to your export sales force. Quick results, in fact, may have counterproductive consequences in the long run. For instance, a big early order could lull you into thinking that foreign business is a piece of cake, causing your export sales force to slow down to a more leisurely pace.

I remember a prefab housing manufacturer who got a $10 million order in the Middle East three short months after first visiting the area. The firm had never done any foreign business before. Convinced that it had plugged into the "right connection" (you guessed it, somebody knew a prince) the company's management sat back and waited for the next order to roll in. Nothing happened for four years. By that time the profits from the first sale had vanished, absorbed in travel, expensive entertainment, and gifts.

The lesson? Don't let quick success go to your head! Stick to your long-range strategy. Keep up the systematic approach to market development. Stay on track!

An export sales force cannot perform effectively if it is under pressure to come up with a specific volume of business in a very short time. Sales quotas are of doubtful value. Use them for general forecasting, not as a threat. Salespeople who feel they have to produce a certain volume "or else" may do ill-advised things, such as appointing an agent purely to get a big immediate order without regard to the agent's long-term capabilities or seriousness.

Quotas can work after you have had a good bit of experience in a country or region, and have established and trained a reliable agent. But meeting a sales quota could also be entirely beyond the control of a regional manager or agent.

Nobody understands the importance of long-range commitment better than the Japanese. Their idea of long-range is at least five years. In this they have a decided advantage over firms in other countries. They develop their international strategy systematically, and they refuse to be fooled by "beginner's luck" orders. Japanese export and regional managers and their salespeople know that they can count on full support back home and that nobody will start making faces when they fail to see streams of foreign orders pouring in overnight.

The value of long-range commitment has yet to be understood by many western firms operating on the international scene.

PATIENCE. Patience goes hand in hand with commitment and is particularly vital if you depend on big projects and orders rather than day-to-day business. Anybody who was exposed to the effervescent Saudi Arabian market in the years after the price of oil went through the ceiling has many stories to tell about the agonies of writing and rewriting offers, waiting weeks and months for decisions, facing delays and sometimes the cancellation of a project, only to be invited again two months later to go through the whole thing one more time. Yet all of it was necessary and important and that's the way the market was. You either had the patience to stick to it or you packed up and went home.

While things in the Middle East have settled down—newcomers now find a steadier, less agitated type of market—the same thing could and indeed will happen again in other parts of the world, whenever countries become suddenly affluent for any reason.

Manufacturers often get impatient with foreign agents who don't start placing orders within weeks of being appointed. The agent may not be any good in the first place, but if that is true the fault lies with you for having picked the wrong one. If you do a reasonably good job of checking out agents before you appoint them, give them a chance. There may be reasons beyond their control why they are unable to place early orders. Instead of applying pressure, find out what you can do to help them.

Foreign agents as a rule operate largely on their own, without the benefit of your immediate support. You must learn to be much more patient with a foreign agent than with a domestic dealer. This is a rule which experienced firms apply consistently in their international operations. Take your time in evaluating overseas agents, but once you appoint them stick by them and help them through thick and thin.

The same measure of patience and understanding is indispensable when becoming involved in major projects. Once you make a commitment to submit a proposal or quotation, see the project through no matter how long it takes.

PERSEVERANCE. The vice-president of a U.S. medical equipment supply company arrived in Riyadh on his first trip to Saudi Arabia and spent two days meeting with various courteous officials in the Ministry of Health. At each meeting there was a great deal of tea drinking in the company of other visitors who kept drifting in and out and were also politely received. Talk was sparse, subdued, and limited to social chitchat. There was little chance to discuss business except for a brief introduction of the company and its product.

After one such meeting a high-level Saudi official made a request of the V.P.: "Would you please return later this week for more talks?"

"Sorry, no way," replied the V.P. "I have meetings in Abu Dhabi, Dubai, Bahrein, Kuwait, and Amman in the next ten days," he went on importantly.

Having thus missed his cue to what probably would have been the start of serious business discussions, the V.P. went on unhappily hopping from country to country, listening to more chitchat and drinking more tea.

When he got back to the office his report to the company's president was very succinct and unequivocal: "Total waste of time. Can't talk to those people. All they do is drink tea. Forget the Arab World."

Which the company did, to the delight of its U.S. and foreign competitors, considering that in the following five years Saudi Arabia and its neighbors spent billions of dollars developing the health sector and purchasing almost every conceivable type of medical product.

An extreme example? Not really. I have seen the same impatient response in many other situations and countries. I have also known persistent international sales executives who kept going back to the same markets in spite of initial setbacks and finally saw their perseverance rewarded with substantial orders. I know executives who went back to Saudi Arabia twelve, fifteen, twenty times in two years, carefully building up business and personal contacts, taking a serious interest in the country's development, and in the process proving to their Saudi prospects that they meant business, while learning to appreciate the revitalizing qualities of Arabian tea and coffee!

I am not advising you to knock your head against a wall. If, in spite of research and the advice of consultants, a country does not look right for your product after you have given it your best, you may have to drop it after a while.

But if you are reasonably certain of a market, stick to it and keep coming back.

FLEXIBILITY.   The world marketplace is widely diversified and always changing. Markets that are modest today become explosive tomorrow. Product needs which were never recognized before suddenly materialize during major development projects. Countries which were ignored in your strategy turn out to be worthy of high-priority treatment.

You find that the model or version of your product which you decided to market in certain countries is in fact far less attractive to agents and end users than one you had labeled as unsaleable. You discover, also, a demand for subassemblies, components, and services which you had never dreamed of marketing abroad.

One regional manager's territory is too small, another's too large. In both cases this is not realized until several months after you start going after the territories.

Your policy of seeking exclusive agents in each country works out in some of the more centralized countries, gets bogged down in others.

These are only some of the situations which may develop as you go into international markets, some of the ways that the real world can clash with your international strategy. These situations will indeed come up, and you will be smart to be alert to them and ready to respond to them. Don't put your export operations in a straightjacket. Going by the book is fine, up to a point. Ignoring changing markets and opportunities is a serious mistake at home and abroad.

Flexibility in your pursuit of international markets gives you a strength and vitality which can put you ahead of competitors who are either too large and cumbersome or too slow to respond to the challenge of new sales opportunities.

ACCEPT YOUR MISTAKES;
PRESS YOUR ADVANTAGES. A positive attitude, commitment, patience, perseverance, and flexibility together constitute a frame of mind which must be developed from within. Developing this frame of mind is just as important as gathering the nuts-and-bolts information that will help you to understand and evaluate world markets and then to formulate and carry out a marketing plan.

Having the right spirit is particularly important if your company is taking its first steps in the international marketplace. International traveling salespeople for multinational conglomerates know that with or without them international operations will go on.

A firm which is new to international business has to convince its own export staff, overseas agents, and end users that it is seriously committed to a sustained marketing effort.

Developing the proper spirit means, in part, realizing that mistakes cannot always be avoided, regardless of how much research has gone into formulating an international strategy. This fact must be understood particularly by a company's board of directors, many of whose members may be well versed in domestic matters but may not have a clue as to what goes on abroad.

In fact, you may fail completely in some countries which at first looked like winners, for reasons entirely beyond the control of your export department.

Consider Iran, a country which drew thousands of businesspeople from all over the world in the early years of the oil crisis. Iran then looked very good as a large, brand-new, expanding market with ample funds for all sorts of development projects and consumer products. Many companies did very well in Iran, but others had not even started to cash in on their substantial investments in time and expenses when Khomeini took over.

Fortunately for international marketing managers, drastic upheavals of the Iranian variety are not common. In most cases they occur in smaller, less important countries and *business does not necessarily suffer.*

No company can be faulted for having zeroed in on Iran back in the early 1970s. It was the sensible thing to do. The mistake of some firms was to concentrate too heavily on Iran and ignore other opportunities. In other words, their mistake was lack of perspective, putting all their eggs in the proverbial single basket.

As you work to build up the right spirit in international marketing you will also find the following points worth keeping in mind.

First, international marketing is too important to be put on the back burner when domestic business picks up and revived when things back home begin to look bad and new outlets are suddenly needed. This on-again, off-again attitude kills the morale of an export department and its overseas agents and is frequently the reason why a firm never moves beyond an amateur rating in the international market.

Second, if your competition includes large firms with full-fledged international marketing departments, it does not necessarily follow that their executives and salespeople are all crack promoters who will trample all over you. Representatives of large companies usually like to go by the book, and they may lack flexibility.

Large companies are made up of many individuals. The larger the firm, the more limited the scope and authority of each executive and salesperson. Some companies have become bureaucratic dinosaurs in which few people can make or dare to make decisions without referring to a committee. Many committees are intended to enlighten senior executives so far removed from the front lines that they wouldn't know a customer if they saw one.

Third, consider this analogy: When you board a commercial airliner, your attitude toward the carrier is tinted by the kind of service you get from the cabin crew. Nothing else really matters. You really don't care at that point how long the airline has been in business or how many countries are covered or even the name of the captain.

Millions of dollars' worth of advertising will have been wasted on you if the cabin attendant gives you a nasty look when you ask for extra tonic for your gin.

On the international marketing scene an agent or end user may judge a company largely by the caliber, personality, expertise, decisiveness, and personal manners of its export and regional managers. Essentially this is a one-on-one relationship, regardless of how large your company may be.

A small or medium company able to give its export sales force enough room to maneuver without constantly checking back with the home office will have a tremendous advantage over a large, experienced, but cumbersome competitor.

There is ample scope in international markets for small, well-organized manufacturers and suppliers who do not always go by the book.

To conclude: The right spirit in international marketing begins to take shape when you are ready to think of markets in terms of the whole world and not merely your traditional domestic territory. It takes a while to reach the point where you are putting on a professional, polished act. But you can get there a lot quicker when you are convinced that you have a product intended for world consumption.

PART TWO

POLISHING YOUR ACT

CHAPTER

TEN

THE ART OF TRAVEL

Travel is vital to an export operation. Without travel your sales will never get off the ground. Surprisingly, there is no shortage of companies who would like to export without investment in foreign travel. There are export managers in the United States, and no doubt in many other countries, who have never set foot abroad.

That's no way to run an export business. How long could your domestic organization stay in business if you did not make frequent personal visits to dealers and major end users? Internationally the need for frequent direct contact with an agent is even more pressing. Many overseas agents will measure your interest in their markets by how often you call on them.

One of the key elements in an effective international strategy is planning for foreign travel: You must budget for and schedule enough foreign travel to allow you, whether an export or regional manager, to cover your overseas markets frequently. You cannot establish yourself in an overseas market with one or two quick visits a year. You will never be taken seriously.

Effective travel requires meticulous advance preparation. You have to alert your agents to your arrival and work out at least a tentative outline of what you expect to accomplish during your visit. This may involve setting up sales training sessions, meetings with important end users, visits to government offices, and perhaps side trips to other cities.

If you are starting your export operation from scratch, don't be in too big a hurry to hop a plane for foreign lands. Allow yourself two or three months at least to get organized. But don't delay much longer than that.

Each trip abroad ought to be the culmination of weeks of planning. Each three- or four-day visit to an overseas agent is the "moment of truth" when you finally find yourself on the firing line. All the research, planning, and preparation that preceded it should have had the sole objective of making it possible for your agent to sell your product successfully and at a profit to your company.

To repeat: *Plan each visit abroad with extreme care.* Don't leave anything to chance. Avoid wasted motion. Make every visit count.

Your actual planning will depend on the makeup of the markets you have chosen. Are they centralized or decentralized markets? Which cities are dominant in business?

To cover West Germany you may have to visit Berlin, Hamburg, Frankfurt, Dusseldorf, Cologne, Stuttgart, and Munich regularly. No single city is dominant. In France, on the other hand, you can safely concentrate on Paris. In Italy you must include Milan and Rome.

If you do business in Australia, you have to stop in Melbourne and Sydney. This, however, does not guarantee you coverage in Perth, clear across the country and a commercial center in its own right. A similar regional consideration applies to Canada, where you have to include Montreal, Toronto, and Quebec in the east and Vancouver on the west coast as a minimum.

The United States, needless to say, is not a market which can be covered with a simple trip to New York or Chicago.

Business in Japan is largely divided between Tokyo and Osaka. In Latin America there are highly centralized countries such as Argentina, Chile, Mexico, and Venezuela. But trade with Brazil requires visits to Rio de Janeiro and Sao Paulo, and Colombia cannot be properly developed unless you include travel to Bogota, Cali, and Medellin.

THE ITINERARY. Every international traveler develops a personal travel pattern. The one which has always worked best for me is to divide the year roughly into four quarters, each one to include an overseas trip lasting about three weeks.

Four trips of three weeks each adds up to twelve weeks a year. If you cover six countries this allows two weeks per country, which you can divide either into two visits of one week or three of four or five days.

A trip of less than three weeks can be expensive (fewer working days for the same airline fare); a longer one, in my own particular case, becomes boring and tiring. For me each overseas trip is a highly concentrated effort. If I extend it beyond a certain point, the pace begins to lag and it is time to head back home.

If you stay away four weeks or more, you will also face the problems of work piling up on your desk at home and of being too long out of touch with what is happening. The phone or telex makes it easy for you to stay in touch with the office, but international communication tends to be sketchy. It's like reading a newspaper with nothing but headlines. You don't know what's really happening until you get back home.

A three-week trip allows you to spend enough time with three or four overseas agents. With four regular trips a year you should be able to cover your markets and countries well.

The three-week pattern may or may not work for you. You will find out soon enough, probably after you have taken two or three trips. But do try to arrive at a comfortable formula of your own so that you will be able to at least rough out a travel plan for a full year. If you still need time to do additional research on agents when you visit a particular country, you may have to schedule a longer stay, which could easily stretch a trip to four weeks (if it includes stops in other countries in your territory).

A regular travel pattern makes it easier for your agents to have an idea when to expect you and to plan their sales promotions accordingly. Earlier we saw how my old friend Takao Murakami developed the U.S. market through persistent and systematic visits to local dealers across the country. Dealers got used to expecting him every three months. Takao's itinerary was always more or less the same. It probably became an extremely boring routine. But it worked!

Once you have developed your own travel pattern, try to stick to it as much as you can but don't allow yourself to fall into a permanent rut. As in everything else concerning international marketing, retain flexibility.

The more stops you make on a trip, the more time you will waste in airplanes and getting in and out of airports and hotels. It can take you twenty minutes from the time your plane touches down until you're in a cab after clearing customs and immigration (as in Singapore, the world's best and most efficient airport, bar none) to two hours or more (as in Cairo, the world's most chaotic, most crowded, and most maddening one).

Don't plan your itineraries too tightly. On occasion you may want to cut down a visit to three days, but don't make it any shorter. You may have a limited objective in a particular country, but a lot may happen to upset your plans. For instance, the government official you were going to visit may not be able to see you until a day or two later;

a flight may be canceled or delayed; your agent may have scheduled unexpected but important last minute appointments for you.

If you finish your business in a country a day earlier than planned, don't be in a hurry to leave. The extra time may provide a unique opportunity to get to know an agent or a major end user a little better. This works particularly well in the Middle East and some Latin American countries where a visitor is always welcome even without an appointment.

Are you a workaholic with hang-ups about goofing off, someone who is uncomfortable when not busy shuffling papers or punching numbers into your pocket calculator? In the international marketplace this type of behavior is not wise. If you must always be on the move, ready to rush out to another meeting, scheduling four meetings when you only have time for three, you will miss a lot of opportunities. Sipping tea in the office of an Egyptian agent without the pressures of a tight schedule can be a good way to strengthen a business relationship.

Saving the weekend for travel from one country to another is not always a good idea either, even though you may feel this keeps you from using up "productive" weekday time. If you arrive in a country on a Saturday or Sunday, you may be left alone until Monday morning. If, however, you show up on a Wednesday or Thursday, you will make yourself available for weekend invitations—another good way to strengthen ties with local people. Furthermore, a midvisit weekend gives you a breathing spell which can help you sort out impressions, problems, and strategy.

HOLIDAYS. If your itinerary includes Islamic countries, remember that most of them follow the Islamic calendar. (Among the exceptions are Turkey, Indonesia, and Malaysia.) The week begins on Saturday; the weekend falls on Thursday and Friday. Businesses are closed Thursday afternoon and all day Friday. In some countries, such as Saudi Arabia, government officials take the full two-day weekend, but as a rule government and businesses are open Thursday morning.

If you have any Islamic countries in your territory, check with their embassies to find out if they observe the Saturday-to-Wednesday or the Monday-to-Friday workweek.

(Since not all countries in the Middle East follow the Saturday-to-Wednesday workweek, the area is ideal for a workaholic regional manager. For instance, you can work Turkey from Monday to Thursday, fly to Saudi Arabia on Friday and go to work there on Saturday morning. Not a day wasted! Things can also work the other way if you are prone to giving yourself a little well-deserved free time. You can work Saudi

Arabia Monday through Thursday, fly to Istanbul on Friday, and take a three-day weekend.)

National and religious holidays can be a problem, particularly in Catholic countries. Occasionally you will also have to put up with unscheduled, impromptu, surprise holidays—as happens in countries like Brazil or Argentina when the national football team wins the World Cup, for instance.

In Brazil watch out for Carnival, which takes up a weekend plus three working days but in reality brings business to a standstill at least a week earlier. Carnival ends the day before Ash Wednesday.

Italy is the world's most strike-prone country. The Italian *sciopero* is unique. It is seldom nationwide or even unionwide, and therefore usually affects a very specific small group for a limited time, for instance, the drivers of the refueling trucks at Fiumicino (Rome) and Linate (Milan) airports, from 3 P.M. to 7 P.M. on a Friday afternoon. You can imagine the chaos. A general airport and airline strike couldn't do any better.

"Bridge-building" holidays are also popular in Latin countries—like not going to work on Friday if Thursday is a holiday. Not unlike what happens in the United States the Friday after Thanksgiving.

One thing that really upsets a lot of travelers is finding out that their embassies not only observe local holidays but their own as well, a practical way of having the best of both worlds! I have never run into U.S. business travelers in casual dalliance by a swimming pool on the Fourth of July, but try to call the U.S. embassy!

(Incidentally, it is also a bit exasperating to learn that personnel in Western embassies in Islamic countries are often paid a bonus for having to work Saturdays and Sundays, even though they have Thursdays and Fridays off.)

Japan has very few official holidays. There is also no bridge building, and you are rarely inconvenienced by strikes. Much the same situation prevails in Korea and throughout southeast Asia.

Become familiar with official and religious holidays in the countries you plan to cover. Check with government sources. The best thing is to call the embassies of the countries you plan to visit. Try to get a list of all the holidays scheduled for a full year in advance.

When you plan your trips, keep the seasons in mind, as well as the local school year in each country (information you can also get from the embassies).

In the southern hemisphere, the worst time for business visits is from mid-December to early March. This is summer vacation time. If you must go, make sure that the people you want to see will be there, but try to avoid travel to the area at this time if you can. Latin

American countries also observe a one-month winter school vacation in July.

In Europe, four-, five- and six-week vacations are not unusual. July and August are the worst times for travel on the continent. Many companies, particularly in France and Italy, actually shut down in August. Other popular European vacation times are mid-December to mid-January and a two-week period including Easter.

Avoid visiting an Islamic country during Ramadhan, the month of fasting, unless it is absolutely necessary. For thirty days devout Moslems will not eat, drink, or have sex from sunup to sundown. Offices are open short hours during the day and longer hours at night.

The Islamic calendar is lunar rather than solar. Therefore, the year is shorter than that of the Gregorian calendar. This means that Ramadhan comes several days earlier each year than the year before, and so does not coincide with any of the four seasons of the year. (In 1985 Ramadhan was from May 20 to June 18.)

Ramadhan is followed six weeks later by Hadj, the pilgrimage season. Hadj lasts one week, but it can be difficult to get a visa to Saudi Arabia for the two or three weeks before and after the holiday. Hundreds of thousands of pilgrims go to the holy city of Mecca from all over the world, creating for the government of Saudi Arabia a massive logistics and security problem. Authorities try to alleviate it by limiting the number of business travelers, workers, officials, and other nonpilgrims visiting the country during the Hadj period. (In 1985 Hadj was from August 14 to August 20.)

In July and August, the hottest months of the year in the Middle East, businesspeople and government officials take long vacations, preferably in Europe. To visit the Middle East in the summer is a total waste of time, unless you have been specifically summoned by a top-level government official to discuss a pending proposal. Summer, Ramadhan, and Hadj take up altogether about four months during which all business in most arab countries slows down or stops. The problem is less serious when Ramadhan comes in July or August, but this will not happen again until the early 1990s.

What with holidays, differing workweeks, and hemispheric changes of season, planning a travel itinerary can be quite complicated. This is why it pays to develop a long-range plan months in advance.

RESERVATIONS.   Never travel anywhere without confirmed airline and hotel reservations. Vague itineraries, open airline tickets, and hotel bookings that are left to chance are of benefit to nobody except your competitors. You end up wasting too many precious hours finding hotel rooms and booking flights, while losing your temper a bit too often. With hotel chains and airlines offering reservations worldwide, there is no excuse for disorganized travel.

In the early days of the Saudi oil boom, hotel rooms were scarce and every evening you could find dozens of nervous, tired, and frustrated businesspeople willing to pay anything just to get a bed, even if only a folding cot behind a hanging bedsheet in a storage room. The one and only five-star modern hotel in Riyadh was jam packed every evening for weeks in advance. I stayed there three times a year for several years, and never had a problem getting a room.

My plan was quite simple. Before leaving Riyadh at the end of a visit, I would book a room for a specific date three months later, pay a $100 deposit, get a receipt from the hotel's cashier, and personally see that my booking was posted on the reservations board. In fact, the reservations manager would often help me pick out a week when no major delegations were expected to stay at the hotel.

You are probably about to ask something I have been asked dozens of times before: How did I know when I was coming back so far in advance? Simple. If you know you have to come back three months later, why not set up the date now and plan everything else around it? Besides, changing a reservation, particularly after you have paid a deposit directly to the hotel, is easier than trying to fight for one at the last moment. The hotel was always helpful if I had to move up my reservation or delay it for a few days.

Now that chain hotels have worldwide computerized reservations, it is safe to make your bookings by simply phoning the chain's international reservations office. Make sure to get a confirmation number and to guarantee your reservation with your credit card. In Riyadh, by the way, there are now plenty of first-class hotels and no more pugilistic bouts in reception lobbies.

For purely practical purposes I will stay at a standardized, big-chain hotel every time. Reservations are centralized and easy to confirm. I know exactly what type of facilities to expect: usually a large room, a modern bathroom, a firm bed, reasonably good plumbing and lighting, functional furniture, an air-conditioning and heating system that works, a telex, a full newsstand and perhaps a bookstore, a coffee shop, a good dining room for entertaining, a business center, one-day laundry and dry cleaning, airline offices, often a swimming pool and sauna.

I don't need unexpected, unpleasant surprises when checking into a hotel. I don't want to waste time getting resettled if I should land in a mediocre one. For several days my hotel will be my office and my home, and it must have as many conveniences as I can possibly get.

Snide remarks about "plastic hotels" are de rigueur among so-called experienced European travelers. Surprisingly, the "plastics" are usually fully booked and not necessarily by Americans. Increasing numbers of seasoned European travelers have learned to appreciate the facilities of the big-chain hotels. There are, incidentally, a number of French and British chains as well as the American ones.

In Europe there are many small, comfortable hotels offering good accommodations and service. They are not always easy to find and you never quite know what you will get. Get references from other travelers and not from local cabdrivers or local businesspeople who have no reason to ever use a local hotel—or if they do, would rather not talk about it.

If you want to know about Paris hotels, ask someone who does not live in Paris!

VISAS.   Citizens of the United States are able to travel without visas to more countries than anybody else. With nothing but a valid U.S. passport you can go in and out of all Western European countries at will, also most of Latin America, parts of north Africa, and several countries in southeast Asia.

For citizens of other countries travel is not always quite as easy. Visas, by the way, are required for people visiting the United States on business.

If you are a U.S. citizen, Japan, Korea, Australia, and Taiwan will quickly give you a visa good for three or four years which you can use as many times as you want.

Most other countries will give a one-time visa. Usually all you need to do to get one is to send the country's embassy or nearest consulate your passport, one or two photos, and an application form. Sometimes a letter from your company assuming full responsibility for your expenses while in the foreign country and confirming that you will be traveling with a prepaid round-trip airline ticket is also required.

Visas are usually issued overnight. If you need more than one for a particular trip and do not want to waste time sending your passport around to the various embassies, let a visa service do it for you. It will cost you about $25 for each visa. Your travel agent will be able to recommend a visa service.

Most countries give you a choice between a business and a tourist visa. The tourist visa is usually a bit quicker to get and is all you really need since you are not going to earn money in the foreign country.

The most difficult visa to get is the one for Saudi Arabia. An application must be submitted to the Ministry of Foreign Affairs in

Saudi Arabia by a Saudi company who will act as your "sponsor." Within two or three weeks the ministry will confirm the visa by telexing the Saudi Embassy in Washington. At that time you will need to submit your passport to the embassy.

Countries in the Arabian Gulf are easier to get into. You can buy a seventy-two hour visa at the airport in Bahrein. Qatar will also let you in for seventy-two hours if a local company submits a letter to the airport authorities requesting that you be allowed to visit the country (letters from companies are dropped in a tray in the arrivals area at the airport, and it is up to you to shuffle through the pile until you find the one from your sponsor).

In the United Arab Emirates you have to be met at the airport by someone from a local firm, who will then vouch for you during your stay.

Some visas take up a full page of your passport. Make sure to get a forty-eight–page passport, particularly if the countries you plan to cover require visas for each visit. Your passport is good for five years. If in the interim you run out of pages, you can have extra ones added.

JET LAG. You will never get used to jet lag. Crossing twelve time zones between New York and Singapore plays havoc with your biological clock. It may take you ten days to get fully back to normal. Any time you have to reset your watch three hours or more you have a jet lag problem.

There is no way to overcome this nuisance. You can ease it a bit by allowing yourself one full day of rest when you reach a destination after crossing at least four time zones. On a particularly long haul, such as New York–New Delhi, break the trip in London for a day or at least a full night. There are plenty of hotels around Heathrow airport with free around-the-clock pickup at any of the three terminals.

Untiring workaholics love to brag about how they can keep on the move, jet lag or no jet lag. They travel halfway around the world, check into hotels at midnight, and insist on an early "working" breakfast with an agent before getting on with business calls.

A breathless pace is bad for your health, bad for business. In the long run nobody is impressed. Much the opposite, in fact. Creating about oneself an atmosphere of perennial crisis and pressure may in fact cast doubts upon one's efficiency.

SERVICE INCLUDED. In countries you visit frequently try to stay at the same hotel on every visit and make yourself known to key members of the staff as early as possible. The most important is the concierge at the information desk.

This jealously guarded profession is still dominated by men. I have yet to run into a female concierge. The concierge usually handles incoming and outgoing mail, keeps track of messages, helps with local transportation and airline reconfirmations, makes recommendations on restaurants, sightseeing, and shopping, makes sure you are paged, takes care of urgent mail you may want to send out by courier, and sees to it that the morning newspaper is delivered early to your room.

The concierge will do all of these things, that is, if you have been smart enough to "cultivate" him.

Treat the concierge well and you will gain a valuable assistant. Behave roughly, demandingly, and authoritatively, and you will keep running into irritating snags.

Shake hands with the concierge every morning, learn his name (but don't be in a hurry to call him by his first name, particularly in Europe!), stop by his desk for a brief chat when you pick up your key. Leave a generous tip when he has been helpful, and don't come across like so many righteous, tightfisted and unimaginative travelers ("Why the hell should I tip? Service is included, isn't it?").

You can tip a concierge anywhere from $5 to $50 depending on how much he did for you during a four- or five-day stay. This is always money well spent—and money received with gracious appreciation by concierges who are so used to dealing with obnoxious travelers that finding an understanding soul from time to time is a pleasant (and rewarding!) surprise.

Another important person is the telex operator. In a small hotel the job may be performed by the concierge. Larger hotels have a full-time telex room that is open around the clock. If outgoing telex traffic is heavy, the operator invariably will give priority to messages from "friendly" guests who understand the importance of rewarding special favors. This may violate the principle of first come, first served, but quite frankly, when on a business trip I'd rather play Me First.

A tip to a telex operator should be from $1 to $5, depending on the length of your message, how urgently you want it sent, and how big a pile of backlogged telexes you see on the operator's desk. It pays to leave a tip even when you are not in a hurry. Later, when you really need speedy service, the telex person will remember.

The demand for gratuities does become irritating from time to time. In quest of easy tips, the cleaning staff and receptionists in hotels often create problems which at best have a minor nuisance value but which can throw the unsuspecting traveler into a panic. Is there same-day laundry service? Can I have *The Herald Tribune* delivered to my room in the morning? Is it possible to send a telex? Would you have an extra blanket?

This sort of question will produce raised eyebrows, expressions of doubt and gloom: "Well . . . perhaps . . . it depends . . . I don't know . . . At this hour it is difficult . . . I will have to ask."

The nuisance—which was never a problem to begin with—vanishes at the sight of a proffered gratuity. The traveler breathes a sigh of relief, and is grateful that his or her underwear will be back by 6 P.M., proving once again that service is never appreciated quite as fully as when it solves an immediate problem.

The exceptions to this demand for greasing of the palms are Japan, Korea, Taiwan, and China, where you simply do not tip anybody—not even the concierge or the telex operator. It just isn't done and could be taken as a personal insult.

In the United States the concierge system does not work very well anymore. Hotels have become enormous, magnificent palaces that have untold facilities but where personal service is vanishing. Staff, usually young, neat, and friendly, seem trained for narrowly defined jobs, rely too much on computers, and are often not very imaginative. There are still many U.S. hotels without telexes.

CHANGING MONEY. With credit cards accepted everywhere, is there any need to take a lot of cash or travelers' checks on a trip? Up to a point, no. If you plan to be away three weeks, $1500 should be more than enough to cover expenses like cabs, tips, and incidentals that cannot be charged.

The U.S. dollar is accepted everywhere; so are the Canadian dollar, the British pound, the French franc, the Swiss franc, most other European currencies, and the Japanese yen. Throughout Asia and in most European major cities you can also easily change Australian, Hong Kong, and Singapore dollars.

In Western Europe, Australia, Japan, Hong Kong, Singapore, and the Arabian peninsula you can change all the dollars or any other hard currency you want at the airport, where you will usually find one or two bank branches. You can buy dollars back with any leftover local currency when you leave.

In most other countries it is safer to change no more than $20 or $30 at the airport when you arrive—just enough to take care of cabs, tips, and incidentals until you get settled. Exchange rates in hotels may be a bit higher than the official rate.

In countries with shortages of hard, convertible currencies there is inevitably a black market which could bring you from 10 percent to

20 percent more than the official rate. Brazil, Colombia, Argentina, and Egypt are good examples. In Brazil this business is known as the "parallel market," and is usually transacted at travel agencies.

Before you start rushing about to squeeze a few extra percentage points out of your dollars, figure out what this will mean in practical terms. Wasting a valuable hour of your time and $10 in cab fares to dash across town in order to earn an extra $15 does not make much sense, but people do it all the time!

Changing foreign hard currencies in the United States is now easier than it once was, but it is still far from routine. You can do it at some major banks and hotels, also at a few exchange agencies. A visitor to the United States is wise to buy U.S. dollars before arriving.

LOCAL TRANSPORTATION.   Next to traveling without a carefully planned itinerary, one of the easiest ways to waste time and money on your international travels is by renting a car. This can be a disastrous experience in London, Paris, and Rome, even if you know your way around these metropolitan labyrinths.

Business travelers from the United States, used to getting behind the wheel of a "U-drive" the moment they get off a plane in Tampa, Topeka, or Tuscaloosa, do it all the time. Take warning: What happens is that when you lose your way (inevitable in most cases), you end up hiring a cab to lead the way to your destination. Afterward your rental car may sit outside your hotel, unused, for two or three days because everytime you go somewhere you realize it is quicker and easier to take a cab.

There is a time and place to rent a car: when you have to go to a town where other means of transportation are not readily available when you need them.

In twenty-five years and over 120 trips abroad I have rented cars only three times, once from Hamburg airport to Kiel, once from Frankfurt to the small French town of Sarreguemines, once to commute for three days in and out of Lausanne. These were the only times when other and better means of transportation were not available.

Upon arrival in a new city, get a good map to give you an idea of the general layout and locate the places you have to visit. Find out what sort of public transportation is available. Fastest is the subway. There is excellent subway service in London, Paris, Hamburg, Stockholm, and many other large European cities, as well as in Tokyo, Osaka, and Buenos Aires. Many other big cities are building subway networks or expanding their current ones.

Get a subway map at your hotel. Instructions on riding the subway in any country are meant for the barely literate six-year-old, but if in trouble ask an attendant or policeman. The subway is the only way to beat surface traffic jams, now a permanent feature of all major cities around the world.

In some European cities, you should also check the local bus and trolley networks.

Surface transportation is invariably very good throughout Europe. Bus travel elsewhere can be uncomfortable, but there are notable exceptions. Rio de Janeiro has one of the best metropolitan bus systems, including luxury executive commuter buses with piped music, free newspapers, and reclining airline seats. In Chile you can travel overnight between Santiago and Puerto Montt in the magnificent comfort of a double-decker soundproof bus with private cabins, real beds, hot meals, champagne, and closed-circuit TV.

Taxicabs are readily available almost everywhere. Regular cabs are usually painted a distinctive color or easily identified by a "taxi" sign. Watch out for "tourist" or "hotel" cabs, which are usually parked outside main hotels and airports. These are operated by drivers who speak some English (another important clue), and charge you two or three times the regular fare, but offer you the comfort of a clean, air-conditioned ride. I take hotel cabs only when I have to go somewhere in a hurry, don't feel like stepping out onto a polluted street in 110-degree weather to flag down a regular one, or don't want to arrive for an important meeting in a dilapidated antique.

When you don't speak the local language, ask the concierge at the hotel to write down the address for you—or you can show the driver a letterhead of the company you are visiting. The latter, by the way, will not work in Japan, Thailand, the Arab World, and other places which use non-Latin alphabets. In these, don't under any circumstances leave the hotel without clear written instructions for cab drivers. You should also carry a card with the hotel's name and address (printed in the local alphabet).

Picture yourself, a U.S. or European business traveler, in a busy urban intersection, all street signs and billboards around you written in unintelligible characters and not a westerner in sight! This type of situation hits you particularly hard in Japan, where all the major hotels have clerks whose main job is to write down instructions to cabdrivers. I have taken hundreds of cabs in Tokyo and Osaka since my first visit to Japan in 1962, and cannot remember ever finding a driver who seemed to understand even the most rudimentary English. (Come to think of it, I cannot recall ever meeting a New York cabdriver who spoke Japanese either!)

Tourist-cab drivers—and in some countries free-lancers out to make a few extra pesos—like to hang around airports, just outside the customs area, waiting to pounce on unsuspecting business travelers. The longer the flight and the more severe the jet lag, the easier the prey. The thing to do is simply walk right past them. Regular cabdrivers in any country seldom leave their cabs unattended to hustle for passengers. As a rule you will find them lined up at a designated taxi stand.

In some cities there are counters at the airport where you can buy a cab ticket at posted rates to the various main hotels in town. The system is used in Rio de Janeiro, Sao Paulo, Buenos Aires, Bangkok, and several other cities, and works very well.

So-called seasoned travelers like to bore their friends back home with stories of twisting cab detours through dilapidated slums, followed by shouting matches with rapacious drivers, from which Seasoned Traveler always emerges triumphant. During my years of travel I have been ripped off modestly by many cabdrivers in nonmetered countries. On one or two occasions I may have been taken through uncharted suburbs. However, engaging in heated arguments with cabdrivers is not my favorite type of entertainment; it's not worth the aggravation.

WORKING HOURS
AND APPOINTMENTS.
The nine-to-five working day with a brief luncheon break is fairly universal these days, but there are still plenty of variations. The system is prevalent throughout central and northern Europe, and in the United Kingdom, South Africa, Hong Kong, Singapore, Australia, New Zealand, Brazil, and most English speaking countries in east and west Africa.

Companies may open at eight or nine in the morning, and close at five or six in the evening. Executives may not show up until midmorning, and their lunch hours may be erratic. But on the whole, you can count on being able to call on people between 9:30 A.M. and 11:30 A.M., and between 2:30 P.M. and 4:30 P.M. To be safe, check working hours before you start making appointments.

The long lunch hour remains firmly entrenched in Saudi Arabia and its neighbors along the Arabian Gulf coast. Businesses open early, but owners and executives may not show up until ten or eleven o'clock. Everything shuts down at one, when everybody goes home for lunch and a nap, returning to work at four or five. Closing time can be as late as eight. Most arabs like to stay in their offices until well into the evening.

Government offices in the Arab World usually open early in the morning and close for the day at 2 P.M. Since the biggest end user by far is usually the government, most businesspeople will be out all morning calling on ministries and state enterprises, but will then remain in their offices in the afternoon and evening. If you have a business appointment in the morning, be sure to confirm it.

The afternoon and early evening hours can be quite hectic for a Saudi executive who wants to get some work done. All sorts of unannounced visitors will drop in for a chat and tea. Customers, friends, and relatives drift in and out, staying anywhere from fifteen minutes to an hour or two, with no special object other than to pass the time of evening. Arab hospitality requires the host—invariably a man—to receive one and all, but this does not prevent him from taking phone calls, signing letters, and dealing with bookkeepers and other staff.

An uninterrupted meeting with an arab in his office is unheard of. On the other hand, an arab is far more accessible to visitors than his western counterparts. I have yet to be told in the Arab World that someone is too busy and "cannot be disturbed."

An arab businessperson who really has to have an important meeting without interruptions may prefer to meet at a guest's hotel. If the businessperson has to work with staff on an important project like preparing for a bid, the work may be done at home, entirely away from the office. I suspect that more than one Saudi has a secret office, a refuge to retire to when the pressure of work makes it impossible to keep up with visitors.

In Latin America and the Mediterranean area the long lunch hour has ceased to be a sacred institution.

Japanese companies, which once used to work from 8 A.M. to 6 P.M. six days a week, are now switching to a nine-to-six or even a nine-to-five schedule, and some are closed on Saturday.

If you are evaluating potential agents, write or telex them well in advance requesting an early morning or early afternoon appointment at a specific time. This leaves you the rest of the morning or afternoon free for either more talks with the same firm or a second appointment elsewhere.

Set up no more than four or five early appointments in advance and ask for written or telexed confirmation. Try not to fill every time slot. Give yourself some flexibility.

In many countries it is acceptable to make appointments at one's hotel for lunch or dinner. In the Middle East, where business is discussed almost anywhere and at all hours, it is quite permissible to suggest business meetings in the evening and even on Fridays.

In a country where you have not yet appointed an agent and want to look around a bit more, refrain from giving anybody specific details of your arrival. Pleasant and helpful as it may be to have someone waiting for you, you stand to lose a measure of control. A prospective agent who picks you up at the airport may already have laid out a program of calls and meetings, hoping to monopolize your time. Backing out of this type of situation is something that cannot always be done gracefully and may not even be advisable. The agent may be forced to cancel an important appointment, and this could cause serious loss of face.

Stay in control, don't announce your exact arrival, avoid putting yourself under any obligations. Make sure that the prospective agents you plan to visit understand that you have other calls to make. At the same time, don't discourage anybody entirely. It all boils down to a delicate balancing act which you will have to perform pretty much by intuition.

NEVER ON SUNDAY (OR FRIDAY). Everybody is entitled to at least one day of rest, and the export or regional manager is no exception. For some travelers this is difficult to acknowledge, as if being on the road imposed an obligation to work around the clock. At the other extreme is the American tractor salesman I met a few years ago at the coffee shop of the Hilton Hotel in Tehran.

"Weekends are my own," he said. "I refuse to talk business or even to get on a plane between Friday evening and Monday morning. Flying time is company time."

A good thought, but not always practical or feasible to act on. But at least give yourself one full day off during the weekend. This does not prevent you from accepting an invitation to spend Sunday as the guest of an agent or important client, or from asking your agent's key salesperson to lunch. This can be fun, entertaining, and relaxing, and gives you new and more informal insights on the agent's company and personnel.

Getting to know your agents and their staff outside of regular work situations is the best way to make new friends and this, in the long run, can be a valuable asset in your international operation.

CHAPTER
ELEVEN

THE PERSONAL TOUCH

Personal manners in the west have steadily deteriorated since the 1960s. Habits that not long ago would have been considered gross are casually accepted today. In international business this can cause problems. *Bad manners don't travel well.*

Many of today's young business executives haven't had much of an opportunity to learn their do's and dont's. They are thus unaware of behavior that could easily ruin a sale or a long-term relationship.

Manners and behavior which today would be considered archaic in some countries are still very much the norm in others. Yet, many export and regional managers go about blissfully unaware that success or failure in international business has much to do with how one comes across personally.

Selling the product is one thing, but *how well do you sell yourself?*

Your foreign agent may never visit your office or meet anybody other than you, the export or regional manager. Your company is a distant entity represented by brochures, catalogs, a letterhead, and merchandise.

But *you* are real.

You stand before the agent.

You personify your company.

Examples abound of export sales executives who never learned the basic rules of appearance, manners, and behavior. A few years ago a manufacturer of office equipment lost any chance of signing up an important account when the company's export manager arrived in the offices of a Brazilian importer wearing white patent-leather boots, red knit trousers, and an open-necked Hawaiian shirt. It wasn't even Carnival time! What is worse, the man never knew why he was turned down.

Lighting a pipe or a cigar in a customer's office is something your fiercest competitor would love to see you do wherever you go, yet there are plenty of salespeople who will not hesitate to light up. They fail to realize that their host may insist out of politeness that he or she thoroughly enjoys the aroma of cigar smoke, meanwhile making a mental note to be out of town next time the culprit comes calling.

Gum chewing is viewed in most countries as gross, childish, and barbaric.

People are not always eager to be called by their first names and in fact may consider this familiarity a serious lack of respect.

There are numerous other manifestations of bad personal manners which can and often do upset business relationships: for example, being too pushy or too loud and boisterous, talking yourself out of a sale, giving too much detail to an official who is only interested in highlights, asking personal questions.

Peppering one's speech with four-letter words has become standard behavior for many young modern male and female executives. It's like wearing a badge. This does not go over very well in most countries. Furthermore, these wild-card words are used in so many different contexts that they end up seriously restricting a person's vocabulary.

You and your staff can spend frustrating hours trying to find out why you lost a big sale. What went wrong? What did our competition quote? Did we have the right specs? Did we overlook an important detail?

Actually, you may have lost the deal because when invited into the office of the end user your regional manager put his feet on the coffee table. This sort of thing isn't covered in sales training manuals. Companies spend thousands of dollars teaching sales personnel how to overcome objections but totally overlook personal and business etiquette.

Your profit goes up when you increase your sales or when you reduce your costs and losses. Bad manners can cause you serious losses, particularly in international business.

No single country has a monopoly on bad manners. The myth of the Ugly American has been blown up out of all proportion. I have seen my share of Ugly Germans, Ugly French, Ugly Canadians, Ugly Swedes, Ugly Britishers, and even Ugly Japanese. Tourist groups from Bremerhaven and Bordeaux can be just as noisy, ignorant, ill-dressed, and naive as the worst U.S., Canadian, and Australian groups.

Tourists, however, rush through a country, and often don't really care what impression they leave behind. When export and regional managers call on overseas agents and end users, they are putting their names and their companies' names on the line.

Proper behavior in international business depends on common sense and respect. Basic rules are easy to learn. A U.S. business traveler does not have to try to act Japanese when visiting Japan, any more than a Japanese should be expected to "act American" when visiting the United States. In either case the results could be quite ludicrous.

What is important in international business is to come across as a low-key, well-behaved, well-mannered individual and to remember that habits which back home would be perfectly acceptable can be taken for bad manners elsewhere.

We have become so engrossed with computers, satellite communications, and other exciting technology that we often forget that business still revolves around personal relationships. The overall performance of the largest multinational firm is nothing but the sum total of thousands of one-on-one personal contacts between company personnel and customers at home and abroad. Travel books, airline pamphlets, and travel magazines provide ample information on customs and habits around the world. Still, you may have to go back to a country three or four times to learn what to wear, how to address people in business, how to function in formal social situations, how to eat, what topics to discuss or avoid.

Here are two basic, simple rules which will work just about anywhere you go.

First, If in Doubt, Be Formal. Should I wear formal business attire or something more casual? Address my agent as Pedro or Señor Gonzalez? Eat with my fingers? Burp after dinner? If you aren't sure, be formal. The rule is so ridiculously simple that one wonders why it is broken day after day by people who should know better.

Second, Be Low-Key and Restrained. It is easier to loosen up than to try to undo a glaring faux pas. This rule will not appeal to the effervescent extrovert who likes to be center stage. But this is precisely the sort of person likely to come across a bit too strongly for most people's taste.

FORMS OF ADDRESS.   Americans, Australians, and Canadians are among the world's most informal people, unhampered by age-old traditions or class distinctions. Nowhere is this more obvious than in the way they quickly get on a first-name basis with casual acquaintances, business associates, employees, customers, waiters, bartenders, and cab-drivers—even when not running for office.

In other countries, however, this sort of informality can be seen as a lack of respect and an invasion of privacy.

The rules that govern forms of address can be quite complex in countries where the language retains formal and informal versions of the "you" pronoun, as do all European languages except English. It may take months before you can safely start addressing Adrien Leclerc in France as plain Adrien and using the informal pronoun *tu*.

One of the many advantages of communicating in English is that you don't need to know all the social intricacies of formal and informal pronouns and when to use them. It is enough to understand that the process is not quite as simple as shifting from Mr. Sadlowski to John.

However, knowing when to switch to first names can be a delicate matter in itself. In Australia and Venezuela the proper waiting time could be five minutes, in Argentina, Germany, and France one year, in Switzerland three years, and in Japan a decade.

In most Scandinavian countries and the United Kingdom the process has been considerably shortened since World War II. *To be safe, be formal and let others take the initiative in moving to a first-name basis.*

Luis Gutierrez is Mr. or Señor Gutierrez, Ahmed El Natsha is Mr. Natsha, and Mandira Balakrishnan is Mrs. Balakrishnan. However, it is also acceptable and formal to say Mr. or Señor Luis, Mr. Ahmed, and Mrs. Mandira. Spanish speaking countries also consider Don Luis as quite proper and perhaps nicer than Señor Gutierrez.

In many countries employees are so used to addressing a particular boss as Señor Luis or Mr. Ahmed that they often may not know his last name. If in Rio de Janeiro you phone the office of Mrs. Juracy Ferreira and ask to speak with Senhora Ferreira, the operator may come back with, "You mean, Dona Juracy?"

The formal first-name mode (Senhor Pedro, Mr. Ahmed, Mrs. Mandira, and Dona Juracy) prevails mainly in Latin America, Asia, and the Arab World. In Europe you should stay with the formal last-name approach (Monsieur Jacquard and not Monsieur Pierre, Herr Schmidt and not Herr Johann, Madame Arnaud and not Madame Jeanne).

Sooner or later you, as an export or regional manager, will be on a first-name informal basis with your agents even in the more formal countries. It may take time. The trick is not to rush things, even when there is a big difference in age and as the older person you feel you should take the initiative in dropping formalities. The other person may feel that it is awkward and disrespectful to start calling you Annette or Joe.

Avoid nicknames, even when a person's given name may sound a bit formal. Don't get involved in an exchange like this one.

"Hello there, I am Alexander Percival."

"Hi there! What do your friends call you, Alex or Al?"

"Neither, they call me Alexander, of course!"

Be alert to titles. In Italy, Brazil, Argentina, and Mexico every man and some of the women you will meet in business will be either a "doctor" or an "engineer" and to address someone simply as Signor or Signora, Senhor or Senhora, Señor or Señora, could imply that you are talking to someone who did not have the benefit of an education.

The title "Doctor" is the most prevalent and does not always go with a doctoral degree. It is loosely used by lawyers, graduates of business schools, teachers, and liberal arts graduates (or dropouts).

Brazilians—ordinarily the most informal and easygoing of all Latins— are nevertheless very fond of the title "Doutor," which is used in correspondence to address virtually anybody, and in the most exalted terms: Ilustrissimo Senhor Doutor Tancredo Gomes is a perfectly acceptable way of addressing a letter to Mr. Gomes, the manager of the local bank branch.

The title "Engineer" is a bit more precise. You can usually assume that the bearer has had postsecondary technical training.

In Mexico the most common title is "Licenciado" or "Licenciada," supposedly restricted to recognized lawyers but in practice appropriated by virtually anybody who has had some university education.

Titles are also used on business cards (always abbreviated—Dr., Ing., Lic.) and by office staff ("The licenciada will see you now." "Ingeniero Luis is not in his office this morning.") You yourself will be addressed as "Doctor" or "Engineer" by respectful and wise secretaries (who are well versed in the importance of being formal when in doubt).

Outside Latin America and a few European countries, however, you won't have problems with titles. Until recently Sweden had one of the strictest social codes for forms of address and titles. Everybody had one according to his or her job or profession—Accountant Johanssen, Trainengineer Peterson, Nurse Bergstrom, Schoolteacher Eklund. You addressed each person by his or her title at all times, even in casual conversation. "How is Nurse Bergstrom today? Good morning, Schoolteacher Eklund! Does Trainengineer Peterson expect to leave on time?" This has all been dropped in the last fifteen years.

For the pragmatic French, the title Monsieur, Madame, Mademoiselle is entirely sufficient, proper, and distinguished, and is used without any embellishments. A French business letter begins quite simply: *Messieurs. Nous avons l'honneur de. . . .*

WHAT TO WEAR?   Again, in dress it pays to be formal if in doubt. Business dress varies from country to country or even from city to city. In Rio de Janeiro it is common to see businessmen in short-sleeve sports shirts and businesswomen in colorful, cool summer dresses, while one jet-hour away in Sao Paulo more conservative clothing is required. In southeast Asia men may wear a shirt and necktie but no jacket. Scandinavians are becoming very informal. Men may go to work in jeans, baggy corduroy sports jackets and sandals (often worn over socks). Women may be just as casual. Most German and Swiss executives wouldn't be caught in anything but somber business clothes.

At the start of the oil boom, male visitors to Saudi Arabia often went about in desert boots and safari suits. Today it has become increasingly gauche for men doing business there not to wear a tie and perhaps even a suit in Riyadh, Dammam, and Jeddah—cities which boast modern boutiques where you can buy the latest designer fashions from Milan, Paris, and New York. The barring of women from business in Saudi Arabia makes business dress there a moot point for them.

Hot climates are no longer an excuse to dress casually. Air-conditioning is almost universal. You will be no more uncomfortable in Djakarta or Bombay in the summertime than in New York or Chicago.

Until you know the dress codes and system of each particular country, you should play it safe and wear conservative, subdued clothing. A man can always remove his jacket and tie later. Dress conservatively also for social events, particularly dinner.

A female export or regional manager should choose suits and dresses of "classic" cut and conservative hue for international travel and steer away from either an overly casual look or a trendy, high-style one, although in countries where women tend to dress more flamboyantly (such as Italy) she may allow herself somewhat more leeway in dressing for social occasions. Even at very dressy social events, however, it is better to be conservatively well turned out than to try to compete with a very chic Italian, French, or Brazilian hostess. Slacks should be worn only for casual social occasions at which a woman is reasonably certain that the other women present will also be wearing them.

A practical wardrobe for a male export or regional manager will include gray or blue suits, solid-color shirts and discreet neckties. Also indispensable for a man is a navy-blue blazer (without gold or silver buttons) and gray flannel slacks. The latter can be worn for business and almost any social occasion, including casual weekend invitations with or without a tie.

Both women and men should try to invest in good quality, well-tailored clothing. There is nothing dramatic about a well-made woolen or linen suit, but quality shows!

When in doubt as to what to wear, ask yourself what sort of an impression you want to make and who you are seeing that particular day. If you plan to spend the day at an agent's office conducting a sales seminar or going over paperwork, you may decide to show up in a skirt and blouse if you are a woman or slacks and a sports shirt if you are a man. But if you are calling on an agent for the first time, or on an important end user, go formal.

The fact that local executives and officials may go about in casual clothes and sandals is no reason why you should dress the same way. Yes, in many countries you can show up for a business meeting wearing a polo shirt or a blouse and designer jeans. However, it is not a question of how you *can* dress but how you *should*.

Clothes reflect your status and self-respect, as well as respect toward the people you are calling on. Everybody admires a well-dressed person. Nobody is impressed by a slob!

BODY LANGUAGE.   Observing body language around the world can be a fascinating hobby. Customs which prevail in one part of the world may be taboo in another. Not everybody likes to shake hands. The distance at which people of one culture like to stand when engaged in conversation can be a bit too close for comfort for people of another culture. In some countries men will walk down the street hand in hand and even kiss in public. While you need not necessarily adopt local customs, it is important to be alert to them and their meaning.

The handshake is fairly universal among men and women. Notable exceptions are Japan, Korea, and a few other Asian countries where physical contact is shunned. A westernized Asian businessperson may extend a hand when meeting a westerner, but the local custom is to greet people with a bow or a nod.

Elsewhere be prepared to shake hands with one and all, morning and afternoon. *If in doubt, shake it!* The habit is prevalent in Latin America, Europe, Africa, and the Arab World. People who work in the same office, see each other daily, and have known each other for years will still shake hands when coming to work in the morning and upon leaving. Employees walk into managers' offices to shake hands with them—a sign of respect and good manners, and no doubt also good individual public relations.

For twenty-nine years my father drove to and from work every day—including at lunch-time—with his oldest friend. They had met in the

Spanish town of Jerez de la Frontera just before the outbreak of World
War I. They never once failed to shake hands morning and evening,
as well as before and after lunch.

Nobody abroad will be bent out of shape if you greet them with a
casual wave and a "Hi!", but you will score more points if you reach
out and shake hands and greet people with a "Good morning!" or "Good
evening!".

In Latin American countries the handshake is usually accompanied
by an *abrazo*. This ranges from a slight and gentle pat on the shoulder
(with your left hand) to a vigorous hug reserved for relatives and close
friends. The Brazilian version is a mild embrace which is almost
mandatory when you have met someone three or four times and begun
to develop a business relationship. (The *abrazo*, by the way, is *not* a
hard slap on the back!)

The "conversational distance" between two standing people may range
from two to five feet. In countries where people like to touch (Latin
America and the Middle East) the distance can be uncomfortably close
for you if you are used to the U.S. norm. However, if you back away
you may give the impression of being aloof. In Japan and other Asian
countries the distance is much greater, and anybody who tries to move
in closer may give the impression that he or she is trying to become
unnecessarily intimate!

LANGUAGE, HUMOR, AND VALUES. The world's business language is English, but not the English you and I may use every day.
Tell your Turkish hostess that hers is a "cool" house and she may
rush to get you a sweater. Australian, U.S., Canadian, and British
travelers quickly learn that there is a world of difference between
idiomatic English and "correct" English. A non-native speaker may
speak impeccable English and be totally baffled by idioms and slang.

You're in Tokyo and you say to your host: "You know, Mr. Okada,
you are something else."

Mr. Okada stares at you. "Something else? Ah, yes! Something else.
You mean, ah, something else. Yes, of course, I see."

But he really doesn't.

"I think it is important to me and my company to know where you're
coming from," you go on, undaunted.

"Really? Oh, I'm so sorry, I didn't know that. Well, I am from
Sapporo. You know Sapporo?"

Speaking precise, clear, nonidiomatic English is extremely taxing and
tiring; you must constantly keep in mind that your words are likely to

be taken literally. In many countries you must be extra careful how you phrase a question.

Questions with negatives can get you into all sorts of verbal entanglements.

"Shouldn't we visit the Ministry of Transportation tomorrow?"

"Yes, [we shouldn't]. The people we want to see are out of town."

Or, "No [we should indeed visit the Ministry]."

Next time phrase the question in simple, positive terms: "Shall we visit. . . .?"

Try to speak slowly and clearly. Don't despair if you don't quite sound like a TV anchor on the evening news. Just try not to chew up too many syllables. People who are not native English speakers have the most trouble with southern and midwestern American accents, often described as talking around a mouthful of hot potatoes.

Humor does not travel well. The story that cracked them up at the convention in San Francisco or Sydney may drop like a lead balloon in Singapore. People around the world laugh at different things, and it is as useless to try to explain your brand of humor to people of a different culture as it is for them to explain theirs to you.

One of the hardest things to learn while traveling is that not everybody may share your values. This is important when you are trying to find out what motivates an agent. The belief that people everywhere share the western ideals of freedom and democracy is a delusion.

What businesspeople *do* share around the world is the language of making money, although even here, values and customs vary. Long-range job and personal security and lifelong loyalty and commitment to a company may be cherished much more in Europe and Japan than in the United States, for instance.

Growth in business is not always seen as a virtue. For years I have been telling my friend Marcel Duprez, owner of a profitable medium-size business in France, that he should expand into the U.S. market.

"Why?" he asks. "It would mean travel, business decisions, problems, headaches. I am quite happy the ways things are."

AT THE TABLE.   People's lives around the world are organized around mealtimes. The ritual of three regular meals breaks the day up into smaller time segments, making it easier for people to sort out the things they have to do.

Firmly entrenched in the middle of any business day is the lunch hour, to the point that the first concern of many businesspeople, when faced with a suggested appointment in late morning or early afternoon, is to figure out if it would clash with this most sacred of mealtimes.

The lunch hour is an unshakeable ritual in most of Europe, Latin America, and the Middle East, and only a little less rigid in Asia, even if most business executives today no longer take the time to go home for a long break.

An invitation to lunch is in some countries more important than being asked to dinner. As an export or regional manager you will be invited often to both, mainly for business but sometimes for social reasons as well.

If you want to make a good impression abroad, try to develop if not a taste for, at least genuine curiosity about, local cuisine. Traveling can be a real adventure in good eating, provided you stay away from cheeseburgers, french fries, chef salads, and club sandwiches. The more interest you take in sampling local cooking, the happier your host will be. Try everything once! Afterward nobody will fault you if you decide you didn't like this or that.

Eat always in the local style. Thanks to the proliferation of Chinese and Japanese restaurants throughout the world, chopsticks are no longer a mystery to travelers. Eating with fingers is not done in Japan, Hong Kong, Taiwan, and Singapore, but is acceptable and proper in India, Pakistan, and Sri Lanka. It does get a bit messy to dig into a bowl of chicken curry with your fingers, but soon you get the knack of it and learn to keep the sauce from dribbling down to your elbow. Eat always with your right hand, by the way. Never touch food with your left. Your hosts may, out of politeness, set the table western style with knives and forks for everybody or only for you. If you are not sure what to do, watch them and do the same or simply ask.

Eating is informal in the Middle East, where there are few rules to observe except for a rigid separation of the sexes; in most countries in the Arabian Peninsula, particularly Saudi Arabia, women eat separately. Guests eat with their fingers and take what they want from a wide array of dishes laid out on the table. In desert countries they will most likely sit on the floor if the meal is in a private home. A servant will lay out a tablecloth over the carpeting and set down the dishes. Hands are washed before and after eating.

In the Middle East, parts of southern Europe, and a few Latin American countries lunch is eaten anywhere between 1 P.M. and 4 P.M. In these countries you may be invited to lunch more often than to dinner.

A dinner invitation in most countries will be for 8 P.M. or later. Your hosts will take you straight to the restaurant rather than stopping somewhere first for a drink. The Japanese like to go to dinner right after leaving the office, partly because most people have a long commute to their homes, partly because restaurants in Tokyo and Osaka usually close by 10 P.M.

In Europe and Latin America an agent will usually bring his wife or her husband along. In the Middle East and Asia, where the business world remains virtually a closed male domain, wives are seldom invited to a business dinner unless the traveler is a woman. An invitation to a Japanese home is a rare event. I have had only one. Arabs, on the other hand, like to invite visitors to their homes, and if you are a man you will find that they are among the most hospitable and relaxed hosts you will ever meet. Dinner in an arab home follows no rigid protocol or timetable. Guests can take off their shoes, sit on the floor, talk, relax, and eat without having to look at their watches. They are free to stay as long as they want.

ENTERTAINING OVERSEAS AGENTS.   When foreign agents visit you, save your main entertaining for the evening. At lunchtime, if they are spending a few days, have different executives take turns inviting them. This gives everybody an opportunity to get some firsthand information on overseas market conditions and will make it easier for you to get the support of other executives when an issue comes up which requires discussion at the management level.

Never take foreign guests to restaurants featuring their country's cuisine. It will never be as good as back home. The only time I ever had a disappointing meal in Tokyo was when someone took me to a "typical American steakhouse."

Visitors to the United States invariably stand in awe of the size, quality, and taste of a good American steak. Unless your guests are vegetarian (which you should find out as early as possible), you cannot go wrong if you take them to a good steakhouse. A French or international restaurant is also a good bet—except when entertaining a French businessperson. Go to a restaurant where you have been before and are well known to the staff. Avoid unpleasant surprises. If in doubt, stick to what you know!

Entertainment at home is a rare treat for any traveler. It is a welcome break from restaurants and hotels, and provides an opportunity to relax and build up close friendships. Meeting spouses, children, friends, and neighbors is the best way to learn about a country.

If you bring an overseas agent home for dinner, serve what you can do best and don't start looking up fancy recipes or new dishes. Never experiment! In the United States, an outdoor barbecue may be highly appreciated. Be relaxed, put your guest at ease. You would appreciate the same treatment if the roles were reversed.

DON'T BE NOSY.   As a European sees it, it doesn't take a U.S. traveler long to turn to the person sitting next to him or her in an airplane and proceed to play the favorite American game of Nosy Pursuit. This game begins with Three Easy Questions:

"What's your name?"

"Where're you from?"

"Who're you with?"

Give our gregarious traveler (lets call her Mildred Vermont) a few more minutes and she will be going into her own curriculum vitae:

"My husband's name is Pat; we have three children and live in Columbus, Ohio."

This instant familiarity, friendly and well-intended as it may be, is seen by many other cultures as an unnecessary and premature invasion of privacy. Even a simple exchange of names is not something a European will willingly do within minutes of meeting a perfect stranger. But to inquire what one does for a living? *Mon Dieu!*

This is not to say that conversation without being properly introduced is *verboten*. It is more a question of style and approach. Eventually names can be exchanged, careers and families discussed, but slowly, gently, and with tact. It really makes no different to Pierre LeJeune if your name is Jack Texas or Mildred Vermont, until he decides whether you are a person he would like to get to know better.

With these qualifications, however, easygoing American informality, shared by Canadians and Australians, is a valuable asset in international business and is highly appreciated in many parts of the world.

The informal approach to international business is also being fostered by modern communications. The ease with which one can contact an agent clear around the world is leading businesses toward more plain talk, less formality and protocol.

CHAPTER

TWELVE

PLAIN TALK
COMMUNICATIONS One hundred and fifty

years ago a letter from a Boston supplier would have taken six months
to reach an agent in Macao. If the agent answered quickly in order to
make a vessel sailing back to Boston the following day, the entire
exchange would take slightly over a year.

Today, by telex, telephone, or computerized communications you can
send a message anywhere in the world and get an answer back before
you have finished sipping a cup of coffee. Theoretically, that is. Delivery
systems today may operate at the speed of light, but human carelessness,
indifference, inefficiency, and procrastination all too often stand in the
way of smooth communication between a company and its foreign
agents.

The Macao agent who rushed an answer back to Boston on next
day's clipper ship acted a lot quicker than many businesspeople today
who take days to answer a simple telex.

Consider the following examples of human inability to keep up with
the pace of communications technology.

1. Internal procedures in the head office of a large Italian conglomerate
   are so complex that it may take twenty-four hours for an incoming
   telex to find its way to the person to whom it is addressed. The
   telex has to be logged in a big ledger, photocopies must be made
   and filed, and the telex is then routed through three sets of in-and-
   out trays.

2. When, on a Friday afternoon just before the George Washington's birthday three-day weekend, the paper ran out on the telex machine of a U.S. electronics manufacturer, an administrative assistant decided not to bother inserting a new roll. "Who's going to telex on George Washington's birthday?"
3. A Spanish publisher wrote a New York publisher that: "We are not able to accept your proposal." One month later the representative of the U.S. firm called on the Spanish publisher, who wanted to know why it had taken such a long time for New York to respond. Copies of the letter were produced. A typing error was noticed for the first time. The writer had intended to say: "We are *now* able to accept your proposal."
4. The Abu Dhabi agent of a Chicago manufacturer of school furniture failed to qualify for an important bid because the catalogs arrived one month too late. A mailing clerk in Chicago had decided to send them by surface mail and save his company some postage.

These stupid and unhappy mistakes are all the result of inexcusably poor communication. Nobody knows how much a company may lose in sales and profits through miscommunication. Miscommunication is a fifth column within your company, a sneaky competitor seldom given the importance it deserves. These and many other instances of sheer neglect are even more unbelievable when nothing is done to correct the errors.

The communications technology now available to any telephone subscriber in the United States is awesome. Until a few years ago international phone calls had to be placed through operators, often with delays of up to several hours. Voice quality was poor; you ended up shouting in order to make yourself barely understood.

International direct dialing, computerized telexes, and facsimile communications now give you instant access to any city in the world. Courier services deliver your catalogs and proposals anywhere in the world in two working days or less, sometimes overnight.

Because of international differences in time, language, culture, and conditions, it is vital to establish routines and systems that will allow an overseas agent to reach the right person in your export department easily and quickly.

The path from switchboard, telex, or mailroom to the addressee should be as direct and as short as possible, with no intervening stops or delays.

THE TELEPHONE. Seldom used in the past because of cost, the telephone is quickly becoming an everyday means of communication across continents and oceans. The cost of international phone calls is dropping. From the east coast of the United States it costs about $5.40 for a five-minute call to London and $9.85 for one to Tokyo. The rates drop to $4 to London after 6 P.M. and $6.50 to Tokyo after 11 P.M..

Time differences can save you money. From New York you can call an agent in southeast Asia or Japan at 11 P.M. your time. It will be noontime the following day at the other end of the line, and you will have the benefit of the low nighttime rate.

The first rule of good international phone communications is that you, the export manager, must be easily accessible to any overseas callers; they have gone to the trouble and expense of phoning you from Seoul, Singapore, or Stockholm, where it may be the middle of the night.

Nothing should keep you from answering an overseas call, not even a meeting of the board of directors. This principle has to be drilled into the heads of anybody who could possibly stand between you and the caller—particularly switchboard operators, receptionists, and sec-retaries, and whoever is likely to replace them when they are away on vacation, at lunch, or in the bathroom. An uninformed, untrained replacement can quite innocently upset a carefully cultivated relationship with an overseas agent or end user.

The principle of accessibility is violated daily in too many companies, companies that have made reaching an executive as tough as running a Marine Corps obstacle course. The idea seems to be to test the caller's ingenuity, perseverance, and imagination. A number of unpardonable sins are perpetrated daily by careless telephone operators. Some examples follow.

1. "Mr. Jones can't be disturbed, he's in a meeting." Disturbed? Since when am I a disturbance? says the caller. The amount of time some executives spend in meetings, purposely shut off from all outside contacts, including customers, is appalling. The Meeting is another deadly fifth column within your company. How much is it costing you in lost business?

    Far from impressing callers with its aura of high-level, sacrosanct deliberations, The Meeting often ends up driving frustrated customers elsewhere.

    Accessibility to executives is most difficult in the United States, easiest in Japan, where I cannot recall ever being told that the person I was trying to reach was unable to come to the phone because of a meeting.

2. "Mr. Smith will not be able to get back to you all week because he is involved in important management meetings for the next few days."

Usually delivered by condescending secretaries or assistants who are unnecessarily impressed with the status of their bosses, this is, pure and simple, bad telephone manners even when the call is local. It constitutes atrocious behavior when the call is from overseas or from an agent who has flown into town and will be available for only a day or two.

3. "Call back after lunch."

Ridiculous because lunch in Chicago is after dinner in Frankfurt and after midnight in Tokyo.

4. "Your name is what? You are calling from where? Where is *that*? All right, let me check, I'll put you on hold."

Five costly and aggravating minutes of silence later the operator comes back on the line. "Now who was it you wanted to speak to? And what was your name again?"

5. "I'm sorry, Mrs. Epstein is away from her desk." (Or, "not available at the moment.")

This vague answer could mean that Mrs. Epstein is on a trip, has not yet arrived at work, is attending A Meeting, or has gone down the hall to get a cup of coffee or to go to the bathroom. If Mrs. Epstein is not enthroned behind her desk but is indeed in the general vicinity, then someone should look for her immediately. Otherwise, the call should be passed on to the second-in-command without delay.

The telephone can be a useful selling tool or a sales killer. A timid foreign agent whose English is neither particularly fluent nor crystal clear will not stand a chance if he or she falls into the vocal tentacles of an intimidating switchboard operator.

You can avoid embarrassing situations by putting in a direct line to your export department. This will bypass switchboard operators and receptionists who have regular domestic calls to handle *and therefore cannot be expected to remember at all times your instructions concerning overseas calls.*

It will be easier for you or your administrative assistant to control a direct export line than to impress upon a harried switchboard operator the need for tact and diplomacy.

A direct line has two drawbacks. A call may go unanswered. Or the person who answers may want to transfer it to someone else, push the wrong buttons, and lose the call. Both problems can be solved by making sure someone is within reach of the phone at all times, and that everybody in the export department knows how to make a call transfer. Obvious? Then why is it that so many people equipped with direct lines still keep pushing the wrong buttons?

If you must have inviolate inner sanctum meetings, schedule them for a time when there will be the least conflict with overseas working hours. For a U.S. firm the best time is late afternoon. By then your agents in Asia will have gone to bed, while the ones in Europe and the Middle East will be shutting down for the night.

Since the twenty-four-hour day comes to an end in North America long after the rest of the world, U.S. firms can expect to get most of their overseas phone calls in the morning. However, you must set up a system that allows an overseas agent to reach you at any time. The telex is one obvious solution. The other is a telephone answering machine hooked up to the export department's direct phone line. You and your assistant should be able to remote-retrieve messages from this phone at any time.

Some export managers like to make themselves accessible to overseas agents even after regular office hours, including weekends and holidays. You don't have to go quite that far. Even when you tell your agents to contact you only when the matter is very urgent, you will find that their definition of what is urgent will not always coincide with yours.

One way to ensure fairly good accessibility is to tell your agents to record their urgent messages on your phone answering machine on weekends and holidays. You can retrieve them once or twice from your home and decide what is and what is not important.

Agents in countries which follow the Islamic week pose a special problem. Their weekend is Thursday and Friday, yours is Saturday and Sunday. You could be out of touch four days out of seven. Add to this a time difference of from ten to twelve hours, which means that when you get to your office on Monday morning, your agent in Kuwait will have finished for the day.

There may not be much you can do for a Kuwaiti agent on a Saturday or Sunday, but setting up a communications link that assures agents that you will be getting their messages even during the weekend will show your support.

A New York exporter who does a lot of business with arab countries long ago decided to adopt his own version of the Islamic week. He set up a small weekend office and telex in his home, and is able to respond to clients' inquiries and messages on Saturday and Sunday, well ahead of his competitors. In compensation he takes off most of Thursday and Friday.

THE TELEX.   You cannot run an export business without a telex. The use of the telex is universal, but U.S. firms whose business is mostly domestic have seldom felt the need for one. It is so easy to use the phone.

Instant access to a foreign agent by telex is ideal when you have to submit important quotations or shipping details, request changes in letters of credit, send critical product information for major bids, schedule trips, or follow up on pending business, and in many other instances where time is of the essence.

A telex message will cost you a fraction of what you would pay to phone, because by telex you can send short, crisp messages with a minimum of verbiage. The old-fashioned "clunker" telex machine, still the most popular, can send out about sixty words per minute. Sample rates from the east coast of the United States: $1.92 per minute to continental Europe and the Middle East, $1.41 to England, $2.21 to Japan, southeast Asia, and Australia.

Incoming telexes should be delivered immediately to the addressee by whoever is in charge of the telex machine. You will be smart if you place the telex as close to you as possible—in your own or your assistant's office.

An outgoing telex should be sent with dispatch and should never be left in an out tray overnight.

Telexes too often are poorly written and confusing and do not answer all questions. Conversely, a telex may suffer from an excessive number of abbreviations, prompting the receiver to telex you back for clarification and thus defeating the purpose of quick and efficient communications.

Among the many pearls of wisdom attributed to Napoleon is this final sentence in a letter to a friend: "Forgive me for writing you a long letter but I did not have the time to compose a short one." Good advice for anybody who writes business communications, particularly telexes.

The telex offers you a unique opportunity to eliminate unnecessary adverbs and adjectives, in fact, to cut out all embellishments and get to the heart of a message. Write every telex yourself. Look at each one critically. Get to the point, and make sure your message is clear. *Take the time to make it short.* Unnecessary verbiage diffuses the impact of any written communication, particularly the telex.

Some abbreviations are acceptable (PLS, REF, YRLET, USD for U.S. dollars) but don't overdo it. Be careful with dates. The short form 5/2 means May the second in the United States. Elsewhere it stands for the fifth of February. So make it 2 May if that is what you mean, and remember always to spell out or abbreviate the month (Jan, Feb, Mar, Apr).

Here is an example of the type of wordy, sloppy telex that you do not want to send.

To Palace Hotel
Attention telex operator:
Will you be kind enough to bring this to the immediate attention of your guest Mr Percival Williams. Thank you.

Dear Percival,
It has come to our attention that the Ministry of Transportation is contemplating the acquisition of a fleet of seventy-five trucks in the very near future. Will be grateful if you can do your best to look into it and advise us without delay.

All the best,
Charles

Here is the same message, straight to the point.

For yr guest Percival Williams
Min of Transportation may buy 75 trucks soon. Pls look into it and tlx me.
Regards,
Charles

Answer your telexes at once, or within a few hours. Remember time zones. A telex from an Islamic country received on Thursday morning need not be answered until Friday evening, but by all means make sure the answer goes out before you leave your office on Friday so that your agent will get it when the new workweek starts on Saturday morning.

CORRESPONDENCE.   One type of international communication which has not been particularly accelerated in the last decade or two is the mail. It can take a letter from New York to London twice as long today as it did in the 1960s. Where once you could count on a few days' delivery to Europe, today you must allow up to ten days. All the more reason to make sure your overseas mail is handled swiftly, ideally within twenty-four hours.

As with phone calls and telexes, you must set up the simplest and most direct method you can for processing mail. I hope you are not the type of executive who insists on having the morning mail opened by a secretary and brought in all at once. I find this a terrible waste of time and of a secretary's talents. You may not get your mail until midmorning. If the secretary is sick or on vacation, someone else has to be recruited to do the job and may not give it the urgency it requires.

Speed things up. Open your own mail!

Assuming one-week mail delivery each way, an exchange of letters with an agent could take half a month. If each side waits five days to send an answer, the entire exercise will consume more than three weeks. Increasingly, export executives are turning to the telex and the telephone, confining their correspondence to nonurgent matters.

Letters to overseas agents are not always answered promptly. Sometimes they are not answered at all. This is exasperating if you are the sort of person who likes to stay on top of things. The reasons are often legitimate. The agent has limited office staff, perhaps not even a secretary. The agent represents many manufacturers and rather than answer all correspondence prefers to choose only those letters which seem important.

The fault can be yours. Your letter was too vague. Or you overloaded your agent with requests for reports and forecasts—a type of request which most overseas agents will try to ignore.

Keep your letters simple and short. An overseas agent with a small, tight operation should be allowed to focus on the business of getting orders. If you need to know how things are going, call or telex. Send photocopies of unanswered correspondence; ask the agent to jot down short comments and replies and mail them back. The more you can do to reduce your agents' paperwork, the more time they will have to go out and do a job for you.

The use of fast courier service has become very popular in recent years. This service isn't cheap. The cost of sending an envelope or package weighing up to one pound from New York is $36 to London and $40 to Tokyo, for instance. Delivery is within forty-eight hours. When important business is pending and an overseas agent needs a proposal or catalogs in a hurry, there is no other way. Courier delivery is used mainly to meet tight bid deadlines.

You can cut your costs considerably if your agent telexes you complete specs and you have a three- or four-week deadline. You can gather all catalogs and other supporting material and send them off immediately by first-class airmail, then telex your actual quotation later. The risk of your catalogs not making it on time or being held up somewhere may not be worth it. Furthermore, it is always better to put together a proposal and quotation *exactly the way you want to submit it* rather than risk having an agent forget to enclose a pertinent piece of documentation.

WHICH SHOULD YOU CHOOSE ?   The frugal approach to international communications dictates that you write before you telex, telex before you telephone, and use the phone only when absolutely necessary. Don't be excessively frugal.

It may not be absolutely necessary to send a quotation by telex, but if it helps speed up an order it will be worth the extra expense.

It may not be absolutely necessary to telephone Claudia Barroso in Rio de Janeiro to tell her what a good job she is doing, when you can simply send her a nice letter. But the extra thought and personal impact of a phone call will mean much more to Claudia.

You must decide which method of communication is the best suited for each particular message. Look at the choice in terms of speed and impact.

A phone call has the strongest impact.

Next is the telex, particularly if you master the art of writing short, crisp messages and *if you compose them yourself.* They are easily read and invite immediate answers. Telexing is not expensive. A three-minute, 180-word message will cost you less than dictating a letter to a secretary.

A letter has minimal impact, does not invite a prompt response, is usually tossed aside to be answered when time allows.

IN-HOUSE COMMUNICATION.   Efficient communications begin at home. The export manager must have at all times easy access to updated information, including status of pending proposals and quotations, status of orders in process, background data on specific countries, lists of prospective overseas agents, reports on existing agents, and the latest field reports from regional managers.

Regional managers should communicate daily with the home office by telex or phone. This should not add more than $15 or $20 a day to travel expenses—less than the price of an average dinner. The expense is amply compensated if the regional manager has an order or a request for quotation to pass on. When it is 5 P.M. in Zurich, your home office in San Francisco is just getting started, and so will have a full day to take action on the request.

If you call your home office from a hotel, watch out for excessive charges. Some hotels will add exorbitant percentages to normal phone rates. Play it safe. Call your office, tell them where you are, and have them phone you right back.

Information on all international sales activities today can be carried in computer files easily accessible to anybody with a terminal or a personal computer.

Effective communication can give you a sharp edge over your competitors. Go for modern, direct communications with your agents; try to telex as much as you can. Good telephone etiquette will enhance your standing with overseas agents and end users, and minimize the risk of lost sales.

Look at good communications as a direct contribution to your bottom line.

THIRTEEN

PROFITS
AND
COMMISSIONS

The profit you want to make, as a manufacturer or supplier, is fairly well defined when you settle on a net export price—the price to be paid by your overseas buyer, whether an agent or an end user.

The amount of profit to be made by your overseas agent should be largely up to the agent.

Your overseas agents will establish end user prices which will cover their costs, expenses, profit, and other obligations. How closely you can or should work with them in developing a pricing structure depends on your product.

If yours is a fairly fast-moving off-the-shelf item and the market is competitive, you may want to keep the end user price at about the same level as in the United States, after taking into consideration all applicable variables such as freight, import duties, and taxes.

If your product has a fairly high unit value, is not an everyday item, and is sold mainly to government and other large organizations where decisions are made by purchasing agents, committees, and department heads, let the agents set the price on their own and don't question them too closely.

In most cases the final price is determined not by you or the agent but by competition.

A happy agent is one who is making money. You should bend over backward to help your agents earn a good profit. Put a tight rein on them, and they will quickly lose interest in your line. Outrageous pricing will of course put you out of business just as quickly.

As in many other aspects of the export business, flexibility is the key word. You will have to do a lot of playing by ear, augmented by a touch of tactful diplomacy, in order to help your agents find a happy medium between a spartan profit and "all that the traffic will bear."

Comparing a foreign market with your domestic scene is not necessarily wise. However, you can look at the agent's end user prices in terms of what they are back home, figure in the variable costs that go into the foreign price, and decide if the agent is keeping things within reason.

If your agent is doing everything right and is actively pushing your line, but is not getting enough orders, it could well be that *your* price is too high. The agent may be adding a reasonable markup and still not making it.

Check your competition; take a close look at bids and awards you may have lost; examine pricing components. There is nothing you can do about import duties and sales taxes. But perhaps you can save on other variables. Here are a few useful questions to ask yourself anyhow, *even when price has not pushed you into a corner:*

Is airfreight necessary?

Can I consolidate several shipments into a single container?

How can I encourage the agent to carry more inventory and place fewer but larger orders?

Does my export price reflect costs plus export overhead, or is it inflated by expenses which are strictly domestic?

Is my profit excessive? Am I trying to squeeze too much out of foreign sales?

A sharp look at your net export prices on a cost-plus basis should help you trim them somewhat. Your agents should go through the same exercise and see what they can cut out of their own prices. This should not be a one-sided effort. Don't ask agents to bear the full brunt of price adjustments while you keep your export prices inviolate.

If any of your agents insist on making exaggerated profits out of each sale, way out of line in terms of your pricing in other markets, you may have to consider changing them. An end user may blame a local agent for charging too much money for a product, but generally the finger will be pointed at you, the manufacturer. How can you tell the end user that the fault is the agent's for trying to make too much money, without discrediting the agent?

In every company there are individuals who are not particularly happy to see agents making money, especially when the agents are in a foreign country. This negative attitude usually comes out of financial departments and from boards of directors and may surface whenever an overseas agent has succeeded in closing a big sale; it is nearly always unjustified and counterproductive. The fact that agents are located in Indonesia and Tanzania is no reason why they should not make as much money as your domestic dealers.

Excessive local profits can be a problem, but not very often. Competition is tough everywhere; there are no easy pickings for manufacturers, exporters, or overseas agents.

If your product is a high-value item sold to major organizations on the basis of case-by-case quotations, you can always ask your agents to send you copies of quotations, particularly when the sale involves a package deal consisting of several items plus installation and other services. This practice will allow you to keep track of an agent's pricing.

Most agents will not be happy to send you the quotations. Remind them that a major end user may pick up the phone and call you to see if the agent's price is reasonable. Without a copy of the quotation there is no way you can answer the question.

At the end of the day what counts for overseas agents is how much net money they are left with. There are two basic ways an agent can boost profits. One is to raise prices, the other is to buy cheap. Agents can be quite adept at juggling one against the other in competitive markets, particularly when public bids are involved. Consider the following example.

- Kuwaiti agent offers German-made physics instrument to end user at $3500.
- Net export price from German manufacturer is $2500.
- Agent stands to make gross profit of $1000.

The agent then (directly or under another company's name) submits a second offer.

- Similar Indian-made product is offered to end user at $2800.
- Net export price from Indian manufacturer is $1500.
- Agent stands to make gross profit of $1300.

The end user buys a product for 20 percent less, the agent makes a profit of 30 percent more.

This sort of thing happens more often when you deal with nonexclusive agents who are in business to produce a profit regardless of loyalty to any particular supplier. In fact, this type of agent will prefer not to be bound to a single source.

You can anticipate this problem by analyzing your low-cost competitors closely and by emphasizing your features, quality, service, and experience.

THIRD-PARTY COMMISSIONS.

On sales of high-value items to large customers, particularly foreign governments, the question of third-party commissions has to be faced realistically.

Since the Lockheed scandal, U.S. companies have been running scared whenever they are involved in "big deals." Export managers are called on the carpet by company lawyers and questioned about foreign agents' margins and commissions; they often find it more difficult and exasperating to justify an order than to actually get one.

Foreign agents resent the implication that their business relies on shady dealings. Compensating friends, intermediaries, and other third parties for favors is considered as natural in many countries as for a U.S. businessperson to invite an important customer for a social weekend.

A basic rule of life—we've all heard it so many times—is that no one does something for nothing.

In business, nobody *should* do something for nothing.

This rule applies all over the world. If someone can really help you make an important sale, you would be foolish to refuse that help.

How do you compensate favors in international business? This need not be up to you. *Leave it up to your agents.* It's their business. Yours is to deal with your agents in a straightforward fashion, at stated prices and discounts, as you would with any domestic dealer.

Let your agents do what they want with their profits and contingency reserves, and don't be afraid that they will take advantage of special connections in order to charge exorbitant prices.

In most countries, with or without third-party help, your agents will still have to knuckle under to the pressure of competition. The brother of an agent may be the minister of transportation, but he can't buy a fleet of trucks at twice the going market price. A low bid that meets specs cannot be ignored.

Remember also that if your agent has good third-party connections, so does the competition—perhaps even the same ones! There is no such thing as a guaranteed deal, no matter who you know.

What you, the manufacturer or exporter, may have to consider from time to time is the role of consultants and other free-lancers who could help *you* develop new business and who therefore have every right to expect a fee or commission from you.

Large, highly structured companies with elaborate policy procedures and manuals flatly refuse to "pay outsiders." Or they will tell the "outsider" to "give us the information, and if things work out we will find a way to take care of you." A condescending, vague, unbusinesslike, and rather insulting formula.

Small and medium-size firms can and should be more receptive to outside advice on major projects, unique business opportunities, potentially attractive overseas agents, new markets. Nobody can cover all bases. You cannot afford to ignore any leads.

Be prepared to pay a fee or a commission for any business that develops from third-party advice, but make sure you have spelled out the conditions in advance. Make a commitment as to how much you will pay and when. Usually there will be no cost to you until the business is consummated and you have been paid.

Once you make a commission deal with a third-party live up to it. Or, to put it another way, if you or any of your company's other executives are going to have a problem issuing a check to an outsider who puts you on to a good deal, *stay out of the deal*.

Trite and obvious as this bit of advice may sound, it is often ignored, and ignoring it gives companies a bad name. Reluctance to part with a commission can be expressed in many ways. Here is a typical statement: "The person who made the deal is no longer with us and we can't find any record of your agreement." More often there are repeated, seemingly interminable delays, which sometimes can last for months.

Whether you refuse to go into a commission deal or balk at paying up when the business is closed, you stand to lose. Keep an open mind or at least look at things case by case.

Look, also, at other types of "bonus" or "windfall" business outside your regular export operations. These include opportunities to make occasional large sales in the "foreign aid market."

FOURTEEN

BONUS SALES THROUGH FOREIGN AID

The first thing that occurs to many executives when they get into exports is to go after foreign aid business. Here, after all, are hundreds of millions of dollars being spent, so why not get some of this money?

This thinking is usually based on two wrong premises:

1. Foreign aid business is easy.
2. If you can live on foreign aid business, you don't have to waste time or money setting up a network of overseas agents.

Foreign aid is indeed big business, but it is highly competitive, and there is nothing easy about it.

The amount of annual purchasing it generates runs into billions of dollars by the time you add up what is spent by all the international lending institutions as well as bilateral aid from the United States, Australia, Canada, Japan, and almost every West European country.

However, foreign aid business is not something you can develop on your own simply by calling at the offices of a few officials in Washington, Geneva, London, or Bonn. You still need effective, hardworking, local agents, because all purchasing decisions for most foreign aid projects are made within the country receiving the funds.

To go into international marketing purely on the basis of foreign aid business is unrealistic for the following reasons.

1. Foreign aid money comes and goes; the level of expenditure is subject to domestic and international politics.
2. Foreign aid projects are widely advertised nationally and internationally, sometimes attracting hundreds of potential bidders.
3. Foreign aid projects for which you can quietly negotiate an order without competitive bids are rare.
4. Pursuing a foreign aid project is no picnic. It calls for persistence, patience, and long-range commitment.
5. A foreign aid project is a sink-or-swim proposition. You either get the order or you don't.
6. Having participated in a foreign aid project, whether you won or lost, does not improve your chances in the next one except to the extent that you can make use of practical lessons you may have learned.

Any business you can get out of the foreign aid market should be considered a welcome and attractive bonus but not the ultimate goal of your export efforts.

Foreign aid emphasis is on priority areas of development such as agriculture, hydroelectric power, food production, rural living standards, health, population control, education, vocational training, transportation, and telecommunications. Recipients of foreign aid include most nations of Latin America, Africa, and southeast Asia and some in the Middle East. In Europe the only countries receiving assistance are Portugal and Greece—both from the World Bank.

I use the term "foreign aid" loosely to describe outright grants which do not have to be repaid, as well as long-term development loans at low interest rates. Grants are made by major industrialized countries and are usually motivated by foreign policy. This type of aid prevailed in the 1960s and early 1970s, but has been largely replaced by long-term loans.

International institutions committed to Third World development, notably the World Bank, work strictly on the basis of long-term low-interest loans which have to be repaid.

Whether the money is from grants or loans will not make much difference to you, the supplier. What does matter in procurement is where the money comes from.

Aid from an individual nation is "bilateral." Money from the United States is dispensed through the U.S. Agency for International Development (USAID). Other bilateral aid organizations active in overseas development projects are the following.

■ ADAB (the Australian Development Assistance Bureau)

- BMZ (the Bundesministerium fuer Wirtschaftliche Zusamenarbeit, or Federal Ministry for Economic Cooperation, of West Germany)
- CDC (the Commonwealth Development Corporation of the United Kingdom)
- CIDA (the Canadian International Development Agency)
- DANIDA (the Danish International Development Agency)
- FAC (the Fonds d'Aide et de Cooperation of France)
- NORAD (the Norwegian Agency for Development)
- ODA (the Overseas Development Administration of the United Kingdom)
- OECF (the Overseas Economic Cooperation Fund of Japan)
- SIDA (the Swedish International Development Authority)

Most bilateral aid procurement is restricted to products from the donor's country. A USAID education project to equip universities and technical schools in Egypt, for instance, will purchase nothing but U.S. equipment.

Other countries follow similar rules, with occasional exceptions. A bilateral grant or loan may be given with no strings attached, leaving the recipient country free to shop anywhere. The Scandinavian countries usually put no restrictions on procurement. This does not necessarily throw procurement wide open to suppliers worldwide. Bilateral projects are nearly always designed by advisors from the donor country who tend to write specifications around home products with which they are familiar.

To find out about bilateral foreign aid projects a U.S. firm should contact USAID in Washington, D.C., first by phone and then in person once specific opportunities and officials have been identified.

Your agents in the Third World should call on U.S. embassies to identify and meet officials in charge of USAID projects. This can be a complicated and discouraging experience. Embassy personnel have a habit of either being locked up in never-ending meetings or passing the agent on to someone else.

Patience and perseverance are seldom put to a harder test than when an agent tries to track down who is running a foreign aid project and who is in charge of writing specifications! The agent may quickly give up in total frustration, leaving it up to you to visit the embassy and sort things out on your next visit.

You may find that the key person is a local official in whichever ministry the project falls, and that the role of USAID is mainly to advertise the project in the United States (in *The Commerce Business Daily*), eventually issue a purchase order, see to it that the merchandise is delivered, and pay the supplier.

Decisions on what to purchase, in fact, are usually made by local officials. The only limitation, in the case of USAID projects, is that the products be made in the United States.

Similar procedures are followed in bilateral aid projects of other countries, and similar frustrations will be encountered.

The biggest foreign aid projects are those financed by international organizations, particularly the World Bank, the Asian Development Bank, the Latin American Development Bank, the African Development Bank, and the European Economic Community (EEC). Procurement in most cases is open to suppliers from the United States, Canada, Japan, Australia, and most of Western Europe, including Switzerland.

What exactly is an internationally financed development project? Usually it is a comprehensive funding package for a large-scale project, such as building and equipping twenty-five vocational schools or fifty rural clinics, or introducing a regional electrification network.

A project will involve the procurement of dozens, if not hundreds, of items; it is *not* merely a loan to purchase a specific product.

The best source of information on pending and ongoing internationally financed projects, including procurement announcements, is *Development Forum* (annual subscription $250), published twice a month by the Division for Economic and Social Information, Department of Public Information, United Nations, Palais des Nations, CH-1211 Geneva 10, Switzerland. This publication covers the World Bank, the Latin American Development Bank, the African and Asian Development Banks, and the EEC, but carries no news of bilateral projects.

World Bank and other internationally financed projects are usually highly publicized even before their official approval. At what point should you or your agent make an appearance and start promoting your product and company?

Lenders like the World Bank (whose rules have been adopted by most of the other lending organizations) require that specs be broad enough to encourage *international competitive bidding.* Furthermore, the country receiving the loan has to purchase from the lowest bidder meeting specs.

Procurement is open to companies in countries which are "members" of the particular lending institution. A member is a country which lends funds (to the World Bank for instance), funds which are then used to float loans to developing nations. Members of the World Bank include all the major industrialized western nations and Japan. (Switzerland is not a member, but Swiss firms can participate.)

Procurement for projects financed by the major regional lending development banks (Latin American, African, and Asian) is usually also open to the United States, Canada, most Western European nations, and Japan.

Before you decide how soon and how deeply to get into a project, let's take a look at how a project is created and run.

Projects are usually initiated by the borrowing country after priority development areas have been identified. Let's say that Tanzania, through its Ministry of Health, proposes to build and equip two hospitals and applies to the World Bank for a loan for the project.

Tanzania offers to use its own funds to pay for construction, labor, and other in-country costs. The money borrowed from the World Bank will be used to purchase materials, equipment, supplies, and technical assistance abroad.

The World Bank assigns a team to do an in-country survey before approving the request. This preproject evaluation may take months. Meanwhile the Ministry of Health, hopeful of approval, may decide to appoint a team of specialists to start developing lists of all the products which will eventually be purchased.

The specialists could be regular officials appointed from within the ministry or local hospitals. Alternatively the ministry could hire a firm of international hospital consultants to do the job on a contract basis.

When the project is approved, the Ministry of Health will become the "project executing agency" and will invite suppliers to prequalify and eventually to bid.

Procurement notices of all eligible countries will be sent to the embassies in Tanzania's capital of Dar-es-Salaam, perhaps also inserted in major international newspapers as well as the *Development Forum.*

From six months to two years may elapse from the date a project is approved and signed until the date of the first procurement. Decisions on purchasing may take several months more, particularly if the project was widely advertised. Some World Bank projects have attracted as many as 600 curious, though not necessarily legitimate, potential suppliers.

Usually the starting field is drastically reduced through prequalification as well as any fees the project managers may decide to charge for a set of product specifications. (The fee can be as high as $100.) However, even if in the end only twenty or thirty companies remain in the race, the process of evaluating their bids can take months.

This ponderous, plodding process is not likely to be streamlined in any way as long as the World Bank and other lending organizations continue to insist on loose, open bidding with minimal prequalification of suppliers.

So, is it an advantage to try to stick your foot in the door well in advance of your competitors?

Not necessarily.

Project directors will indeed be happy to collect your catalogs, particularly if the information they have is two or three years old. You may succeed in encouraging consultants and specifications committees to include products which they had not considered. You can help them work out budget estimates for specific product categories.

But don't be in a big hurry to lay your cards on the table.

Many months will go by before you have a chance to bid. Any information you give out could help your competitors analyze your game plan. There is no reason why a project officer should keep your data under lock and key. Remember also that the specifications will be broad. Tight specs are against the rules. Another thing to keep in mind is that the main scene of the action is, as most manufacturers and suppliers eventually find out, not Washington, London, or Geneva, but the host country. In the case of our hypothetical Tanzanian project, you would have to make your pitch in Dar-es-Salaam and not in Washington.

The lending organization's main concern is making sure that the borrower follows specifications and procurement rules, and that purchasing is within stipulated budget allocations. The choice of what and from whom to buy is up to the borrower.

Local manufacturers usually get a 15 percent price break on international project procurement. If you quote $1000, a local firm can quote $1149 and be considered low bidder. In countries with fairly developed industry, for instance, Argentina, Brazil, India, and Korea, this can make the local company tough to beat. On the other hand, local manufacturers may have trouble meeting quality standards or delivering on time.

Urge your agents in Third World countries to build up and maintain contact with bilateral and international project officers. Keep after them. Feed them any information you pick up from the *Development Forum* and government publications.

Many international projects are put together with the help of specialists from a number of United Nations organizations. The U.N. specialists act as advisors; they may have a lot to do with writing procurement specifications and may even participate in bid evaluation committees.

The top U.N. advisory groups and their locations are listed below.

- FAO (Food and Agriculture Organization), Rome
- IAEA (International Atomic Energy Agency), Vienna
- ICAO (International Civil Aviation Organization), Montreal
- ITU (International Telecommunications Union), Geneva
- UNFPA (United Nations Fund for Population Activities), New York

- ILO (International Labor Organization), Geneva
- UNESCO (United Nations Educational, Scientific, and Cultural Organization), Paris
- WHO (World Health Organization), Geneva
- IMCO (Intergovernmental Maritime Consultive Organization), London
- WMO (World Meteorological Organization)

Occasionally these organizations will also handle procurement for major international projects. Keep in touch with the ones which may require your type of product, and make sure you provide their purchasing and advisory departments with ample supplies of catalogs and specifications, and with frequent product announcements.

In addition, some of these U.N. units purchase specific products on behalf of Third World nations. This procurement is usually negotiated directly with suppliers rather than put out on open bid.

Be alert to foreign aid projects and possibilities, and do contact foreign aid organizations in person or at least by mail, but don't make foreign aid a prime international target. Be particularly wary of projects in countries where you have no agent, assuming that your product requires after-sales service.

As in all overseas marketing, personal and frequent contact is critical in foreign aid business. Mailing a bid and catalogs is not enough. Of the hundreds of firms who may try to prequalify for an international project, perhaps not more than one in forty will send someone to call on the project director. This shows lack of interest. Procurement can be quite complex, and without a chance to discuss requirements and local conditions with the project staff you could make mistakes that would quickly disqualify you.

Foreign aid business is good business, but developing a solid, overseas network of effective agents is much more important. Go after foreign aid business where you are able to follow up through an agent, or can pursue it directly without roaming too far afield.

CHAPTER
FIFTEEN

THE SAUDI EXPERIENCE

Throughout this book I have referred frequently to Saudi Arabia because for a few years during the 1970s it was where the action was, *or seemed to be.* There are many lessons to be learned from the successes and mistakes of the manufacturers, exporters, and consultants who tried to make a killing in the Saudi market. The lessons are not new. They were just learned one more time.

What was new was sudden, unprecedented, explosive affluence in a country which had been totally removed from the international business scene except for dealings with a few major oil companies.

Thousands of businesspeople from all over the world were drawn to Saudi Arabia, many of them entirely inexperienced in international markets. Saudi Arabia became an arena where everything was blown up beyond all reasonable proportions and perspective was quickly lost.

Many companies were quickly turned off by the frenzied competition and by the complexities of the Saudi market. It made no sense to dash over to Jeddah or Riyadh if you had had no exposure whatsoever to international business, knew next to nothing about the Saudi market in particular, and made no effort to do a bit of research ahead of time. Yet this was done many times.

A marketing executive once asked me if Riyadh was a separate country and if so would he need a visa to go there after he finished his business in Saudi Arabia. Now I don't expect everybody to be able to recite the capitals of the arab countries either alphabetically or at random, but if you are flying to the area next week . . . ?

To make it to the desert kingdom *right now* became an obsession with businesspeople who felt that if you didn't claim your slice of the pie then and there, it would be too late.

Some companies closed big orders early in the game and then sank into a state of smug complacency, convinced that they had it made. For them the lessons were costly. As months went by without any orders they relearned a principle as old as the history of trading: *Don't take customers or markets for granted, because there is always someone a bit more aggressive, a bit hungrier, trying to grab them away from you.*

The manufacturers and exporters who did well in Saudi Arabia realized very early that success there, as in any other market, in the long run depended on a steady, persistent, systematic, businesslike sales effort, and on being ready to spot extraneous influences which could get them hopelessly sidetracked.

What are some of the lessons of the Saudi experience?

First, sudden access to billions of dollars does not result in easy, quick sales. At first, the big end users in Saudi Arabia made many reckless, rush decisions. Money was plentiful, needs were boundless for almost everything imaginable, and purchasing experience and selectivity were sadly lacking.

Local merchants and their friends wanted to make money in a hurry, and lots of it. So did foreign suppliers.

Soon, however, as competitors from all over the world began to fill the waiting rooms outside their offices, Saudi purchasing agents and decisionmakers began to see the advantage of holding back to consider alternative offers; as their attitude changed, the traditional give-and-take of trading, at which the arabs have always excelled, again became the norm.

In Saudi Arabia local buyers had no problem finding visiting businesspeople with whom to negotiate. Competition soon became fierce, and eventually eliminated anybody who was not prepared to stick it out.

Although the rewards may not be quite as attractive, it is easier to negotiate and get an order in a smaller, poorer country where competition is weak and the buyer seldom sees a foreign businessperson.

Second, when a country becomes suddenly affluent, sales will rise sharply for a few years, but eventually they will slow down to a less breathtaking pace. In the beginning there was a rush in Saudi Arabia to sign construction contracts, purchase vast quantities of merchandise, and acquire technical assistance to meet needs which had been postponed or had gone unrecognized for decades. For instance, hundreds of schools and clinics had to be built and equipped from scratch in a few years.

But there are only so many ministries, military bases, schools, and clinics which one can reasonably build and equip in a country, no matter how much treasure may lie in the national coffers.

Beware, therefore, of sudden big sales in a country going through a temporary, explosive boom, as Saudi Arabia did in the 1970s. Be happy, but don't count on this business as a steady diet.

Don't let excessive purchasing in the early years of a sudden boom cloud your views concerning a country's real, year-to-year potential. When buying eases off, the general impression is that the market is finished, when actually all that has happened is that it has finally settled to a more reasonable level, one that can be sustained over the long term. If you were wise enough to have gone into the market with a systematic, long-range plan, you are at a decided advantage at this point.

Third, high-level connections are no guarantee of success. This is perhaps the biggest lesson anybody learned in Saudi Arabia. There are more than 3000 princes in the Saudi royal family. So many of them lent their sponsorship to local business enterprises that it became rare to find a manufacturer who did not claim to be represented "by a member of the royal family" whose uncle or cousin was a minister or a deputy minister or the head of any one of a number of major government departments.

The Saudi firms themselves would use the magic words when advertising their services in trade publications throughout the world.

The problem is that this vast family pyramid had a very small tip— at the top was a narrow circle of decision-making officials to whom everybody was related. The same minister had other brothers, cousins, uncles, and nephews, and there was no reason to expect the minister to grant favors to one and all.

Princes could and still do establish and sponsor business firms but are seldom involved in the firms' day-to-day affairs. A Saudi firm is nearly always run by Lebanese, Palestinian, Egyptian, Syrian, Jordanian, or Pakistani managers. The prince who sponsors the firm will not necessarily intercede with end users unless a major project is involved. This in turn has a lot to do with his status and prestige. Remember what happened to our friend Pierre LeJeune when he appointed a prominent prince as his agent!

Unwise manufacturers who are convinced that their own or their agent's connections at the top are immaculate will be tempted to pad their prices a little. This can be deadly. The competitor quoting a lower price may walk away with the order.

"What happened?" asks the bewildered manufacturer.

"Your price was too high."

"But I thought we had been promised the deal."

"Yes, but your price was too high."

This unpleasant ending to a lengthy project was all too frequent throughout the Middle East. The same thing will keep on happening to firms who ignore the fact that no matter how important "good connections" may be in securing orders, one should always play it safe and avoid counting on them.

Assume the worst-case scenario—that all your competitors have good top-level connections and that you have none. Then settle down to promoting your product as you would in any competitive market. Make every proposal stand on its own merits. Then, if someone is able to give a helping hand at the top, so much the better!

Fourth, major projects and tenders flush out all sorts of agents, intermediaries, and others who eagerly claim to know the right person and to be able to guarantee you the order. This was often true in the Middle East, as in any country which has just received multimillion-dollar infusions of funds for major projects. Throughout the world, particularly in developing countries, there are hordes of individuals who bide their time waiting for big projects to pop up and then rush out to find suppliers. In the Saudi Arabia of the 1970s nobody had to sit around waiting too long, because projects were popping up almost by the hour.

Numbers of manufacturers and suppliers responded eagerly to telexed inquiries which were often sent by the same individual to half a dozen competing firms. In most cases the eager agent was never heard from again.

Companies who took the trouble to send someone over to Riyadh or Jeddah in response to this sort of request either ended up making a trip for nothing or chalked it up to experience and went on to try to build up a more solid local presence.

Fifth, there is no point in putting pressure on a foreign agent when your business depends on government decisions. How many times have I heard a manufacturer griping about an overseas agent who takes forever to get a particular order? When you deal with an off-the-shelf consumer item, you can expect quick results. When the order has to come out of a large organization, particularly government, your agent has no control. The order will be issued when and if the buyer is ready.

Some projects in Saudi Arabia took months to be resolved. A ministry would announce the procurement of hundreds of items by public tender.

Firms from all over the world would submit offers. Quantities were usually mind-boggling. Weeks and months would go by without any hint of a decision.

There was nothing any agent could do to speed things up. In fact, I suspect that the more local agents tried to stir things up by prodding the officials in charge, the more confusing the whole issue became, until eventually the project was thrown out the window and a new version written up.

Sixth, if you have expertise in preparing turnkey package deals, don't give it away for nothing. The lure of multimillion-dollar projects and the "guarantee" of a high-level connection led many firms to spend hundreds of hours and thousands of dollars writing up complete turnkey specs for major end users in Saudi Arabia. In the end what happened in most cases was that a competitor who had sat on the sidelines without spending a nickel was able to come in, pick up their specs from the end user, and offer to do the project at a much lower price.

There is no foolproof way to protect yourself against this practice. The initial temptation is to trust the end user. Don't! The particular individual with whom you are dealing may be perfectly honorable and have every intention of following up with an order. But what happens if this person is replaced by someone who hardly knows you? Or if the project is canceled? Or suppose that the project, which originally was to have been negotiated privately between your firm and the end user, is suddenly thrown wide open to public bids?

Yes, you're out of luck.

On turnkey projects you can do either of two things.

1. You can sketch out a project without going into detail. In this case you give bare bones scenario-type descriptions, tell your end user what you will accomplish, and give details of exclusive services and particular products that the end user can obtain only from you, but without going into final drawings or revealing precise information on products which the end users (or your competition) can then obtain on their own.
2. You can offer to do a complete presentation, with final drawings, equipment lists, and other details—for a price which covers your time and expenses and a reasonable profit, just in case you don't get the order for the project itself.

Too many companies gave their expertise away for nothing in Saudi Arabia. You cannot fault the end users for it. In fact, many major organizations in the Middle East and elsewhere in the world will continue to welcome all the free advice they can get from willing, but often ill-advised and overoptimistic companies.

Seventh, make every deal pay. How often have you heard these familiar words: "Look, let's get one or two sales at cost, just to break the ice, and from then on we'll have it made"? How often do you think this advice was given to eager western businessmen by their Saudi friends and agents?

As you know, "breaking the ice" simply does not work. You give merchandise away at cost today; an eager competitor new on the scene will do the same tomorrow. There is always someone who will use the lure of rock-bottom prices to try to take business away from you.

Stick to your best prices. Sell your product on its merits, promote its features, your service, your agent's capabilities. Earn a reasonable profit on every possible sale. And remember that an end user, in Saudi Arabia or in Sweden, who tells you that your price is too high is probably asking for reasons that will justify buying your product.

Saudi Arabia today has become an affluent, steady, reliable market for imported products. In spite of dire predictions by some business-people that the market would be dead in a few short years, Saudi Arabia offers excellent opportunities for consumer and professional products, and most likely will be on your list of priority markets.

The boom-town atmosphere is not entirely gone, but on the whole the country has settled down. There are now dozens of Saudi firms with ten or more years' experience in pursuing projects as well as day-to-day business. Members of the royal family continue to sponsor business firms, but their role and the role of their managers is now better understood by foreign businesses.

Support services in Saudi Arabia have reached high standards of performance; the situation in this respect is a far cry from the chaos which prevailed in the mid-1970s. In fact, businesspeople arriving in Saudi Arabia today will find facilities and a business climate much more modern than in many western countries. In other ways, however, Saudi Arabia has not changed much.

PART
THREE
WHAT NEXT?

CHAPTER
SIXTEEN

NEW
TECHNOLOGY
AS AN
EXPORT TOOL   In the air-conditioned comfort of his
modern home in Trincomalee, Ashok Subasinghe has just received a
request from the Ministry of Public Works for a robot-operated road-
paving machine. It is 10 A.M., Sri Lankan time. The quotation is needed
by 10:45 A.M.

Ashok's office is in his comfortable study. There are no filing cabinets,
no catalog racks or in-and-out trays. Not a sheet of paper in sight. On
a small table within reach is a low lamp and an ivory-inlaid mahogany
box not much bigger than a paperback. One entire wall is covered with
a magnificent mural of the New York skyline.

Without budging from his chair Ashok says: "Access SPEEDEX-
FIVE. Password SHAKO."

The New York skyline vanishes, and the wall-size mural becomes a
giant computer screen. Ashok's voice-activated computer, in the mahogany box, has simultaneously accessed Ashok's main commercial
online database service in the United States, a service which provides
information on all the products and services offered by the dozens of
U.S. companies Ashok represents in Sri Lanka.

A question appears on the screen: "Product?"

"Road-paving machine, robot-operated," Ashok answers.

Three seconds later a list of four U.S. manufacturers is displayed on the upper left corner of the screen. Other sections of the screen become windows showing detailed specifications of the fifteen models produced by these firms and high-resolution color graphics depicting the actual machines. One window displays the FOB factory price of each model, along with shipping weight and dimensions, type of packaging, the insurance and freight charges to Sri Lanka by ocean and air (Ashok's password identifies the destination of the merchandise, allowing the Speedex-Five computer to calculate all charges automatically), and the estimated delivery time.

"Match specs," Ashok orders.

His computer retrieves from its memory the specifications transmitted by wireless microlink less than five minutes before by the Ministry of Public Works. Two of the fifteen U.S. machines match the ministry's specs and are pinpointed by red flashing arrows on the screen. Five machines which meet 80 percent of the specs are indicated by non-flashing arrows. Specs on the other machines remain on the screen but are shaded down.

Ashok studies the display for a few moments. A few more voice commands modify the prices so that they will include Ashok's 3.5 percent commission. Utilizing built-in translation software and a pro-grammed form for Ministry of Public Works quotations, the computer prepares an immediate quotation in English, Sinhalese, and Tamil. The quotation is transmitted to the Ministry of Public Works in Colombo. The time: 10:17 A.M.

At 11 A.M. Ashok's computer receives the order, processes it, and passes it on to Pave-O-Matic Inc. in Helgenberg, Nebraska. The computer also instructs Ashok's New York bank to open a confirmed, irrevocable letter of credit and to advise the manufacturer. Computers at the bank and at Pave-O-Matic take over, opening and transmitting the L/C, setting up the order for production, scheduling shipment, reserving space on a vessel, and finally sending an order confirmation to Ashok, complete with shipping details and dates. The whole business is done in minutes.

This scenario could become reality in 1998. Or in 1991. Or next year. Informatics and telematics are already sufficiently developed to make the scene in Ashok Subasinghe's office technically possible even today.

But don't hold your breath.

For an international business transaction to be handled as swiftly as this hypothetical request for a road-paving robot for Sri Lanka implies intricate worldwide computer networks involving manufacturers, im-porters, exporters, databases, shipping companies, researchers, freight forwarders, banks, and many other professional individuals or organizations.

This futuristic scenario also assumes the existence of extensive and very sophisticated computerized support services which someday will constitute a highly lucrative industry but which do not exist *now*.

What is indeed within reach of any export organization, no matter how small and modest, is the computer. Properly used it can be a powerful tool for export and regional managers, researchers, foreign agents, and support staff.

An effective international marketing organization relies on accurate intelligence. You need day-to-day updating of information on markets, business developments, competitors, your own agents' performance, pending sales and projects.

You have to make available to your agents and major end users accurate data on product, specifications, prices, terms and conditions, and delivery and shipping schedules.

You must be able to produce quotations quickly and accurately.

Having information is useless unless it can be accessed by your export executives and staff, including your traveling regional managers.

When you computerize your export operation, you should do more than set up procedures to handle orders, shipping, payrolls, and other conventional administrative functions. You should make full use of computers in active and aggressive marketing, in functions from research to on-the-road communications.

Market intelligence that is filed away in folders and cabinet drawers is eventually forgotten, and you will find yourself making strategic and tactical errors which could have been avoided if only someone had taken the trouble to dig up a few facts and figures. The computer can help you avoid this, by providing you with a practical and easy-to master-means of keeping your market intelligence 'live" and handy.

Another tool which will soon come to dominate export marketing as never before is the telephone. By 1990 there may be 800 million telephones throughout the world. International direct dialing (IDD) is already offered in almost every country.

Combine the telephone with a portable, battery operated computer and your regional manager becomes a powerful one-person sales force who has the full support capabilities of your company readily available, even while calling on an agent 10,000 miles away from the home office.

The scene in Ashok's office is a distant and nebulous dream (or nightmare).

The computer and the telephone are real tools *today*. Use them. Your competitors most definitely will.

But don't count on the computer and the telephone to conquer export markets for you. This is still a very personal business. Even if the time ever comes when one can manipulate international transactions by simply talking into a gadget the size of a cigar box, the winners in the export game will still be those who have the wisdom to remember that success lies in cultivating face-to-face human relationships with agents, end users, and the many others who in one way or another are involved in the international marketplace.

CHAPTER

SEVENTEEN

THE BOTTOM LINE

You are now ready to swing into action. You have all the tools you need to launch your own export operation from scratch, or to take a critical look at the one you already have and make sure you are headed in the right direction.

THE SIX DECISIONS. The process involves a step-by-step series of six decisions, none of them earth shattering, none of them requiring massive commitments of capital and personnel, each of them a modest calculated risk with everything to gain and very little, if anything, to lose.

Decision 1: Go International. This decision costs you nothing. It is a statement of commitment to find new profit opportunities. You can make this decision right now, without having to go into extensive meetings or protracted periods of meditation and agonizing.

Decision 2: Hire a Consultant. You will have to pay consultant fees, but you can keep them within reason. No need to get a high-powered person. Get names from government and trade association people. You need make only a few phone calls. Set a top figure you are willing to pay, or set up an open-ended deal allowing you to use the consultant as needed. The fees are money well spent; the consultant can show you many time- and cost-saving shortcuts and speed up the business of building up sales and profits.

Decision 3: Identify Markets. Draw up, without too much fuss, a broad list of likely markets. Do this simply by looking up trade statistics and getting advice from your consultant (who, by the way, from now on should be involved in all phases of your export activity). Don't be too concerned if you end up with twenty or thirty countries. The list can be trimmed later.

Implementing this decision will take no more than a few hours of your and your consultant's time as long as you keep it simple and don't get involved in fancy feasibility studies.

Decision 4: Appoint an Export Manager. Putting this person in place will involve a minimal investment if you consider suitable in-house candidates. Your consultant will have some ideas and should talk to the people you have in mind.

Decision 5: Draw up an Export Budget. Work up the budget with your consultant. Stick to major items and avoid going into a lot of detail. The point is to establish an overall figure. Later the export manager can break it down.

Decision 6: Approve an Export Marketing Plan. When you do this, you will be giving the final go-ahead and making the first real commitment. The plan should be drawn up by the export manager and the consultant.

The first five of the six decisions can be made and carried out within thirty days and without taking more than four or five working days of your consultant's time. The process, however, can go on for weeks if you start writing up memos to other company executives, asking them for written "inputs," and referring the whole business to staff meetings and committees.

If you are an Australian, Canadian, European, or Japanese business executive, you will have one major, overpowering question to answer: What to do about the United States market?

You will not have to do much research to come to the conclusion that the United States should be one of your top foreign markets. Because of its complexity and size, the United States will be large enough to absorb all of your export resources and efforts.

In the early decision-making stages, however, it is not necessary to spell out in detail how you will penetrate any particular market, even a large one like the United States, Canada, Germany, or Japan. The final strategy can be worked out when you have appointed an export manager. This will depend on your budget and your personnel resources.

Once your six decisions are made, it is up to the export manager to carry the ball. Export managers perform best when able to make decisions with the smallest amount of interference from other executives. (You should also leave it up to the export manager to decide when to delegate authority to regional managers, particularly when it comes to selecting and appointing overseas agents.)

Organizing the export department will take a lot of the export manager's time. It will help to have some simple guidelines, particularly during the first year. Here is a twelve-point organizational checklist for the export manager.

One: Prepare an Export Budget. Work up staff, travel, promotion, and other estimates, keeping in mind first-phase markets and the overall budget limits established by the company.

Two: Contact Exporters and Trading Companies. Get lists from government, trade associations; obtain directories. Create mailing list. Schedule mailings and assign responsibility for getting the jobs done.

Three: Pinpoint First-Phase Priority Markets. Gather market statistics and other available reports from government, embassies, and trade associations. Identify five or six markets (or more if you, the export manager, plan to hire a regional manager from the very beginning).

Four: Plan Your Promotion. Evaluate and sign up for promotions aimed at your priority markets; select specific literature for overseas agents; develop lists of important trade publications to whom you will send press releases and other PR material.

Five: Identify Agents in Priority Markets. Get lists of agents. Write and send questionnaires to potential agents. Begin the process of evaluation.

Six: Identify Foreign Aid Projects. Contact foreign aid organizations, get details of projects now underway or planned in first-phase markets.

Seven: Set Up a Good Communications System. Make sure of quick and effective phone and telex connections.

Eight: Prepare a Twelve-Month Travel Plan. The plan should include at least three visits to each first-phase priority market.

Nine: Appoint Agents. Complete on-the-spot evaluation of first-phase markets and agents and make agency appointments.

Ten: Identify Second-Phase Markets. Start preparing for sales expansion in second year; figure on two or three additional countries for each person on the road.

Eleven: Identify Potential Agents in Second-Phase Markets. Assign responsibility within the export staff for obtaining lists of agents, sending out initial mailings, and following up.

Twelve: Start Planning Second-Year Promotion. Get details of overseas promotional schemes scheduled for first- and second-phase markets.

If you are a business executive outside the United States and the United States is your top-priority market, you will have to adapt your checklist somewhat although you will still have to go through the conventional steps of identifying, evaluating, and appointing manufacturers' reps, distributors, dealers, and whatever other types of agents your product may require.

As your export operation develops, you will have to set up some criteria to evaluate performance. The bottom line, of course, is profit. However, you cannot expect miracles in one year. Too much pressure to produce early sales and profits the first year will detract from the more important goal of getting organized. The larger a particular market, the more complex it will be, and therefore the longer it will take you to get it firmly established.

If you go after export sales systematically, without undue rushing and with the intention of establishing a lasting operation, your profits will eventually come through.

At the end of the first year the best yardstick of your initial success will be how well you were able to meet the tasks in the twelve-point checklist. Evaluation of this must be accompanied by an evaluation of the performance of export and regional managers, not so much in terms of actual sales as of ability to adapt to overseas sales situations and accept the burdens of foreign travel.

You also have to decide if any of the original markets have to be dropped and which agents may need special help. One year is not enough to judge the performance of any agent, particularly since some will not be appointed until several months after you start your export sales operation. Certainly one year is far from enough to allow you to evaluate an agent's performance in a major market like West Germany, Japan, France, the United Kingdom, Canada, or the United States.

However, if things look promising, you will be ready to start moving into a few additional markets in your second year. They will have been identified, you may even have narrowed down your list of possible agents.

If the new markets are in the vicinity of the initial ones, your regional managers may already have made one or two brief stops to take a first look at opportunities. For instance, a side trip to Bahrein, Qatar, the United Arab Emirates, Oman, and Kuwait is a logical extension of a regular visit to Saudi Arabia. If you find these nearby markets receptive, add them to the territory.

Your initial penetration of a major market may have been limited to a particular state, province, or metropolitan area. Expansion into other regions in the same market would therefore make sense. This will require more time, investment, and personnel, but you will have the advantage of enlarging an existing sales operation rather than starting in a new country from scratch.

Go into new markets with the same basic plan you adopted for the original ones. Check government promotional events such as catalog shows, trade missions, Trade Center shows, and trade fairs. Take advantage of them early.

As you go into second-phase markets, continue to operate on the basis of concentrated repeat visits. Be careful not to neglect the agents in the original markets. Those who were not appointed until well into the first year of your export activities will still require considerable help. Your move into second-phase markets will have to be gradual.

Your overseas agents have to be kept sold at all times, no matter how experienced they may become, or how well you may get to know them personally. There is always a competitor behind the nearest bush, ready to pounce and woo your agent away from you if given a chance.

A major item due for revision at the end of the first year is your budget. No drastic changes are needed, but you should allow enough funds to add one regional manager to the sales team. This will help you open up a few more markets.

Don't forget the exporters and EMCs as you plan your expansion into new markets. If they have started to open up markets of their own, discuss ways of supporting them. Should you send a technician or a regional manager to an exporter's territory to help with special presentations or technical training? How can you give a boost to the exporter's own overseas agents?

Sooner or later you will have to face a major decision: whether to continue working with exporters in some markets or to assume total marketing responsibility on your own. Hopefully you will be able to find a formula that combines both types of organization.

Continue to promote the rest of the home-for-export market, in particular the large trading companies, through frequent mailings and personal visits.

Keep total control over your export activities at all times. In the final analysis nobody can do a better job of promoting your product than you and your sales force, in your home market or abroad. Pick your export markets carefully; use your export sales force and your other resources where they are likely to bring you the highest returns.

Getting into exports means expanding your horizons. The whole world is your oyster. Develop a universal outlook; free your thinking from the confines of a narrow domestic market.

Make exports pay off.

APPENDIX

USEFUL ADDRESSES

International Corporations

To identify the major U.S. international corporations and get on their vendor lists order a copy of the *Directory of American Firms Operating in Foreign Countries* (World Trade Academy Press, 1 West 39th Street, New York, NY 10018).

U.S. Department of Commerce (DOC)

The export service arm of DOC is the International Trade Administration (ITA). ITA's Foreign Commercial Service maintains offices in 120 foreign cities in sixty-three countries considered "principal trade partners of the United States." Among the functions of overseas offices are gathering data on export opportunities and country trends, and identifying and evaluating local importers, agents, distributors, and other business organizations.

Business leads dug up by the ITA's Foreign Commercial Service are published in *The Commerce Business Daily.* They include trade leads as well as information on foreign government procurement notices.

Another useful DOC publication is *Business America,* a biweekly. It carries articles and statistics on foreign trade developments, markets, and trends, and regularly lists all upcoming promotions abroad sponsored by the U.S. government. Annual subscription rate is $57.

To subscribe to either publication, contact the Superintendent of Documents, U.S. Government Printing Office, Washington, DC 20402 or telephone (202) 783-3238.

In Washington, ITA maintains an Export Counseling Center worth contacting (call (202) 377-3181).

To newcomers, ITA offers a number of useful services. An Automated Information Transfer System links small computers in ITA district offices in the United States with 43 overseas posts, making market information accessible worldwide. The system creates computer files of U.S. exporters and foreign importers and tries to match them.

TOP Bulletin, a weekly publication, lists all trade leads received by ITA the week before from all countries. The information is now available on computer tape.

An Agent Distributor Service helps you identify foreign agents, and will provide you a report on up to six possible candidates.

"World Traders' Data Reports" give background information on individual foreign firms.

To subscribe to these services contact the nearest ITA District Office or write Client Service, Trade Information Services, U.S. Department of Commerce, P.O. Box 14207, Washington, DC 20044.

District Offices

Albuquerque, 87102, 505 Marquette Ave. NW, Rm 1015. (505) 766-2386

Anchorage, 99513, P.O. Box 32, 701 C St. (907) 271-5041

Atlanta, 30309, Suite 600, 1365 Peachtree St., NE (404) 881-7000

Baltimore, 21202, 415 U.S. Customhouse, Gay and Lombard Sts. (301) 962-3560

Birmingham, 35205, Suite 200–201, 908 South 20th St. (205) 254-1331

Boston, 02116, 441 Stuart St., 10th floor (617) 223-2312

Buffalo, 14202, 1312 Federal Bldg., 111 West Huron St. (716) 846-4191

Charleston, WV, 25301, 3000 New Federal Office Bldg., 500 Quarrier St. (304) 343-6181, Ext. 375

Cheyenne, WY, 82001, 6022 O'Mahoney Federal Center, 2120 Capitol Ave. (307) 778-2220, Ext. 2151

Chicago, 60603, Room 1406, Mid-Continental Plaza Bldg., 55 East Monroe St. (312) 353-4450

Cincinnati, 45202, 10504 Federal Bldg., 550 Main St. (513) 684-2944

Cleveland, 44114, Room 600, 666 Euclid Ave. (216) 522-4750

Columbia, SC, 29201, Federal Bldg., 1835 Assembly St. (803) 765-5345

Dallas, 75242, Room 7A5, 1100 Commerce St. (214) 767-0542

Denver, 80202, Room 177, U.S. Custom House, 721 19th St. (303) 837-3246

Des Moines, 50309, 817 Federal Bldg., 210 Walnut St. (515) 284-4222

Detroit, 48226, 445 Federal Bldg., 231 West Lafayette (313) 226-3650

Greensboro, NC, 27402, 203 Federal Bldg., West Market St., P.O. Box 1950 (919) 378-5345

Hartford, 06103, Room 610-B, Federal Bldg., 450 Main St. (203) 244-3530

Honolulu, 96850, 4106 Federal Bldg., 300 Ala Moana Blvd., P.O. Box 50026 (808) 546-8694

Houston, 77002, 2625 Federal Bldg., 515 Rusk St. (713) 226-4231

Indianapolis, 46204, 357 U.S. Courthouse and Federal Bldg., 46 East Ohio St. (317) 269-6214

Jackson, MS, 39201, Suite 550, 200 East Pascagoula (601) 960-4388

Kansas City, MO, 64106, Rm. 1840, Savers Federal Bldg., 601 East 12th St. (816) 374-3142

Little Rock, AR, 72201, Rm. 635, 320 West Capitol Ave. (501) 378-5794

Los Angeles, 90049, Rm. 800, 11777 San Vicente Blvd. (213) 824-7591

Louisville, KY, 40202, Rm. 636B, U.S. Post Office and Courthouse Bldg. (502) 582-5066

Memphis, 38103, Room 710, 147 Jefferson Ave. (901) 521-3213

Miami, 33130, Rm. 821, City National Bank Bldg., 25 West Flagler St. (305) 350-5267

Milwaukee, 53202, 605 Federal Office Bldg., 517 East Wisconsin Ave. (414) 291-3473

Minneapolis, 55401, 218 Federal Bldg., 110 South 4th St. (612) 725-2133

New Orleans, 70130, Room 432, International Trade Mart, 2 Canal St. (504) 589-6546

New York, 10278, Federal Office Bldg., 37th Floor, 26 Federal Plaza, Foley Sq. (212) 264-0634

Newark, 07102, Gateway Bldg., 4th floor, Market St. and Penn Plaza (201) 645-6214

Omaha, 68102, Empire State Bldg., 1st floor, 300 South 19th St. (402) 221-3664

Philadelphia, 19106, 9448 Federal Bldg., 600 Arch St. (215) 597-2866

Phoenix, 85073, 2950 Valley Bank Center, 201 North Central Ave. (602) 261-3285

Pittsburgh, 15222, 2002 Federal Bldg., 1000 Liberty Ave. (412) 644-2850

Portland, OR, 97204, Room 618, 1220 Southwest Third Ave. (503) 221-3001

Reno, NV, 89503, 777 West 2nd St., Room 120 (702) 784-5203

Richmond, VA, 23240, 8010 Federal Bldg., 400 North 8th St. (804) 771-2246

St. Louis, 63105, 120 S. Central Ave. (314) 425-3302

Salt Lake City, 84101, Rm. 340, U.S. Post Office and Courthouse Bldg., 350 South Main St. (801) 524-5116

San Francisco, 94102, Federal Bldg., Box 36013, 450 Golden Gate Ave. (415) 556-5860

San Juan PR, 00918, Room 659, Federal Bldg., Chardon Ave. (809) 753-4555, Ext. 555

Savannah, 31412, 222 U.S. Courthouse, P.O. Box 9746, 125-29 Bull St. (912) 944-4204

Seattle, 98109, 706 Lake Union Bldg., 1700 Westlake Ave., North (206) 442-5616

If you have a consumer product, register with In-Store Promotion Program, U.S. Department of Commerce, Office of International Marketing, Washington, DC 20230.

Official export statistics of the United States are published by the Bureau of the Census. The report, entitled "FT 410: U.S. Exports of Domestic and Foreign Merchandise, Commodity by Country of Destination," is available through ITA district offices.

Table A1 summarizes the services and information available from the U.S. Department of Commerce and indicates how you can make use of each one in your export planning.

Private and Government Organizations of Interest to U.S. Firms

The Business Roundtable, 200 Park Avenue, Suite 2222, New York, NY 10017 (212) 682-6370

Table A1
Services and Information Available from the U.S. Department of Commerce

DOC Service	Potential Markets	Market Research	Direct Sales Leads	Agents and Distributors	Export Counseling	Export-Import Regulations	Overseas Contract Opportunities	Marketing Plans
Foreign Trade Statistics	x							
Global Market Surveys	x	x						
Market Share Reports	x	x						
Foreign Economic Trends	x	x						
Commercial Exhibitions	x	x	x	x				
Overseas Business Reports	x	x						
Overseas Private Investment Corp.		x						
New Product Information Service								
Trade Opportunities Program			x	x			x	
Export Contact List Services			x	x				
Agent Distributor Service				x				
U.S. Commercial Service	x	x			x	x		
ITA Business Counseling	x	x			x	x		
Export Seminars					x			
U.S. Foreign Commercial Service	x	x	x	x	x	x	x	
International Economic Indicators	x	x						
Country Market Sectoral Surveys	x	x						
Office of Country Marketing	x	x	x	x				
East-West Trade	x	x				x	x	x
Office of Export Administration					x	x		x
Small Business Administration					x	x		
Major Projects Overseas							x	
Worldwide Information and Trade System	x	x	x	x				
Product Marketing Service	x	x	x	x			x	

Chamber of Commerce of the United States, 1615 H Street, N.W., Washington, DC 20062 (202) 659-6000

Department of State Bureau of Economic and Business Affairs, 2201 C Street N.W., Washington, DC 20520 (202) 632-0354

East-West Trade Council, 1700 Pennsylvania Avenue N.W., Suite 670, Washington, DC 20006 (202) 393-6240

The National Council For U.S.-China Trade, Suite 350, 1050 17th Street N.W., Washington, DC 20036 (202) 828-8300

National Foreign Trade Council Inc., 10 Rockefeller Plaza, Room 530, New York, NY 10020 (212) 581-6420

U.S. International Trade Commission, 701 E Street N.W., Washington, DC 20004 (202) 523-0161

U.S.-Korea Economic Council, 88 Morningside Drive, New York, NY 10027 (212) 749-4200

State Economic Development Offices with Responsibility for International Trade

Alabama Development Office, 3734 Atlanta Highway, Montgomery, AL 36109 (205) 832-6980

Department of Commerce and Economic Development, Pouch D, Juneau, AK 99811 (907) 465-3580

Director of International Trade, Office of Economic Planning and Development, 1700 West Washington St., Room 505, Phoenix, AZ 85007 (602) 255-3737

Department of Economic Development, 1 Capitol Mall, Room 4C-300, Little Rock, AR 72201 (501) 371-2052

Office of International Trade, 350 South Figueroa, Suite 550, Los Angeles, CA 90071 (213) 620-3474

Department of Commerce and Development, 1313 Sherman St., Room 500, Denver, CO 80203 (303) 839-2552

International Division, Department of Economic Development, 210 Washington St., Hartford, CT 06106 (203) 566-3842

Economic Development, Box 1401, 630 State College Rd., Dover, DE 19901 (302) 736-4254

Bureau of Trade Development, Division of Economic Development, Department of Commerce, Collins Building, Tallahassee, FL 32301 (904) 488-6124

International Trade Division, Department of Industry and Trade, 1400 North Omni International, Atlanta, GA 30303 (404) 656-3746

International Services Agency, Department of Planning and Economic Development, Financial Plaza of the Pacific, No. 910, 130 Merchant St., Honolulu, HA 96813 (808) 548-3048 or 548-4621

Division of Economic and Community Affairs, State Capitol, Boise, ID 83720 (208) 334-2470

Business Services Division, Department of Commerce and Community Affairs, 222 South College, Springfield, IL 62706 (217) 782-6861

International Trade Division, Department of Commerce, 444 North Meridian, Indianapolis, IN 46204 (317) 232-8845 or 232-8846

International Division, Iowa Development Commission, 250 Jewett Building, 924 Grand St., Des Moines, IA 50309

International Trade Development Division, Kansas Department of Economic Development, 503 Kansas Ave., 6th floor, Topeka, KS 66603 (913) 296-3483

International Trade Division, Kentucky Department of Commerce, Capital Plaza Tower, Frankfort, KY 40601 (502) 564-2170

International Division, Office of Commerce and Industry, 343 International Trade Mart, New Orleans, LA 70130 (504) 568-5255

State Development Office, State House, Station 59, Augusta, ME 04333 (207) 289-2656

Office of Business and Industrial Development, Department of Economic and Community Development, 1748 Forest Dr., Annapolis, MD 21401 (301) 269-3514

Massachusetts Foreign Business Council, 600 Atlanta Ave., Boston, MA 02106 (617) 973-3774

International Operations Division, Michigan Department of Commerce, Law Bldg., 5th floor, Lansing, MI 48909 (517) 373-6390

Department of Economic Development, 480 Cedar St., St. Paul, MN 55101 (612) 296-2755

International Business Development, P.O. Box 849, Jackson, MS 39205 (601) 354-6707

International Business Office, Division of Community and Economic Development, P.O. Box 118, Jefferson City, MO 65102 (314) 751-4855

Governor's Office of Commerce and Small Business Development, State Capitol, Helena, MT 59601 (406) 449-3923

Industrial Development Division, Department of Economic Development, P.O. Box 94666, Lincoln, NE 68509 (402) 471-3111

Department of Economic Development, Capitol Complex, Carson City, NV 89710 (702) 885-4322

Foreign Trade and Commercial Development, Department of Resources and Economic Development, 6 Park St., Concord, NH 03301 (603) 271-2591

Department of Labor and Industry, John Fitch Plaza, Trenton, NJ 08625 (609) 292-2323

Office of International Trade, One World Trade Center, Suite 86161, New York, NY 10048 (212) 775-1330

International Trade Development, Department of Commerce and Industry, Bataan Memorial Building, Santa Fe, NM 87503 (505) 827-5571

Department of Commerce, Twin Towers, 99 Washington Avenue, Albany, NY 12245 (518) 474-4100

Division of International Commerce, 230 Park Avenue, New York, NY 10169 (212) 949-9290

International Division, Department of Commerce, 430 North Salisbury St., Raleigh, NC 27611 (919) 733-7193

Business and Industrial Development, 523 East Bismark Ave., Bismark, ND 58505 (701) 224-2810

Division of International Trade, Department of Commerce, 30 East Broad St., 25th floor, Columbus, OH 43215 (614) 466-5017

International Trade Division, Department of Industrial Development, 4024 North Lincoln Blvd., Oklahoma City, OK 73105 (405) 521-3501

Department of Economic Development, 921 Southwest Washington, Suite 425, Portland, OR 97205 (503) 229-5625 or (800) 452-7813

Bureau of International Development, Department of Commerce, 408 South Office Building, Harrisburg, PA 71720 (717) 787-7190

Department of Economic Development, 7 Jackson Walkway, Providence, RI 02903 (401) 277-2605

Business and Economic Development, P.O. Box 927, Columbia, SC 29202 (803) 758-2235

Industrial Development Expansion Agency, 221 South Central, Pierre, SD 57501 (605) 773-5037

Office of Export Promotion, Andrew Jackson Bldg., No. 1021, Nashville, TN 37219 (615) 741-5870

Texas Industrial Commission, P.O. Box 12728, Capitol Station, Austin, TX 78711 (512) 472-5059

Industrial Development Division, Office of Community and Economic Development, 165 Southwest Temple, No. 200, Salt Lake City, UT 84101 (801) 533-5325

International Business and Industrial Training, Economic Development Department, Agency of Development and Community Affairs, Pavilion Office Building, 109 State St., Montpelier, VT 05602 (802) 828-3221

International Trade and Development, Division of Industrial Development, 1010 State Office Building, Richmond, VA 23219 (804) 786-3791

Trade Development, Department of Commerce and Economic Development, 312 First Avenue North, Seattle, WA 98109 (206) 464-7076

Trade Administration, Department of Commerce, Charleston, WV 25304 (304) 343-6181

Department of Business Development, 123 West Washington Ave., No. 650, Madison, WI 53702 (608) 266-3222

Industrial Division, Department of Economic Planning and Development, Barrett Building, Cheyenne, WY 82002 (307) 777-7285

International Commodity Codes

You can get a directory of SITC codes with correlated BTN equivalents from the United Nations, Sales Section, U.N. Plaza, New York, NY 10017. Order "Standard International Trade Classification, Revision 2." Sales No. E.75.XVII.6, ST/ESA/STAT/SER.M/34/Rev2.

Military PX and Commissary Organizations

If you have a product to offer the PX and Commissary market, get a copy of "Vendor Facts," Army and Air Force Exchange Service, Red Bird Plaza, Dallas, TX 75222; subscribe to *Exchange and Commissary News,* P.O. Box 788, Lynbrook, NY 11563, and *Military Market,* 475 School Street, Washington, DC 20024

The largest military reps belong to the Armed Forces Marketing Council, 955 L'Enfant Plaza North, Washington, DC 20006. Write for a list, specifying your type of product.

Headquarters for the PX System

Army and Air Force Exchange Service, Red Bird Plaza, Dallas, TX 75222 (214) 330-3721

Marine Corps Exchange Service Division, Headquarters, U.S. Marine Corps, Bldg. No. 3074, MCB Quantico, VA 22134 (703) 640-2917

Navy Resale System Office, Third Ave. and 29th St., P.O. Box Drawer 12, Brooklyn, NY 11232 (212) 965-5000

Navy Resale System Office, West Coast, Building 310, Naval Supply Center, Oakland, CA 94625 (415) 466-5733

Headquarters for the Commissary System

Air Force Commissary Stores, Director of Supply and Services, Personnel Support Branch, Department of the Air Force, Washington, DC 20330 (202) 697-5672 or 697-7446

Army Commissary Stores, Commissary Branch, Troop Support Division, Department of the Army (DALO-SMT-C), Room 1E-573A, The Pentagon, Washington, DC 20310 (202) OX5-9001 or OX7-4322

Coast Guard Commissary Stores, Resale Programs Branch Headquarters, U.S. Coast Guard, 400 7th St. S.W., Room 7124, Washington, DC 20590 (202) 426-2094

Marine Corps Commissary Stores, Commissary Store Branch (Code LFS-1), Headquarters, U.S. Marine Corps, Washington, DC 20380 (703) 694-8616, 694-1622, or 694-8369

Navy Commissary Stores, Navy Resale System Store, Third Ave. and 29th St., Brooklyn, NY 11232 (212) 965-5000.

Overseas Companies Selling to PXs and Commissaries

Associated Brands International, P.O. Box 20513, Causeway Bay, Hong Kong

Loyal Trading International Ltd., 507 Dragon Seed Blvd., 39 Queens Rd., Central, Hong Kong

Siber Hegner & Company Ltd., P.O. Box 164, Hong Kong

Thaiviet Sales Co., 906 Sutherland House, 3 Charter Road, Hong Kong

Fareast Service Co., P.O. Box 14, Urasoe, Okinawa, Japan

Frank Beach, P.O. Box 85, Ginowan City, Okinawa, Japan 901-22

Harold W. Hipp, Hipko Associates (Far East) Ltd., Suite 411, Villa Parto, 109 Yamati-Machi, Naka-ku, Yokohama 231, Japan

H.E. Winters & Associates, P.O. Box 278, Yokohama, Japan

Omni International, Port P.O. Box 90, Yokohama, Japan

Tradeship (Japan) Ltd., Yoyogi, P.O. Box 38, Tokyo, Japan

Western Pacific Corp., Central P.O. Box 42, Naha, Okinawa

Williams International of Japan Ltd., Central P.O. Box 807, Tokyo, Japan

Olivares Associates, P.O. Box 77, Tangier, Morocco

N.A.A.F.E.X.C.O. Freeport, P.O. Box 27, 6830 Chiasse 3, Switzerland

Phil Hoerr, Jr., P.O. Box 28-51 Shihlin, Taipei, Taiwan

Associated Sales and Marketing Corp., Suite 601, 588/3 Petchburi Rd., Bangkok, Thailand

Webco S.A. (England) Ltd., 17C Curzon St., London W1Y 7FE, England

Comex Service Corp, 7 Franz-Lenbackstrasse 6, Frankfurt/Main S 10, West Germany

Tasco Marketing International, Wolfsgangstrasse 132, 600 Frankfurt/Main, West Germany

Trans-European Marketing, 25 Feldbergstrasse, 6 Frankfurt/Main, West Germany

Foreign Embassies

Subscribe to *Diplomatic List.* This quarterly publication contains the addresses of all foreign embassies in Washington and the names of the members of diplomatic staffs. Annual subscription rate: $3. Order from Superintendent of

Documents, U.S. Government Printing Office, Washington, DC 20402. Refer to Department of State Publication No. 7894.

Associations of Export Management Companies in the United States

Contact these associations for names and addresses of U.S. exporters and export management companies. Ask also for names and addresses of similar associations in major industrialized countries, particularly in Western Europe, since some of their members could be good outlets into specific markets.

The Association of New England Export Management Companies, P.O. Box 5, Moodus, CT 06469 (203) 873-8968

Export Managers Association of Southern California, 1537 Pontius Ave., Los Angeles, CA 90025 (213) 479-3911

National Association of Export Management Companies Inc., 65 Liberty St., New York, NY 10005 (212) 766-1343

Overseas Sales and Marketing Association of America Inc., P.O. Box 45446, Chicago, IL 60645 (312) 583-6060

Pacific Northwest Association of Export Managers, 5316 Southwest Westgate Dr., Portland, OR 97211 (503) 292-9219

Foreign Chambers of Commerce in the United States

Contact foreign chambers of commerce for advice on possible overseas agents, and to get names and addresses of counterpart chambers of commerce in their countries.

U.S.-Austrian Chamber of Commerce Inc., 120 Broadway, New York, NY 10005 (212) 571-0340

Belgian-American Chamber of Commerce in the United States Inc., 50 Rockefeller Plaza, Suite 1003/1005, New York, NY 10020 (212) 247-7613

The Finnish-American Chamber of Commerce, 540 Madison Ave., 15th floor, New York, NY 10022 (212) 832-2588

The Finnish-American Chamber of Commerce of the Midwest, 35 East Wacker Dr., Suite 1900, Chicago, IL 60601 (312) 346-1150

French-American Chamber of Commerce in the United States, 1350 Avenue of the Americas, New York, NY 10019 (212) 581-4554

German-American Chamber of Commerce Inc., 666 Fifth Ave., New York, NY 10019 (212) 582-7788

German-American Chamber of Commerce of Chicago, 77 East Monroe St., Chicago, IL 60603 (312) 782-8557

German-American Chamber of Commerce of Los Angeles Inc., One Park Plaza Building, Suite 2212, 3250 Wilshire Boulevard, Los Angeles, CA 90010 (213) 381-2236

German-American Chamber of Commerce of the Pacific Coast Inc., 465 California St., Suite 910, San Francisco, CA 94104 (415) 392-2262

German-American Chamber of Commerce, One Farragut Square South, Suite 606, Washington, DC 20006 (202) 347-0247

Hellenic-American Chamber of Commerce, 25 Broadway, Room 1145, New York, NY 10004 (212) 943-8594

Ireland-United States Council for Commerce and Industry Inc., 460 Park Ave., New York, NY 10022 (212) 751-2660

Italian Chamber of Commerce of Chicago, 327 South LaSalle St., Chicago, IL 60604 (312) 427-3014

Italy-America Chamber of Commerce Inc., 350 Fifth Avenue, Suite 3015, New York, NY 10001 (212) 279-5520

The Netherlands Chamber of Commerce in the United States Inc., One Rockefeller Plaza, 11th Floor, New York, NY 10020 (212) 265-6460

Portugal-U.S. Chamber of Commerce Inc., 5 West 45th St., New York, NY 10036 (212) 354-4627

Spain-U.S. Chamber of Commerce, 500 Fifth Avenue, Room 4220, New York, NY 10036

Spain-U.S. Chamber of Commerce of the Pacific Coast, World Trade Center, Suite 944, 350 S. Figueroa St., Los Angeles, CA 90071 (213) 489-4459

Swedish-American Chamber of Commerce Inc., One Dag Hammarskjold Plaza, New York, NY 10017 (212) 838-5530

Swedish-American Chamber of Commerce of the Western United States Inc., Suite 268, Ferry Building, World Trade Center, San Francisco, CA 94101 (415) 781-4188

British-American Chamber of Commerce, Room 2805, 10 East 40th St., New York, NY 10016 (212) 889-0680

British-American Chamber of Commerce and Trade Center of the Pacific Southwest, 350 S. Figueroa St., Suite 562, Los Angeles, CA 90071 (213) 622-7124

Agencies of the United Nations and Other International Organizations

At the very least write each of these organizations and ask to be placed on their mailing list for any project announcements pertaining to your product category. Send catalogs and prices for reference.

UN: United Nations, Chief Purchase and Transportation Service, New York, NY 10017

ILO: International Labor Organization, Chief Bureau for the Coordination of Operational Activities, International Labour Office, Geneva 22, Switzerland

FAO: Food and Agriculture Organization, Chief Purchasing and Control Branch, Administrative Services Division, Food and Agriculture Organization of the United Nations, via delle terme di Caracalla, Rome, Italy

UNESCO: United Nations Educational, Scientific, and Cultural Organization, Director UNESCO Field Equipment Division, UNESCO, 7 Place de Fontenoy, 75700 Paris, France

ICAO: International Civil Aviation Organization, Director Technical Assistance Bureau, International Civil Aviation Building, 1080 University St., Montreal 101, Canada

WHO: World Health Organization, Deputy Director General, World Health Organization, Avenue Appia, Geneva 22, Switzerland

ITU: International Telecommunications Union, The Secretary General, International Telecommunications Union, 1211 Geneva 20, Switzerland

IAEA: International Atomic Energy Agency, Division of Technical Assistance, International Atomic Energy Agency, Kaerntnerring 11, A-1010 Vienna 1, Austria

UNIDO: United Nations Industrial Development Organization, Chief Purchasing and Contracting Services, UNIDO, P.O. Box 707, A-1011 Vienna, Austria

IMCO: Intergovernmental Maritime Consultive Organization, Director Technical Cooperation Division, 101-104 Piccadilly, London WiV OEA, England

WMO: World Meteorological Organization, Director Technical Cooperation Department, World Meteorological Organization, P.O. Box No. 5, CH-1211 Geneva 20, Switzerland

UNDP: United Nations Development Programme, Director Office for Projects Execution, United Nations Development Programme, New York, NY 10017

ADB: Asian Development Bank, P.O. Box 789, Metro Manila, Philippines

ADFAED: Abu Dhabi Fund for Arab Economic Development, P.O. Box 814, Abu Dhabi, United Arab Emirates

AfDB: African Development Bank, B.P. 1387, Abidjan 01, Ivory Coast

Arab Fund for Economic and Social Development, P.O. Box 21923, Kuwait

BADEA: Banque Arabe de Developpement Economique en Afrique, P.O. Box 2640, Baladia Road, Khartoum, Sudan

BOAD: Banque Ouest Africaine de Developpement, P.O. Box 1172, Lome, Togo

CABEI: Central American Bank for Economic Integration, Apartado Postal 772, Tegucigalpa, Honduras

CDB: Caribbean Development Bank, P.O. Box 408, Wildey, St. Michael, Barbados

IFC: International Finance Corporation, 1818 H Street N.W., Washington, DC 20433

IMF: International Monetary Fund, 700 19th St. N.W., Washington, DC 20431

Islamic Development Bank, Al-Niaba Palace, Jeddah, Saudi Arabia

KFAED: Kuwait Fund for Arab Economic Development, P.O. Box 2921, Kuwait

OAS: Organization of American States, General Secretariat, 1889 F Street N.W., Washington, DC 20006

OPEC: Organization of Petroleum Exporting Countries, Special Fund, P.O. Box 995, A-1011 Vienna, Austria

Saudi Fund for Development, P.O. Box 5711, Riyadh, Saudi Arabia

UNICEF: United Nations Children's Fund, 866 U.N. Plaza, New York, NY 10017

USAID: United States Agency for International Development, 320 21st St. N.W., Washington, DC, 20520

World Bank (IBRD), 1818 H Street N.W. Washington, DC 20433

Purchasing Offices in the United States of Non-U.S. Department Stores

Aaron Schwab International, 208 West 8th St., Los Angeles, CA 90014

Arkwright Inc., 50 West 44th St., New York, NY 10036

Associated Merchandising Corp., 1440 Broadway, New York, NY 10018

Felix Lilienthal & Company, Inc., 417 Fifth Ave., New York, NY 10016

Independent Retailers Syndicate, 33 West 34th St., New York, NY 10001.

Kirby Block Marketing Service, 292 Seventh Ave., New York, NY 10001

McGreevey, Werring, & Howell, 225 West 34th St., New York, NY 10001

Maricent International Inc., 200 Park Ave., Suite 5305, New York, NY 10017

Metasco Inc., International Division of Allied Stores Corp., 1120 Avenue of the Americas, New York, NY 10036

Mutual Buying Syndicate, 11 West 42nd St., New York, NY 10036

Products Exchange Company Inc., 330 Fifth Ave., New York, NY 10001

R.W. Cameron and Co., 420 Lexington Ave., New York, NY 10017

Retailers Representatives Inc., 1372 Broadway, New York, NY 10018
Sears Roebuck International, 7401 North Skokie Blvd., Skokie, IL 60076

U.S. Branch Offices of Non-U.S. Trading Companies

Asahi Bussan Company Ltd., 16 West 22nd St., New York, NY 10010
East Asiatic Company Inc., 110 Wall Street, New York, NY 10005
C. Itoh & Co. (American), 270 Park Ave., New York, NY 10017
Kanematsu-Gosho (U.S.A.) Inc., World Trade Center, New York, NY 10048
Marubeni Corp., 200 Park Ave., New York, NY 10017
Mitsubishi International Corp., 277 Park Ave., New York, NY 10017
Mitsui & Co. (U.S.A.) Inc., 200 Park Ave., New York, NY 10017
Nichimen Company Inc., 1185 Avenue of the Americas, New York, NY 10036
Nissho-Iwai American Corp., 80 Pine St., New York, NY 10005
Sumitomo Shoji America Inc., 345 Park Ave., New York, NY 10017

INDEX

Abrazo, 154
Accessibility, 161–163
ACHEMA, 98
Address, form of, 148–151
Advertising, 100, 106
Africa:
  as export region, 73
  travel in, 135–136
  women as export managers in, 59
  (*See also specific countries*)
African Development Bank, 19, 178
Airway bill, 118
Algeria as market, 43–44
Appointments, 145–146
Asia:
  as export region, 73
  handshake in, 153
  (*See also specific countries*)
Asian Development Bank, 19, 178
Attitude of company, 120–121
Australia and New Zealand:
  as markets, 42, 73, 75
  travel in, 132, 135–136

Bahrein, visas and, 139
Banks:
  development, 19, 176, 178
  information from, 49
Bidding specifications, 102
Bill of lading, 118
Biotechnology, 18–19
"Bird dog fees," 111
Black market, changing money on, 141–142
Body language, 153–154
Brazil:
  titles in, 151
  travel in, 132, 143
Brochures (*see* Literature)
Brussels Tariff Nomenclature (BTN), 40
  directory of, 207
Budget, 77–80
  for promotion, 78, 106–107
  three-year, 79
  for travel, 78
  use of, 196
Buses, travel and, 143
Business periodicals, 26

Canada:
  as target market, 42
  travel in, 132
Car rental, travel and, 142
Catalog shows, 96–97
Centralized countries, 70
Certificate of origin, 118
C&F price, 113
Chambers of commerce:
  foreign, in U.S., 209–210
  as source of prospect information, 26
Chile, buses in, 143
China:
  as market, 42–43
  tipping in, 141
CIF price, 113
Clerical help, cost of, 77
Clothing, 148, 152–153
Colombia, travel in, 132
Commerce Business Daily, The, 27
Commercial attaché, 27
Commission(s), 169–173
  within net export price, 111
  overseas agents and, 172–173
Commission representatives, 63–66
Commitment of company, 121–122
Commodity codes (*see* Trade codes)
Communication, 159–168
  budget for, 78
  choice of method of, 167
  correspondence and, 165–166
  importance of, 159–160
  in-house, 167–168
  telephone and, 160–163, 193
  telex and, 164–165, 167
  time required for, 10
Company support, need for, 120
Components, demand for, 19
Computer(s), 191–194
  communication and, 167
  organizing data with, 40, 46, 47
  quotations and proforma invoices and, 114
  value of, 40, 62, 65–66, 193
Computer-aided design, 20
Computer-aided engineering, 20
Computer-aided manufacturing, 19
Concierge, tipping, 140
Consulate, 89–90

Consultant:
  in direct sales market, 24–25
    to guide initial international steps,
      53–54
  for market research, 51
  reasons to use, 195–196
  roles of, 66–67
"Conversational distance" in foreign
    countries, 154
Correspondence, appropriate use of, 165–
  167
Cost(s):
  in home-for-export market, 35–36
  of market research, 50–51
  minimizing, 79–80
  of salaries, 77
  of shipping literature, 103–104
  of trade fair, 98
  (*See also* Budget)

Decentralized countries, 70
Delivery times, 115
Department stores:
  in direct sales market, 27
  displays in, 16
  foreign, 211–212
Developing countries as markets, 7, 43
  table, 8
Development Forum, 178, 179
DIDACTA, 98
Direct mail, 101
Direct sales market, 24–28
  consultants in, 24–25
  department stores in, 27
  embassies in, 27
  foreign visitors in, 28
  governments in, 26–27
  international companies in, 25–26
  military, 26
  United Nations in, 27–28
Dock receipt, 118
Dress, 148, 152–153

Education:
  of export manager, 60–61
  export opportunities in, 20–21
Electrical requirements, 17
Electronics, 19
Embassies:
  in direct sales market, 27
  holidays observed by, 135
  listing of, 208–209
  as sources of information, 30, 46, 49–
    50, 89, 92

End users:
  caution regarding, 187
  use of data on, 48
  visits to, 90
English language, usefulness of, 10, 56
Entertaining of overseas agents, 157
Europe:
  export apathy in, 2
  as market, 42–43, 75
  trading companies in, 30
  travel in, 136, 143
  (*See also specific countries*)
European Economic Community (EEC),
  19, 178
Export(s):
  destination of, 47
  sources of data on, 44–46
  total, 46–47
Export apathy, 1–5
  European, 2
  Japanese, 29
  prevalence of, 5
  reasons for, 3–5
Export assistant, 62–63, 77
Export documents, 117–118
Export license, 117–118
Export management company (EMC),
  31–33
  advantage of, 31–32
  associations of, 209
  dangers of, 32
  how to work with, 33
  in international strategy, 76
  selecting, 32
Export manager:
  checklist for, 197–198
  female, 57–60
  hired from outside, 56–57
  organizational location of, 54–55
  promoted from within, 55–56
  as regional manager, 65
  requirements for, 55, 60–62
  responsibilities of, 54
  salary of, 77
  selection of, 53, 196
  timing of hiring of, 54
  travel required of, 61–62
Export sales:
  decisions basic to, 195–196
  reasons to pursue, 6–10
  ways to get into, 23–24
Export salesperson, 33
Exporters:
  advantage of, 31–32
  directory of, 30
  disadvantage of, 30
  in home-for-export market, 30–35

Exporters (*Cont.*):
  in international strategy, 76
  policy toward, 31
  to United States, table, 45

Firms:
  international: in direct sales market,
    25–26
    directory of, 201
    size of, 126–127
Flexibility, need for, 124–125
FOB price, 111–112
Foreign agents (*see* Overseas agents)
Foreign aid, 175–181
  danger of relying on, 175–176
  selection of markets and, 44
Foreign visitors in direct sales market,
  28
Formality in foreign countries, 149, 158
France, travel in, 132
Frankfurt Book Fair, 98
Freight forwarder, 114

Government(s):
  foreign, in direct sales market, 26–27
  promotions available from, 95–96
  publications of, 27, 30, 90, 201–203
    table, 204
  as source of prospect information, 26
  trade statistics from, 39
Government organizations of interest to
  U.S. firms, 203, 205
Gum chewing, 148

Hadj, travel and, 136
Handshake, 153
Hanover Fair, 98
Health improvement projects, 19
Holidays, travel and, 134–136
Home-for-export market, 24
  costs in, 35–36
  direct mail in, 101
  exporters in, 30–35
  outlets in, 76–77
  trading companies in, 28–30
Hong Kong as market, 43
Hotels:
  choice of, 137–138
  information available from, 89
Humor, 155

Imports:
  country-by-country, 47–48
  history of, 49
  sources of data on, 44–46

Industries:
  indigenous, demand for components
    and, 19
  U.S., with highest predicted growth, 20
Inspection certificate, 118
Insurance certificate, 118
International lending agencies, 19, 176,
  178
International organizations, agencies of,
  210–211
International strategy, 69–80
  budget for, 77–80
  ingredients of, 69
  liaison with home-for-export outlets
    and, 76–77
Invoice:
  commercial, 118
  consular, 118
  proforma, 109, 114
Islamic countries:
  travel in, 134–136, 163
  (*See also* Middle East; Saudi Arabia)
Italy, travel in, 132, 135

Japan:
  export apathy in, 29
  as market, 42
  trading companies and, 29, 76–77
  travel in, 132, 135, 141, 143, 145, 153
  women as export managers in, 59
Jet lag, 139

Korea, travel in, 135, 141, 153

Language:
  brochures and, 105
  English, 10, 56
  foreign, need for, 56
  of target countries, 48
  travel and, 154–155
Latin America:
  as market, 73, 75
  travel in, 132, 145, 154
  women as export managers in, 59
Latin American Development Bank, 19,
  178
Letter(s):
  appropriate use of, 165–167
  of intent, 115
Letter of credit (L/C), 7, 115–118
  amendments to, 117
  charge for, 117
  irrevocable, 116
    confirmed, 116
  quotations and, 113

Literature:
    for agents, 103–105
    language of, 105

Mailings:
    direct mail, 101
    for home-for-export market, 36
Manners (*see* Personal manners)
Maps, travel and, 142
Market(s):
    identifying, 37–52, 196
    size and complexity of, 17
    U.S. as, 44, 196
    of U.S., 15, 41
        table, 41
    women barred from, 59–60
    (*See also* Direct sales market; Home-
        for-export market; Target markets)
Market intelligence, 193
Market research:
    consultant to carry out, 51
    cost of, 50–51
    free of charge, 51
    gathering data for, 39–46
    organizing data for, 46–48
    resources for, 49–52
Market share, 48
Marketing executives, requirements for,
    120
    (*See also* Export manager; Regional
        manager)
Marketing plan, 196
Mealtimes, personal manners during,
    155–157
Mediterranean area, working day in, 145
Mexico:
    as market, 43
    titles in, 151
Middle East:
    as market, 43, 73, 75
    travel in, 139, 143–145, 156
    women as export managers in, 59
    (*See also* Saudi Arabia)
Military attaché, 27
Military market, overseas, 26
Military PX and commissary organiza-
    tions, 207–208
    companies selling to, 208
Military representatives, 26
Mistakes, 125–126
Money, changing, 141–142
Morale of export department, 126
Morocco as market, 43

New Zealand (*see* Australia and New
    Zealand)

Newsletter for agents, 102
Nigeria as market, 43

Office automation, 20
Organizational checklist for export man-
    ager, 197–198
Overseas agents, 81–93
    bidding specifications for, 102
    cautions regarding, 87–89
    commissions and, 172–173
    commitment to, 91–93
    direct mail and, 101
    entertaining of, 157
    foreign aid projects and, 181
    information on, 84, 92
    legal requirements on, 92
    literature for, 103–105
    locating, 83–87
    need for patience with, 123
    newsletter for, 102
    prices and, 169–171
    sales manual for, 102
    videocassette shows for, 106
    working conditions of, 92–93
Overseas development, 7, 19, 25, 44,
    176–178
    table, 8

Packaging for export, 16
Paris Air Show, 98
Patience, need for, 122–123
Perseverance, need for, 123–124
Personal manners, 147–158
    body language and, 153–154
    clothing and, 148, 152–153
    degree of formality and, 158
    entertaining and, 157
    form of address and, 149–151
    language, humor, and values and, 154–
        155
    at mealtimes, 155–157
    women and, 60
Personal service, 126
Personnel, 53–67
Postage, budget for, 78
Press release, 100–101
Price(s):
    CIF and C&F, 113
    cost-plus, 111
    delivered, 112–113
    FOB, 111–112
    identical, 111
    list or end user, 110
    net export, 110–112
    overseas agents and, 169–171

Price(s) (*Cont.*):
   quoting, 109–110
   resisting changes in, 188
Private organizations of interest to U.S.
      firms, 203, 205
Product(s), 15–22
   changing for export, 17–18
   difficult to export, 16–17
   with high demand, 18–21
   need for, 107
   successfully exported, 16
Profanity, 148
Promotion(s), 95–107
   advertising and, 100, 106
   bidding specifications and, 102
   budget for, 78, 106–107
   in department stores, 16
   direct mail, 101
   functions of, 95
   government-sponsored, 45–46
   literature and, 103–105
   newsletter and, 102
   press release and, 100–101
   product needs and, 107
   sales manual and, 102
   sales meetings and, 103
   U.S. Department of Commerce sponsor-
      ship of, 95–100
   videocassettes and, 96–97, 106

Qatar, visas and, 139
Questionnaire for foreign agents, 85–86
Quotations, 113–114

Ramadhan, travel and, 136
Regional manager, 63–66
   base location of, 64–65
   export manager as, 65
   functions of, 64
   need to use computers, 65–66
   number of markets for, 74–75
   personal contact by, 64
   reasons to use, 64–65
Reservations, travel and, 136–138
Restaurants for entertaining overseas
      agents, 157

Sales expansion, 75
Sales manual, 102
Sales meetings, 103
Sales quotas, value of, 122
Saudi Arabia:
   lessons learned in, 183–188
   as market, 43

Saudi Arabia (*Cont.*):
   travel in, 134, 136, 138–139, 144
   unpredictability of market in, 122–123
Shipping:
   of literature, 103–104
   options for, 112
Singapore as market, 43
Smoking, 148
South Africa as market, 43
South America (*see* Latin America)
South Asia and Southeast Asia:
   as market, 72–73, 75
   travel in, 135
   women as export managers in, 59
Southern hemisphere, travel in, 135–136
Standard International Classification
      (SIC), 40
Standard International Trade Classifica-
      tion (SITC), 40
   directory of, 207
State economic development offices, in-
      ternational trade and, 205–207
Subway, travel and, 142–143

Taiwan:
   as market, 43
   tipping in, 141
Target markets:
   clustering by region, 71–74
   criteria for, 48–49
   to develop at one time, 70
   first-phase priority, 69–74
   foreign aid and, 44
   making good working territories, 71–
      72
   optimum number of, 74–75
   second-phase priority, 74–75
   small countries as, 41–42
   of United States, 15
Tariff Schedules of the United States, 40
Taxicabs, travel and, 143
Technical installation, 34–35
Telephone:
   making best use of, 160–163
   value of, 193
   when to use, 167
Telephone directories, 50, 84, 89
Telex:
   making best use of, 164–165
   when to use, 167
Telex operator, tipping, 140
Thailand, taxicabs in, 143
Third World as market, 7, 43
   table, 8
Tipping, 139–141
Titles in foreign countries, 151

Trade associations, 39, 49, 84
Trade center show, 97–98
Trade codes, 39–40
  directory of, 207
Trade fairs, 50, 98–100
Trade mission, 97
Trade publications, 85
Trade statistics:
  to determine markets, 40–41
  government as source of, 39
Trading companies:
  developing list of, 30
  European, 30
  in home-for-export market, 28–30
  in international strategy, 76–77
  Japanese, 29, 76–77
  U.S. branch offices of, 212
Training:
  export opportunities in, 20–21
  sales that require, 34–35
Transportation, local, travel and, 142–
    144
Travel, 131–146
  activities during, 89–91
  budget for, 78
  changing money and, 141–142
  by export manager, 61–62
  holidays and, 134–136
  for home-for-export market, 36
  itinerary for, 132–134
  jet lag and, 139
  local transportation and, 142–144
  need for, 70, 131
  preparation for, 131–132
  reservations and, 136–138
  rest time during, 146
  time required for, 10
  tipping and, 139–141
  visas and, 138–139
  working hours and appointments and,
    144–146

Union of Soviet Socialist Republics,
    (U.S.S.R.) as market, 42–43
United Nations:
  advisory groups of, 180–181
  agencies of, 210–211
  in direct sales market, 27–28

United Nations Children's Fund
    (UNICEF), 28
United Nations Educational, Scientific,
    and Cultural Organization
    (UNESCO), 27–28, 181
United States:
  chief exporters to, table, 45
  export markets of, 15, 41
    table, 41
  industries with highest predicted
    growth in, 20
  as market, 44, 196
  1984 trade deficit of, 1
  tariff schedules of, 40
  travel in, 132
U.S. Agency for International Develop-
    ment (USAID), 25, 176–178
U.S. Army Corps of Engineers, 24, 25
U.S. Department of Commerce (DOC), 25
  promotions available from, 95–100
  publications of: directory of exporters,
    30
    services and addresses of, 201–203
    table, 204
  trade, 27
  as source of information, 49
    on foreign agents, 84, 92
    trade data, 39, 45
U.S. State Department, 25

Values in foreign countries, 155
Videocassette shows:
  for overseas agents, 106
  U.S. Department of Commerce sponsor-
    ship of, 96–97
Visa(s), 138–139
Volume potential of target countries, 48

Weekend, travel and, 134, 146
West Germany, travel in, 132
Women:
  acceptance of, overseas, 58–60
  as export managers, 57–60
Working hours, scheduling appointments
    and, 134, 144–146, 163
World Bank, 19, 176, 178